praise for

A LINE IN THE SAND

T0152021

"With *A Line in the Sand*, Ray Wiss has given us a moving and personal account of his second tour of duty as a doctor with the Canadian Forces in Afghanistan. Frank and thoughtful, the book brings into sharp focus the day-to-day doings of the interesting array of characters among whom he finds himself. We get a feel for the strange stresses of war . . . the pain and uncertainty, as well as the humour and camaraderie that make the awful reality bearable. The lines in the sand are clearly drawn with humanity and grace. This is a book for anyone who cares about the human face of mankind's oldest activity. Highly recommended reading!"

BRUCE COCKBURN, OC, *singer/songwriter*

"Volunteer paramedic with the Sandinistas in Nicaragua, Canadian infantry platoon commander, emergency-department director and combat doctor, Ray Wiss has never compromised in his brave and distinctly Canadian idealism. Now as a battle diarist, Wiss is every bit as uncompromising in his devotion to the unadorned truth about life and death in the merciless heat and amid the bombs and bloodshed of the Afghan front. This is a gripping, heartbreaking and inspiring book. It's about ordinary Afghans and ordinary Canadian soldiers whose humbling, everyday bravery will take your breath away. The Afghanistan you will encounter in *A Line in the Sand* is not the country you've read much about in your newspapers. The Afghanistan in the pages of this book is the one that matters. It is about the cause that matters, and why so many young Canadians have died fighting for it."

TERRY GLAVIN, award-winning journalist and author

"A doctor with an infantry background, Captain Ray Wiss gives us a unique insight into the lives and sacrifices of Canadian soldiers 'outside the wire' in Afghanistan. Read on and be proud to be Canadian."

MAJOR-GENERAL (RET'D) LEWIS MACKENZIE, CM, OOnt, MSC and Bar, CD

"Captain Wiss captures the soldiers' view on the ground and in the thick of it. Just as they did on the muddy battlefields of Europe in the First and Second World Wars, the steep hills of Korea and numerous peacekeeping missions around the globe, Canadians distinguish themselves today on the dusty roads of Afghanistan. Words like valour, commitment and sacrifice are just as apt today when describing the current generation of Canadian heroes. Thankfully our nation has awakened to this reality, and within these pages you find the stirring stories to keep their memory alive."

THE HONOURABLE PETER MACKAY, Minister of National Defence

A LINE IN THE SAND

A LINE IN

Captain Ray Wiss, M.D.

THE SAND

Canadians at War in Kandahar

Douglas & McIntyre
D&M PUBLISHERS INC.
Vancouver / Toronto / Berkeley

Copyright © 2010 by Captain Ray Wiss, M.D.
First paperback edition 2011
First U.S. edition 2011

11 12 13 14 15   5 4 3 2 1

All rights reserved. No part of this book may be reproduced, stored in a retrieval system or
transmitted, in any form or by any means, without the prior written consent of the publisher
or a licence from The Canadian Copyright Licensing Agency (Access Copyright).
For a copyright licence, visit www.accesscopyright.ca or call toll free to 1-800-893-5777.

Douglas & McIntyre
An imprint of D&M Publishers Inc.
2323 Quebec Street, Suite 201
Vancouver BC Canada V5T 4S7
www.douglas-mcintyre.com

Cataloguing data available from Library and Archives Canada
ISBN 978-1-55365-592-3 (cloth)
ISBN 978-1-55365-926-6 (pbk.)
ISBN 978-1-55365-654-8 (ebook)

Editing by John Eerkes-Medrano
Cover and text design by Naomi MacDougall
Front cover photograph by Shah Marai/AFP/Getty Images
Back cover photos courtesy Ray Wiss

All illustrations courtesy of the author, except p. 15, courtesy Eric Leinberger; pp. 34 (top), 119, 122, 161,
191, 194, 250, 408, courtesy Master Corporal Julien Ricard; pp. 56, 237, 278, © Louie Palu/ZUMA Press,
reprinted with permission; p. 387, courtesy Deb Ranson, official photographer for the
prime minister; pp. 395–405, courtesy Combat Camera Team, Department of National Defence (DND),
reproduced with the permission of the Minister of Public Works and Government Services,
2010; p. 407 (top), courtesy Master Corporal Ken Fenner, Combat Camera; and
p. 407 (bottom), artwork by and courtesy of Silvia Pecota.

The lyric quoted on page 345 is excerpted from the song "If I Had A Rocket Launcher," written
by Bruce Cockburn, © 1983 Gold Mountain Music Corp. (SOCAN). Used with permission.

Printed and bound in Canada by Friesens
Text printed on acid-free, 100% post-consumer paper
Distributed in the U.S. by Publishers Group West

We gratefully acknowledge the financial support of the Canada Council for the Arts, the British
Columbia Arts Council, the Province of British Columbia through the Book Publishing Tax Credit and
the Government of Canada through the Canada Book Fund for our publishing activities.

For my daughters, Michelle and Julianne.
Why do soldiers risk their present, if not for their future?

And in memory of Nico, Conan, Boomer, Glen,
Michael, Colin, Kristal and, most of all, Andrew. These combat
medics lived and died by the words Militi Succurrimus (We aid
the soldier) and provided the finest battlefield medical care this
planet has ever seen. It is an honour to wear the same badge they did.

On ne lâchera jamais.
We will never quit.

Motto of Bravo Company Combat Team
Second Battalion, Royal 22e Régiment / Royal 22nd Regiment
Les Van Doos
Kandahar, Afghanistan, 2009

CONTENTS

Foreword

THROUGHOUT CENTURIES OF conflict, ethicists have struggled to determine when a war may truly be said to be just. Occasionally, one occurs whose circumstances leave little room for argument. Such is the international intervention in Afghanistan, on behalf of that troubled country's government—sanctioned by the United Nations organization, undertaken by NATO and fully supported by Canada.

We all know the story. Nearly fifteen years ago, the Taliban regime seized power in Kabul and imposed its reign of horror upon a nation already wearied by many years of war. The regime brutalized Afghan society. Men were forced to conform to the arbitrary dictates of often-illiterate religious leaders. Women were deprived of all rights as human beings. Few children received even a basic education. And in stadiums where once people played soccer, summary public executions—often for modest offences—became a frequent occurrence. It was a detestable and nihilistic regime, dedicated only to destruction—of art, of anything Afghans took pleasure in, of any hint of personal choice that deviated from its own narrow strictures, of human life itself.

Hidden away in the remote mountain fastnesses of Asia, east of Iran and north of Pakistan, the Taliban might nevertheless have stumbled along for years, but for its leadership's fatal alliance with al Qaeda. However, by making common cause with Islamist terrorists determined to take their self-declared jihad to the West, the Taliban transformed itself into a present danger to the international community. It sheltered the al Qaeda organization, even as al Qaeda planned and perpetrated multiple outrages against Western interests abroad over a period of several years.

Then, on September 11, 2001, terrorists used hijacked airliners to destroy New York's World Trade Center and to attack the Pentagon. A total of 2,976 people died that day in the two attacks and in the related crash of Flight 93. Among the casualties were twenty-five Canadians. These actions were conceived and planned in Afghanistan.

The Taliban could no longer be ignored: the justice of the world's prompt and vigorous intervention in the Taliban homeland in response to the 9/11 provocation was, and remains, unassailable.

International law blesses self-defence. The moral tenets of every major religion endorse it. Common sense demands that when attacked, we remove the threat. And, even had time raised doubts, the lessons of the campaign would have settled them.

What we have now learned through fighting the Taliban revealed how deep was the chasm between our world views. There is a fundamental difference between Canada and our allies, and those we fight. The Western world view cherishes life and, however imperfectly, ascribes value to individuals.

Not so, this enemy.

This has been a widely reported war. However, there are valuable additional insights to be gathered from these writings of Dr. Ray Wiss. A Sudbury doctor who rejoined the army as an officer in early middle age specifically to serve on the front line in Afghanistan, he reveals through his vivid descriptions a layer of detail about the character of the enemy that horrifies, even as it informs.

It is not news, of course, that the Taliban place little value upon human life, although Dr. Wiss's description of their specific atrocities is no less chilling for being carefully understated. It is in the more mundane cruelty, however, that the mist clears on the chasm that separates us. Wiss writes, for instance, of a teenager who dies, despite all that he could do, from injuries inflicted by a Taliban explosive—an event of a type "so common as to be barely worth mentioning." And of a young boy whose broken leg becomes a lifelong impairment because, to the Taliban, taking him to a hospital would be an act of collaboration with the government.

It is true that there are accidents in war, but these were not accidents. Wiss expresses it with clarity: "[W]hen Afghan civilians are hurt by Coalition weapons, it is because we screwed up. When they are hurt by Taliban weapons, it is a direct and predictable result of intentional Taliban tactics."

Canadian doctors—like Ray Wiss—treat even the enemy. Canadian soldiers strive to protect Afghans, even at great personal risk. And Canadians, and their allies, provide the conditions under which reconstruction projects—such as the Dahla Dam, which I visited in May 2009—are able to be developed.

Thanks to Ray, we have the chance to understand what Canadian troops experience on Afghanistan's front lines, and why what they're doing is worth it. Canadians should be very proud of our men and women in uniform, and of the extraordinary job that they are doing.

Importantly, he also reminds us of something we should never forget: yes, this is a just war.

Above all, it is also a war that we are fighting justly.

It is the Canadian way.

Just as with his previous book, FOB *Doc*, all royalties go to support the Military Families Fund, established by General Rick Hillier to assist the families of our service people.

I am delighted to provide this foreword.

THE RIGHT HONOURABLE STEPHEN HARPER, M.P., P.C.

Prime Minister of Canada

Introduction

I **WENT TO AFGHANISTAN** in 2007 to serve my country. Canadians had been attacked by adherents of an ideology who considered our way of life abhorrent. It was clear that those ideologues intended to continue attacking us. Our choice was, and remains, to fight them now in Afghanistan or later closer to home.

I also went to fight for human ideals that are primordial. Idealism of this kind is often derided in modern society, but it is at the core of who I am.

My decision to go to war nonetheless shocked everyone who knew me. Interrupting a successful career was bizarre; putting myself in harm's way in my late forties, while I had a wife and young daughter at home, was incomprehensible. It was to explain my actions to my friends and family that I began writing a diary.

Readers of that diary felt I had done a good job of explaining what was at stake in this war and why our country should participate in it. By a series of serendipitous events, my diary became a book, FOB Doc. This was a completely unexpected development, but one that had great potential benefit. To have more Canadians read my words would give these ideas greater exposure. That book, however, was an outgrowth of a conversation I had been having with those I was close to; my own experiences were the focal point.

When the Canadian Forces asked me to return to Afghanistan in 2009, I was determined to write a very different book. This second effort would be a conversation with all Canadians. I would look outwards, this time, and focus on the extraordinary men and women who were with me. I also wanted to write much more about the Afghans: those who were fighting to rid their country of the Taliban curse, those who fought against us, and the ordinary people caught between the warring camps.

This book is also an act of remembrance, and not only for our fallen. I hope that, by reading in detail about the experiences of one deployed group, Canadians will learn what life was like for all those who served in Afghanistan. To this end, I asked many veterans to read my various entries. They offered clarifications when I asked for them, and corrections when my all-too-human memory lapsed. I hope that, with their help, I have succeeded in being accurate. I will know I have succeeded when my fellow veterans tell me that I got it right, and that I helped them to explain to their own friends and families what they experienced. That will be the highest accolade.

Lastly, this book seeks to raise the awareness of Canadians about a tiny piece of ground halfway around the world, a piece that most of them have never heard of. Many of our citizens will recognize Kandahar as the Afghan province in which we have been fighting for the past four years. Very few will recognize the names of Shah Wali Khot, Arghandab, and especially Panjwayi and Zhari. Those are the province's districts where virtually all the combat in which Canadians have been involved has taken place, an area roughly the same size as the Greater Toronto Area.

Why did we expend so much blood and treasure in such a small area? Because it is the birthplace of the Taliban, and the area where they have the most support. In 2006, with the Taliban resurgent, Canadians took on the toughest assignment there was. We paid a heavy price to do so: on a per capita basis, Canada has suffered more casualties than any other nation in the Coalition. For over three years, Canadian soldiers held the line against the worst the Taliban could throw at us. That is something all Canadians need to know.

As I write these words, the outcome of the Afghan war is still in doubt. I worry not only about what the outcome will be, but also about how Canadians will perceive our participation in this conflict.

Defeat is an orphan. If the war ends in some kind of fiasco, there is the chance that Canadians will turn their backs on this memory.

But what if we win? Victory has a large extended family, all of whom want to come to the celebration. The British and the Dutch deserve to be there—they did their share of the heavy lifting in Helmand and Uruzgan provinces respectively. Our other European NATO allies were conspicuous by their absence in the violent southern provinces during the difficult years, but they are sure to come out from their hiding places and demand a place in any victory parade.

In either scenario, there is the possibility that Canada's accomplishments will be downplayed. That would be a grave injustice. Canadian soldiers have fought and continue to fight in Kandahar with as much tenacity as their forebears did at Vimy Ridge and at Juno Beach. It is essential that the names of Panjwayi, Zhari, Arghandab and Shah Wali Khot become as much a part of our nation's collective memory as those storied places.

That is the true goal of this book.

The Diary
May 31 to September 27, 2009

MAY 31 | Departure

Going to war, a second time. How did I feel on this day? A lot different from the first time.

The last time I went, my preparations were rushed and my emotions were completely focused on the task at hand. Like a lot of soldiers, I disconnected from my family before I left. I particularly did not attend to my daughter very much. Michelle was only two then and not very verbal. My civilian job often took me away from home for days at a time, and Michelle's lack of a sense of time seemed to protect her from any feelings of missing me. I thought the same thing would happen during my deployment. I was wrong. In the second week of that first tour my wife, Claude, found Michelle crying silently one night in bed. She asked her if she was crying because she missed her daddy, and Michelle nodded yes. It would not be the last time she cried during that tour.

As happens with a lot of men, my connection to my daughter deepened after she turned three and began to interact in what I considered a meaningful way. I knew Michelle would react even more negatively to my absence this time, so I took a number of steps in hopes of lessening her pain. The most helpful thing was purchasing a high-quality video camera to record myself reading bedtime stories for her. I spent the first minutes of my last day at home recording a few more.

I had been videotaping for about half an hour when Michelle woke up and came looking for me. This is her normal practice, as we both wake up earlier than Claude. Michelle and I will often spend an hour or more together in the mornings.

For a couple of months before my departure, our routine had been the same: I would put Michelle in a backpack and work out on our Stairmaster while we watched a movie. This was the only time that Claude and I would allow Michelle to watch TV, so she looked forward to our morning sessions quite a bit.

For the past several weeks, she always asked for the same movie: *Monsters, Inc.*, an animated film whose central plot revolves around a father-daughter relationship. Michelle quickly learned that DVDs can be controlled, and she would ask for her favourite segments to be played over and over. By far the part she liked best was the ending, a rousing chase scene where the father figure struggles to save his "daughter" from an evil monster. She never seemed to get enough of that.

This scene is followed by a sad one in which the father figure must leave his "daughter" behind. Every time we viewed this scene, I explained to Michelle that her daddy would soon have to go away as well, for "a lot of sleeps." I explained that it was okay to be sad and that Daddy was going to come back. She took this in very thoughtfully.

We had almost finished breakfast when Claude got up. Our conversation was cordial, with only a trace of the strain that had been all too evident before my previous tour of duty in 2007.

I was much more present for Claude in the period leading up to my deployment this time. I spent more time at home, and I tried to keep things as normal as possible. I never wore my uniform around the house, and I even let my hair grow longer. Most importantly, I remained emotionally focused on Claude as much as possible.

This is not to say that this deployment has been easier on her. What I am asking of Claude goes way beyond anything she imagined she would have to do when she entered into this relationship. Many of my friends have told me that their marriages would not have survived one combat deployment, much less a second.

I had finished packing the night before, so we were able to have a leisurely morning together as a family. But all too soon, it was time to put my bags in the car and head off. I spent one last minute looking around my neighbourhood before we left. Quiet, peaceful, prosperous. It seemed unbelievable that I was leaving this behind.

We first drove to my parents' home. Claude chose not to come in, partly to give my parents and me some time to ourselves, partly because she felt it would be stressful to watch me say goodbye to them. She was right—it was an awkward moment.

My father is one of only two true pacifists I have met in my life, individuals who would be incapable of harming another human being even if they were being attacked. We have discussed the various crimes of the Taliban, and he recognizes that they are horrible abusers of human rights. It does not follow for him that Canadians in general—and his son in particular—have to go to war to stop them.

As for my mother . . . well, she's a mom. Her spontaneous reaction, the first time I told her I was thinking of volunteering to go to Afghanistan, was: "If you do that, I'll shoot you myself!" Although I knew six months ago I would be going back, I did not tell my parents until four weeks ago. This time, my mother said: *"C'est une bêtise!"* ("That's really stupid!"). You could say that things are improving.

My mother's initial reaction—motivated by her concern about my safety—was replaced within minutes by unconditional support. During my last tour, she e-mailed me every day and her messages were invariably upbeat and encouraging. I drew strength and comfort from those e-mails, more than my mom will ever know. I have no doubt she will do the same thing this time.*

Addendum, back home after the tour: Sure enough, Mom came through big time. She wrote to me every day, expressing her support and pride. Those messages kept me going.

We had a brief discussion about the mission and my role in it. It ended with my mother telling me that she would always support me, no matter what I did, as long as I always came back. I promised that I would, both of us knowing full well that might be a promise I would be unable to keep.

By the time we got to the airport, there were only a few minutes left before boarding. There is nothing good about being at the airport in this situation, so it is best if it is short and over with quickly. Claude and I shared a few more hugs and I love yous and it was time to go. Michelle was happy as I said goodbye to her and hugged her. She did not even seem perturbed when she called out to me, after I had gone through security, that "Mommy's crying." From where I was standing, I could see that Claude's cheeks were dry. Michelle, sensitive as all children are to a parent's distress, had noticed her mother's shiny eyes. I replied to her that Mommy was crying because Daddy was going away for a lot of sleeps but that Daddy would come back. I repeated "Daddy will come back" at least four times.

After an uneventful flight to Toronto and a quick stop to get a regulation haircut, I called up a taxi company the army uses to ferry soldiers from Toronto to Canadian Forces Base (CFB) Trenton. You have almost certainly heard of this base, as it is also the place our fallen return: the "Highway of Heroes" leads from Trenton back to Toronto.

The ride to Trenton is a sombre one. You can't help but think of the Canadian soldiers whose return to Canada was followed by a trip down this road. You can't help but desperately wish you will not join them.

I got to Trenton in time for dinner. I reported in to the base accommodations (which were—by army standards—superb, like a good roadside motel), called Claude to let her know I had arrived, then went out for one last restaurant meal. I then went for a long walk by myself before turning in for the night. I tried to reflect on what I was doing, but I couldn't focus.

I have given so many presentations since returning from

Afghanistan that I am usually clear about why I am going back. But it is difficult to remember those motivations when I think about my wife crying, my daughter saying goodbye and the risks ahead.

I am going to war, again.

JUNE 1–2 | Getting to Kandahar: The Easy Way

My first flight from Canada to Kandahar had been a painful, prolonged and exhausting ordeal. Things were much better this time.

The trip began with a civilized wake-up at the unmilitarily congenial hour of eight o'clock. I threw on a pair of jeans and a T-shirt, revelling in my last chance to wear normal clothing. A short walk to the mess hall (cafeteria) next door was all that was needed to acquire breakfast. I then had to call a taxi to get from the sleeping quarters to the air terminal. And that's where the civilian part ended. Waiting for me in the terminal were several dozen other individuals with short hair and military packs.

The plane we boarded was a gigantic Airbus model, owned and operated by the Canadian Forces (CF). When we boarded—via the forward hatch—we were met with some extraordinary institutional insensitivity. What was in the first-class section for all to see? Generals in comfortable seats? Politicians with their entourage?

Stretchers.

These same planes ferry seriously wounded Canadian soldiers home from the tertiary care hospital in Germany to which they are evacuated if they cannot be treated at Kandahar Air Field (KAF). We were on the outbound flight, so the stretchers were empty. Yet seeing these stretchers was sobering. I'm sure the administrators who organize these flights only consider the aircraft layout in terms of seating availability. They have probably never been on the aircraft itself, so they have never thought that it would be easier for all concerned if passengers entered only from the rear of the aircraft. This is not because of any discomfort I or other Canadian soldiers feel at the sight of our wounded. Rather, it is out of a desire not to intrude on them when they are so vulnerable.

After a couple of hours, I got up to stretch my legs and ran into an air force nurse named Rhonda Crew. We had worked together for a few weeks at KAF in 2008, and she had impressed me with her competence and collegiality. She was also pretty gutsy: she had volunteered to fly on the medevac helicopters, landing on battlefields to pick up our wounded. She had even been under small-arms fire during several missions. This means that Taliban soldiers were shooting at her with rifles and machine guns from a distance of a few hundred metres. As I said, gutsy.

Rhonda was in charge of the medical evacuation component of these flights. She was on her way to Germany to pick up a couple of our guys. I commented on the layout of the aircraft, and she agreed that it was far from optimal.

We compared notes about our activities since we had last seen each other, and I got updates on friends we have in common. We were soon joined by the nurse and medic who made up the rest of the medevac team. As frequently happens in our small army (including reservists, the CF has fewer than 100,000 people in uniform), we all knew people in common. The medic had served on Roto 2 and had been on the scene when Glen Arnold and David Byers, two soldiers from my part of northern Ontario, were killed in 2006. The nurse had served in the 1990 Persian Gulf War with a doctor who had been my roommate at KAF during my first tour.

The stopover in Germany lasted an hour and a bit. We all piled into a special military waiting area graced with the presence of a Subway restaurant, where I got one last dose of North American junk food. Six hours later we landed at a small, isolated civilian airport in the "host nation," the Middle Eastern country that allows us to maintain a logistics base close to Afghanistan. After a short bus ride, we arrived at "Camp Mirage," our pseudo-secret base in the aforementioned host nation.

Before I racked out, I called home. I had promised to call every day. To make sure that I would be able to do so no matter what happened, I had bought my own global satellite phone. Voice communication with Canada, even from here, can be a little iffy. It was wonderful to be able to simply reach into my backpack and talk to my wife and daughter. Expensive, but worth it.

With things settled back at home (as much as they could be) I was able to focus on what was coming next. "Battlemind" preparation, getting oneself emotionally prepared for exposure to combat, is an essential process for any soldier to go through. I had done very little of this before departure, for a number of reasons. As a veteran, there was no need for me to repeat many parts of the training process I had gone through the first time. Although this allowed me to spend more time with my family, it cut me off from my military brethren.

The military flight had not contributed much to my preparation. The host nation is extremely sensitive about having Canadian soldiers on its soil, so the trip is done in civilian clothing. You don't feel very soldierly when you're unarmed and wearing jeans and a T-shirt. And upon landing in the Middle East, the pilot wishes good luck to those who are "going up north." No one seems to want to say "Afghanistan."

After I got settled into my room, I went for a walk around the base to try to "get my head in the game." Halfway around the world, alone and in the dark, having left a much-loved family behind and heading towards possible death or dismemberment, it can be hard to feel the clarity of purpose that was so strong a few months ago. The heart aches for peace and a soft, warm embrace.

JUNE 3 | Afghanistan Again

I woke up at 0900, dragged my gear over to the baggage loading area, then headed over to the weapons shack to draw my rifle, pistol and ammunition. This area is no longer a sea container but a real building; in the daylight I could see that the base had expanded considerably.

As we climbed aboard the Hercules, the transport gods (who had so cursed my last trip to KAF) smiled upon me yet again: the aircraft was only half full. There was ample room to stretch out. I tried hard not to sleep, to get over the jet lag quickly.

When we got to KAF, I went to the orderly room to get the routine in-clearance paperwork done.* I then reported to my company commander, Major Annie Bouchard, a little dynamo whom I had met during my pre-deployment phase.

Major Bouchard began by congratulating me on the impact that ultrasound has had on the ability of her medical company to provide cutting-edge emergency care. In the months before the company's doctors and physician assistants (PAs) deployed, I had given them a basic Emergency Department Echo (EDE)† course and conducted advanced training for three of them. I had also gotten the SonoSite company to donate (Yes, donate! For use in a war zone!) three brand-new systems for the duration of the rotation for use on the FOBs, or forward operating bases. The guys I trained have been making excellent use of this gear, detecting injuries that would have been missed otherwise.

Major Bouchard then briefed me on my mission. It's going to be a busy summer. A lot of enemy activity is expected, which we will do our best to counter. We will also continue to support reconstruction as much as possible. The "operational tempo" (military-talk for how hard we will be working) will be extremely high.

---

* The clerks who took care of my "in-processing" were razor sharp. The fact that they had processed my paperwork in a heartbeat already made them aces in my books. Then one of them, Master Seaman Carole Dubois, noticed that the danger and hardship bonuses I was entitled to in 2007–08 had not been paid. I'll be getting that on my paycheque next month!

† This is a course on ultrasound for emergency physicians that I designed in 2001. It has been given to over five thousand Canadian physicians since then, and has strongly influenced the way emergency medicine is practised in our country.

One thing hasn't changed: this is still a civil war, and it is still the Afghans who are enduring most of the suffering. Since the current rotation (Roto 7) began in late March, only one Canadian soldier has been killed: twenty-one-year-old Karine Blais, the second Canadian woman to die in combat in Afghanistan. Casualties among Afghan troops and Afghan civilians have been high.

Major Bouchard then said something that struck me as very odd. It seems that, at the FOBs, I will be treating Afghan casualties almost exclusively. The helicopter evacuation system has become much more efficient in the eighteen months since I was here last, and wounded Canadians are almost invariably picked up from the battlefield by air medevac. Helicopters have also changed the way non-medevac functions are accomplished. Since February of this year Canada has had its own helicopter squadron at KAF for transportation and air assault missions. We no longer depend on our allies to fly us around. This should have a positive impact on our casualty rate, since most of our deaths have occurred as a result of roadside bombs striking our vehicles.

The major adroitly anticipated my next question. The Afghan army and police, she said, can call for helicopter evacuation, but to date they have not been fully integrated into the Coalition communication network. If they are not accompanied by a Coalition mentor, communication with the medevac choppers is extremely arduous. It is therefore more efficient for the Afghan forces to load their wounded, and even their dead, into the back of a truck and bolt for the nearest FOB.

I also learned that I will be joining this war very soon: I head for my first FOB at dawn tomorrow. That being the case, I had to draw additional ammunition as well as a desert-pattern flak jacket this evening. The ammunition was no problem, but getting my flak jacket proved to be a challenge because the clothing store where these items are kept is run by civilians and closes at 1800, and it was well past 2100 when I arrived. The clothing store supervisor explained that it was inconceivable—inconceivable!—that he would wake up one of his people to allow me to get the gear I needed. We had to get Captain François Aziz-Beaulieu, one of the senior officers of the medical company, involved. Captain Aziz-Beaulieu, who can bark with the best of them, resolved the problem. It seems that not everybody here accepts that we are at war.*

With all my gear collected, I went back to my room to pack. I started by loading my rifle ammunition into the (many) additional magazines I had been given. My infantry background shows when I do this. At the top of the magazine I load a few ordinary bullets, to be fired off quickly if a firefight starts unexpectedly. This gives the enemy something to think about, and gives me something proactive to do. That helps to calm you down, even if the shots are only vaguely aimed. By the time those shots are away I hope to be in good cover, trying to locate the source of the enemy fire. Once I figure out precisely where the bad guys are, I want some tracer rounds ready to go to indicate to my comrades where the enemy is. Finally, I leave my mags slightly underfilled, because mags filled to capacity are more prone to jamming.

I finished loading my two backpacks with what I would need for the next four months: clothing (which, given the heat, is pretty limited), my laptop, my DVDs and some books. I learned during my previous tour that the boredom of the FOBs needs to be countered with more than movies. After the first month, I was desperate for something to read.

By midnight I was done, and I stepped outside to call home. I couldn't bring myself to tell Claude that I was headed outside the wire the next day. This meant that I could also avoid talking about the

---

* And yet the war has definitely touched KAF. The medical company headquarters was hit by a rocket a few weeks ago. It landed right outside the building, but it broke apart instead of detonating. The fuse flew through the sergeant-major's window, and the high-explosive warhead crashed through a wall. Far more seriously, another rocket detonated on the camp and seriously wounded two Coalition soldiers.

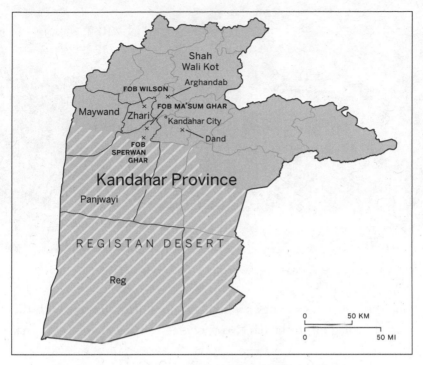

Afghanistan's Kandahar province, showing three Canadian FOBs

worst part of the next day's activities: I will be going by road rather than helicopter. There is a convoy headed to my first FOB, and it makes more sense to send me now than to wait for a helicopter. The helicopters are so occupied with medevacs and combat operations that routine KAF-to-FOB transfers are unpredictable. It is essential that I get to my first FOB to provide coverage, so I have to go tomorrow. I will be going with the Bison (armoured ambulance) crew from my FOB. They returned from vacation today and are headed out tomorrow.

Going down the roads of Zhari-Panjwayi, the threat of roadside bombs and ambushes are ever-present. The place where most Canadian deaths have occurred.

The worst thing you can do.

After Major Bouchard told me that, she sent me to get my picture taken. I went to pack my gear instead. The picture in question is the

Kandahar street scene: dilapidated building . . . with satellite dish*

one they show on the news when you are killed, the one with the Canadian flag off to the left. No way was I letting anyone take that picture.

JUNE 4 | Back to the FOB

I woke up at 0500 and spent the next half hour finishing my packing. The Bison crew arrived in front of my quarters half an hour later to pick me up. I jumped in the back and took my usual position in the right rear (starboard) "air sentry" hatch, and we drove off to the area where the convoy was being marshalled.

The pre-convoy briefing began with a description of enemy activity in the area we will be traversing. The briefer began with a map

---

* Under the Taliban, all manner of entertainment was banned, including television, movies, music, dancing, most sports and even kite flying. This last was particularly cruel, since it is historically the most popular activity among Afghan children, and one that can be done even by the very poor. Ironically, the Taliban now use kites as a means to communicate.

The view from Northeast Observation Post, looking south

indicating the locations where the Taliban had planted bombs or had sprung an ambush in the past week. I couldn't believe how much activity there had been between Kandahar City and the FOB. Things were not nearly this bad when I was here during Roto 4, a "winter tour." There has always been an increase in the fighting in Afghanistan in the summer, and it was clear that the "fighting season" was upon us.

There are a number of routes you can take to get to Zhari-Panjwayi from KAF. The one we chose took us through Kandahar City. This is a strange experience. You're driving through a city of a half-million people that looks like many other communities in the developing world. This should be a cultural experience to be savoured. But here you're riding in an armoured vehicle, part of a convoy bristling with heavy weapons. Every vehicle that crosses your path might contain several hundred kilograms of high explosive accompanied by an individual convinced that he will go to heaven if he blows himself up beside you. Your attention is focused on vehicles that are within fifty metres of your own. The city itself goes by in a blur.

Away from the city, the likelihood of suicide bombers decreases. That leaves the possibility of improvised explosive devices (IEDs) that are either remote controlled or wire controlled or that blow up when you drive or step on them. The correct term for this is VOIED—victim-operated improvised explosive device. I hate that term: it implies that it will be my own fault if I step on one of these things.

In the end, the trip was a quiet but nonetheless unpleasant drive.

At 1100 we arrived at the first FOB I will serve at: FOB Wilson. It lies at the northern edge of Zhari district and at about its east-west midpoint. It is the northernmost of our FOBS. It was named for Trooper Mark Wilson, who was killed in action near here on October 7, 2006.

FOB Wilson is the only FOB I did not serve at during my first tour. Its layout is striking: whereas our other FOBS are built on heights of land, Wilson is flat. It is a big square of Hesco Bastions (gigantic sandbags) plopped down in the desert. This explains why it has been hit by only two rockets in the past three years: it is difficult for these devastating but inaccurate weapons to hit a target that is flat on the ground.

This is not to say that the area around FOB Wilson is safe. Enemy activity is high, and one can watch Canadian and Afghan soldiers engage in close-quarters gun battles right outside the FOB's walls. IEDs have even been placed no more than a hundred metres from the main guard post. Be that as it may, life inside the FOB walls is quite safe. Everyone walks around in T-shirts—no helmets, no frag vests, no ballistic glasses. Things are a lot more relaxed than they were at either of the FOBS I served at in 2007–08.

As for creature comforts, things have improved considerably since my first tour. We get two hot meals a day, breakfast and supper, served in a wide-open area with handwashing stations that make it easy to be hygienic. At lunch, the cooks lay out all kinds of salads, cold cuts and warmed-up leftovers from the previous night's meal. The grub is fantastic. No more ration packs!

There are two "shower cans," each with *three* washing machines and dryers! No more washing by hand!

"Triple-7" in action

We have the same kind of communications shack I remembered from FOB Ma'Sum Ghar last time, with three Internet connections (mostly reliable) and three phones (somewhat reliable).

Right beside the Internet shack we have an amazing gym. It is named "Greener's Gym" in honour of Sapper* Sean Greenfield, who was killed in action on January 31 of this year. There had been a gym at the first FOB I served at in 2007, but it was a dark, dusty place with only a small amount of gear. I think I went twice before deciding that pumping iron in that place was too depressing.

And get this. There is also a "Rock House," a wooden structure the size of a large room with a climbing wall on the outside and a music studio on the inside.

In the UMS, the unit medical station, we have a wall of munchies, a large coffee maker (permanently filled), a toaster, a microwave oven and a fridge. And outside we have a large freezer, filled with water bottles that have been frozen—ice in the desert!

---

* The equivalent of a private in the combat engineers.

Instead of being in a bunker with five guys, I am in a "sea can" that has three curtained-off "rooms" and a central area that serves as an office. My bed has a mattress (no canvas cot!) and my "room" has an air conditioner.

The FOB is home to a combat team centred on a company of infantry, Bravo Company of the Second Battalion of the Royal 22nd Regiment, the "Van Doos"—the same French Canadian outfit I spent most of my tour with last time. They left for an operation this morning, so the base is deserted.

The only downside of living at FOB Wilson is that the M777 155 mm cannons are located less than a hundred metres from my quarters. They often have to fire right over my shack. This isn't dangerous, but the noise and the concussion wave of the shot makes sleeping pretty much impossible.

The cannons can't fire very close to the FOB—even with a minimum of propellant, the shells go too far. For close-in bombardment, the artillery has some 81 mm mortars. These weapons "arc" their bombs, making it possible for them to hit targets that are very close.

"The guns" (as everyone refers to the artillery) were busy today. Before the day was out, they would fire over eighty rounds in support of Bravo Company's operations in the Panjwayi. This was one of the largest "fire missions" executed by Canadians since arriving in Afghanistan. The combat team had encountered an unusually high number of enemy while they were on foot and away from their vehicles. They had used the artillery to blast a path back to their "leager."* After eight years of war, it is disappointing that there are still so many Taliban targets to shoot at—another disturbing indicator that things are not going as well as we would like.

But as badly as things might be going, I learned two things at the

---

* An area in flat, open terrain where the vehicles of the combat team will set up in a rough circle, with the heavy guns of the vehicles facing outwards, much like the wagon trains of old.

end of the day that convinced me we are doing the right thing here. Two things that got my battlemind to where it needed to be.

First, on the national scale. In 2007, the Taliban burnt or blew up 130 schools in Afghanistan, while forcing another 300 to close by threatening the teachers. They also murdered at least 105 students and teachers. Convinced of the correctness of this course of action, they have continued in the same vein since then.

If you look at everything written about Afghanistan in the news, you can catch a glimpse of this,* but it is something else to get a briefing that shows you, on a local map, all the schools that have been destroyed.

Locally, I learned that there is an Afghan medical clinic within sight of the FOB. This is the last functioning clinic in the area. Four others farther away have closed their doors because of Taliban threats. Apart from this last clinic and our UMS, there are no health care facilities of any kind in Zhari district. This does not seem to matter to our enemies.

Regardless of the challenges, regardless of mistakes we may have made, whatever our chances of success, Canada is in the right place. I am in the right place.

I am here to help defeat the Taliban. Let's get on with it.

Addendum, June 9: Major Bouchard, ever mindful of the morale of the people in her company, called me tonight to see how I was doing. She asked how I was getting along with "the bayonets," the slightly derogatory term used by the medical services to refer to the combat arms. I answered that I was getting along with them quite well, and I left it at that.

If I had known her better, I would have told her that I felt I was back with my brothers, and that I saw myself more as one of them than as a member of the health services. I am a bayonet.

---

* For example, "Battle for Afghanistan a Fight for Young Minds," *The Globe and Mail,* May 25, 2009.

Battlemind set—good to go

JUNE 5 | The Shop

Another night of lousy sleep, thanks to artillery fire over my head during the night and the first call to Muslim prayers from the Afghan National Army (ANA) compound ten metres away at 0430 (first light). I take over as FOB Wilson medical officer today—time to go to work.

The UMS is across the street from my quarters. There is also a four-stretcher tent close to it that can hold four more minor casualties. All told, the UMS can handle three times more patients than it could in 2007.

As a doctor, my first reflex was to be pleased with the improvements. I have spent a good part of my career in Canada pleading for more resources for emergency medicine, so I was chuffed to see that I would have more of everything with which to do my job than I'd had during my previous tour.

The FOB Wilson UMS

As a soldier, though, I was troubled. Those with access to far more information than I, our leaders and decision makers, believe that we are going to need these resources to care for a larger number of wounded. It seemed the major's briefing two nights ago was bang on.

The UMS itself shows the effects of the lessons learned over three years of warfare in Kandahar province. Again, I was pleased to see that many of the recommendations I made after my last tour have been put into effect. The place functions like a small community emergency department in Canada onto which the resuscitation area of a Level 1 trauma centre has been grafted. The specialized medications and gear that I'd had to request for myself last time are already in place. The military medical staff may not be familiar with all this stuff, but at least it is here. This makes me as functional as possible, and it will give me the chance to do a bit of teaching with the person I am replacing.

The communications have vastly improved. We now have e-mail right in the UMS, a land line to the key places on the camp (command post, district centre, etc.), and a phone that can make a call to KAF or Canada as easily as a call across town back home. We also have secure communication devices that allow us to monitor what is going on with the units in the field so that we can anticipate their medical requirements. And my desk has drawers! We had none of this on Roto 4.

Wounded Afghans—who so far have represented 100 per cent of the casualties treated here—arrive via the main gate, regardless of whether they are military, police or civilian. This places them close to the UMS. Since they almost invariably arrive by vehicle, the warning call we get from the gate coincides with the arrival of the patients at the UMS door. For some reason, the Afghan soldiers and police rarely use their radios to alert the FOB of the arrival of their wounded.

It is therefore not unusual for a load of casualties to arrive at the doors of the UMS with very little warning. This is not unlike what I have been dealing with in emergency medicine for over a decade now, and it is something I have had a lot of experience with in the developing world. The worst MasCal (mass casualty) incident I ever dealt with occurred during the Nicaraguan Contra War and involved eighty patients, worse than anything Canadians have had to deal with in Afghanistan.

Rather unusually, the FOB had been covered for the past few weeks by a doctor, rather than by a PA. She has had additional training to prepare her for the trauma patients who dominate the caseload here, but she remains what the army calls a general duty medical officer, an office-based general practitioner.

The arrival of unscheduled patients was something she seemed to have found very surprising. She kept repeating over and over, "Patients will just show up!" as if to warn me of the probability of these anomalous events. I tried to reassure her that I had lived through these events many times before. As an emergency specialist, that is what my career entails: if bad things happen to people unexpectedly, I want to be there to take care of them.

Let me now introduce the crew of the Bison armoured ambulance based here.*

Master Corporal Nick Beaulieu (centre in the following photograph) is the crew commander. At the age of forty-one, Nick should be much further along in terms of rank. He is not lacking in courage—he still goes out on foot patrols when the combat units are short a medic—but he is one of those guys who is more comfortable with less responsibility and therefore less authority. You get the impression he has almost engineered various disciplinary incidents—some of them quite funny—so that he will not be promoted.†

The driver (left) is twenty-three-year-old Corporal Pierre Yves ("P.Y.") Lavoie. P.Y. is on his second tour in Afghanistan, having been a convoy driver during Roto 4. P.Y. went down the roads of Zhari-Panjwayi—what I said yesterday was "the worst thing you can do"—almost every day for six months. He signed up for this tour two months before it was scheduled to go. Although he had never driven a Bison before, he quickly mastered the vehicle. He seems to be a natural around heavy machinery.

The Bison medic is twenty-nine-year-old Private Dominic Vaillancourt-Larose (even he laughs about the length of that surname). Like all our medics, he is extraordinarily competent when it comes to caring for a trauma victim. Dominic is also one of the most eager learners I have ever met in medicine: he is constantly asking me questions. There is also a medic assigned to the UMS proper, but he will

---

* My work brought me into close daily contact with the CF medical personnel of the FOBS I served at. Since these characters reappear regularly, I've placed descriptions of them at the beginning of each section, even though these words were written several weeks later, after I had gotten to know them well.

† *Postscript, July 27:* Nick has kept up with his antics on this tour. He recently shot the FOB Wilson UMS fridge, mortally wounding a diet Coke, two pineapple yogurts and a litre of milk. The CF takes a pretty dim view of "accidental discharges." Although the consequences were humorous, they could have been far worse.

The FOB Wilson Bison crew

not arrive for another week. Currently, that position is filled by Master Corporal Sylvie Guay.

Only one trauma patient today. An Afghan convoy guard was shot through the top of his foot. Through-and-through, no major damage, but ultrasound confirmed a fracture of one of his metatarsals (the bones that connect the toes to the foot), so I sent him to KAF for an orthopedic consultation. The helicopter arrived to take him away within thirty minutes. Cool!

There's another positive aspect about being assigned to the FOB Wilson UMS. During my last roto, a Taliban rocket detonated about two metres from the UMS. The two medics inside were very fortunate: they survived with minor injuries.

I like to think that this makes it unlikely the UMS will get hit by another rocket while I am here. Statistically, that is incorrect. The odds of a rocket strike on a particular spot are always exactly the same, regardless of where one hit before.

In a war zone, superstition trumps statistics.

The jet lag was still beating me up this morning, and after a couple of hours I collapsed back into bed. The UMS is only ten metres from my shack, but I brought the UMS radio with me so that I would be immediately available. Emergency physicians never stray from their resuscitation area when they are on duty. And I am on duty here 24/7.

That turned out to be a good move: as I was entering REM sleep, Master Corporal Guay radioed that I was needed immediately. I staggered over and was still prying my eyes open when I came to the door of the UMS. Inside, I was confronted with something that is all too common in this war. Two children, one of them eight years old and the other one in his mid-teens, had set off a Taliban IED. They were "collateral damage," a horrible term that tries to gloss over the fact that civilians are often killed and maimed in war.

The younger child had been hit by a half-dozen small pieces of gravel that had been thrown off by the explosion. His wounds were trivial, but he was very upset. Like most children who go through such events, all he needed was to sleep in the arms of someone who cared for him.

The older child was far worse off. The detonation had taken place no more than three metres from him. From the pattern of his injuries, it seemed that the mine had been placed in a soft plastic container. (Plastic jugs, not unlike the things you see at campgrounds in Canada, are used by the Taliban to store their explosives.) I drew this conclusion because the patient was shredded from his groin down to his calf on both sides, but there were none of the amputations or deep penetrations that occur when the explosive is encased in metal.

About a third of the soft tissue on both legs had been lost, giving the limbs the appearance of raw, bloody hamburger. The nerves remained at least partially intact; the patient was still moving both his limbs, although not purposefully. His abdomen and chest were untouched, but his face looked like it had been sandblasted. Both corneas were coated with grains of sand that had been forced into the tissue. His eyes must have been open when the blast occurred.

He was still breathing on his own, but he was semi-conscious, barely moaning when I tried to stimulate him by rubbing hard with my knuckles on his breastbone. He was also in shock: we could detect a pulse in his neck, but not in his wrist or in his groin. This meant that his blood pressure was somewhere around 70/nothing.

We proceeded with a straightforward resuscitation. We started two IVs, one on each arm, and gave the patient large amounts of fluids to bring his blood pressure back up. Meanwhile we prepared him for evacuation. Both his legs were swathed in pressure bandages and we administered two medications, etomidate to put him to sleep and rocuronium to paralyze him. Intubating—putting a breathing tube from the mouth down into the lungs so that we can take over breathing for the patient—can make patients vomit. If this happens when they are semi-conscious or unconscious, the vomit can be sucked into the lungs and choke them to death. Paralyzing the patient makes it far less likely that this will happen because the stomach can no longer contract and expel its contents back up into the throat.

The destination for this patient was none other than Camp Hero, an Afghan army hospital that opened its doors in February 2008 and at which I had done some teaching on my last tour. It is functioning at a high level now and is accepting a large proportion of the Afghan civilian and military casualties.

Addendum, June 7: The teenager is dead. No life-threatening injuries were missed; he had spent too long in shock before getting to us. This delay damaged the internal organs, notably the liver and kidneys, so badly that the patient died even though his injuries had been repaired and his lost blood had been replaced.

Events like these are so common as to be barely worth mentioning. The Taliban do not hesitate to plant their weapons in populated areas because they know our patrols go there to interact with the locals. Most civilian casualties in this war are caused by these incidents.

Remember that when you hear about American air strikes going astray. Yes, these incidents are tragic. They need to be investigated, and we need to do a better job to reduce these casualties. But when Afghan civilians are hurt by Coalition weapons, it is because we screwed up. When they are hurt by Taliban weapons, it is a direct and predictable result of intentional Taliban tactics.

JUNE 8 | Every Body Goes Home

It could have been a lot worse.

One of the platoons of Bravo Company, the company based at my FOB, had been clearing a dirt road, searching for IEDs. The four troopers who were leading the advance had come to an intersection. The road running to the left had mud brick walls on either side. Another wall of similar construction ran along the left side of the road leading straight ahead.

Three walls needing to be cleared, four troopers. The trooper in charge directed one of his men to start clearing the left-hand side of the side road while he sent the other two to the other side. Once there, these two split up. One headed farther down the main road, following the wall on the left side. The other one, Private Alexandre Peloquin, took the right-hand side on the side road and started moving away from the intersection.

He had not gone far when the IED detonated—but far enough that his partner was shielded from the blast. The trooper supervising the team from the other side of the road was knocked off his feet and temporarily lost his hearing, but was otherwise unhurt.

His buddies rushed to Private Peloquin's side and started administering first aid. They were joined in less than a minute by the platoon medic, who did a superb job. But Private Peloquin's injuries were devastating. Every part of his body that had not been covered by the fragmentation vest was torn apart. He was a big man, and very strong, but he lost consciousness almost immediately and died soon after.

This is the first fatality for this FOB and this company, and everyone is taking it pretty hard. Nothing can prepare you for this, not even having gone through it several times before. Unfortunately, I am not in a position to help the troops very much. As I am the "new guy" on the FOB, it would be awkward to reach out to them. For their part, the soldiers are unlikely to seek me out for support unless they are severely affected.

Our jobs as battlefield medical personnel did not end with the evacuation of the victim. We had one more important task to accomplish. Last December, Warrant Officer Gaëtan Roberge of Hanmer (a small village in Greater Sudbury) was killed by a roadside bomb. As with Private Peloquin, he suffered devastating injuries, including the loss of an arm. The soldiers with him that day, under enemy fire, had focused on trying to save their comrade and, failing that, extracting his body. We will never know for certain if the missing limb was vaporized, which seems likely, or thrown far away. Either way, the arm never made it home.

Warrant Roberge's parents found this very hard to accept, and complained bitterly about it in a front-page story in the *Sudbury Star*. This was noticed by the CF, which tries to do the best that can be done for casualties and their families. It is now standard operating procedure to ensure that all human remains are collected. The combat team commander and the medics made sure, personally, that this was done.

Sounds grim, doesn't it? It was. But by the time Private Peloquin gets on the Hercules, he will be whole.

Through the ages and in all cultures, there are stories of soldiers taking insane risks and sometimes even losing their lives to retrieve the bodies of their comrades from the battlefield. "Everybody goes home" is part of the soldier's code. We are taking it one step further.

Every body goes home.

JUNE 9 | Pashtunwali

Some of the injuries I treated today were due to local societal norms, so this is a good time to delve into the subject of tribal society.

Most of the population of southern Afghanistan belongs to the Pashtun tribe. This is the largest tribe in Afghanistan, comprising some 42 per cent of the country's population. Because the Taliban are drawn almost exclusively from this tribe, some Canadians believe the tribe is opposed to us. This is incorrect: most Pashtuns oppose the Taliban to varying degrees, often with very good reason. The current president of Afghanistan, Hamid Karzai, is a Pashtun who fought the Taliban for years before 9/11. Like so many of his countrymen, he too had a family member murdered by the Taliban, in this case his father.

The Pashtuns live by a strict tribal code of honour and behaviour called Pashtunwali. There are three key elements in Pashtunwali, the first two of which are closely related. *Melmastia* refers to the obligation to extend hospitality to anyone who arrives in one's home. Pashtuns will deprive their own family of basic nutrition to be able to provide a meal to the visitor. Closely related to *melmastia* is *nanawati*, which mandates that hospitality can never be denied to any fugitive.

Afghanistan's geography has had a large role to play in this. Since the time of Alexander the Great, this area has been transited by invading armies. No one cared about Afghanistan per se. The country is mostly rocks and desert—only about 20 per cent of its land mass is arable. It is the topography of the region—the high mountain ranges of the Himalayas and the Karakoram and the deserts of what is now southern Afghanistan and southwestern Pakistan—that has funnelled invaders through here as they headed somewhere else. Depending on which way they were going, these invaders sought to reach the wealth of the Middle East, the markets of Central Asia or the ports of the Indian Ocean. Several empires were built on any one of these prizes, and those same empires often tried to conquer the other two. An area that spent most of its time dealing with foreign invaders developed a social code that supported anyone who was fleeing, since the chance that they were fleeing a common oppressor was high.

But since good-news stories never have much traction, the existence of *melmastia* and *nanawati* are relatively unknown outside of

Afghanistan. And since violence gets you on the evening news, a lot more people have heard about the third component of Pashtunwali: *badal*—the right of revenge.

The tribe takes this so seriously that it is not an exaggeration to say that crossing a Pashtun is one of the unhealthiest things you can do on this planet. There is even an ancient Hindu incantation to the gods, asking to be saved from various natural disasters and one human one: "The revenge of the Afghan."

You might think that this cannot bode well for any kind of national reconciliation after so many years of civil war, but armed conflict between large groups doesn't seem to trigger an intense need for *badal*.

To really make a Pashtun crazy, you have to go after his *zar* (gold), *zan* (women) or *zamin* (land). Then you have a blood feud on your hands. In every reference I have read on the subject, the order of these three is always the same: *zar, zan, zamin*. First gold, then women, then land. You can infer from that what you will.

On to today's medical misadventures. Two young men arrived with stab wounds. One had a single wound to his upper arm which, though it was squirting arterial blood, was easy to control and to bandage. The other one had three small wounds in his upper back. One of these wounds was trivial, but the other two—one on each side of the chest a few centimetres below the shoulder blade—proved to be quite deep.

A quick look with ultrasound determined that the patient had a pneumothorax, popularly called a "collapsed lung," on the left. In this situation, air has escaped from the lung and gone into the chest cavity. This air does not move in and out of the body with respiration, and as it accumulates it can exert so much pressure that the lung can no longer expand—hence "collapsed lung." This is a Bad Thing: the patient's oxygen saturation (a test that allows us to determine how well the lungs are functioning) was worrisomely low.

The treatment for this condition is to make a small hole above the fifth rib, in line with the middle of the armpit, and to insert a plastic tube into the chest cavity to allow the trapped air to escape. I punched through the chest wall and was rewarded with a satisfying "hiss" of pressurized air escaping. The patient's oxygen saturation improved.

I then switched the probes on the ultrasound machine to look for bleeding in the chest and in the abdomen. The abdomen was fine. There was bleeding in the left chest, but I already knew that—it was coming out of the chest tube on that side. I discovered that there was also bleeding on the right, caused by the stab wound on that side of the chest. Blood can do the same thing as air: if too much of it accumulates in the chest cavity, it can also collapse the lung and provoke the same kind of breathing problems. So I zipped a second chest tube into him and managed to secure it as the medevac helicopter landed.

Lots of blood, lots of life-saving procedures, everybody alive at the end. The perfect emergency medicine interaction!

The unique aspect of the case was the "mechanism of injury." It turns out that the two patients are cousins. They live in one of the ubiquitous mud brick dwellings that house most of the population here in the hinterland. These structures, called "compounds," are designed with Afghan history in mind: a country constantly at war prepares for defence in even the most mundane of circumstances. Each compound resembles a small fort. The walls are thick enough to stop even a modern rifle bullet, and there is often a well in the centre of the compound. Add some food and ammunition, and you are ready for a siege.

Back to our story about the cousins. The compound they live in has two doors, one on the front and one on the side. Persons exiting from the side door are in a position to look into the neighbour's backyard for a few seconds before they turn a corner. As said neighbour is unable to afford a high enough wall around his yard, there is the possibility that his women will be seen by someone exiting from the side door. These women would be in full burka, but would be unaccompanied by a male relative.

This was unacceptable to the owner of the house in question. He had warned the cousins that exiting through their side door was

View of several Afghan family compounds
(Photo courtesy Master Corporal Julien Ricard)

Close-up of corner of compound (the well is visible)

Graduation day

intolerable to him. This intervention failed to achieve the desired result: the cousins kept exiting via their side door. Their neighbour then took things to what was, for him, the next logical step: physical violence, with at least the possibility of killing the target.

This kind of behaviour will have to be moderated if Afghanistan is to evolve. While a functioning government and legal system, backed up by a professional police force, will help, the lasting solution is education. Far more than any legal means or coercive system, it is education that rids humans of their baser instincts.

More precisely, we must focus on the education of women. Those of us involved in developing-world work have known for decades that the highest return on investment comes from educating women. It is much more likely that the skills acquired will remain close to the family and village of the person receiving the training.

Addendum, October 15: Under the Taliban, there were 600,000 students and 1,500 schools in Afghanistan. In 2007, those numbers were 6 million students and 9,000 schools. Despite the Taliban's out-and-out war on the educational system, that system has grown by leaps and bounds: in 2009, there were 8 million Afghan children in school.

JUNE 10 | The Contractor

There is a man here who could be said to be performing both the oldest and the newest function in warfare. Let's call him "the contractor." In reality, the contractor is a composite of a few different people who are doing the same job. I have commingled them to protect their anonymity.

The contractor is a Canadian who has had extensive military experience in the CF, both in Canada and on various deployments. He was approached by a fellow veteran and asked to return to Afghanistan to work for a private security company. He agreed. For all intents and purposes, he is a mercenary, a soldier for hire.

The Iraq war saw the advent of companies that, for a hefty fee, would take over functions that previously had been the sole purview of the military. These included perimeter defence of bases, escorting supply convoys and even limited, but nonetheless aggressive, patrolling. The rationale was that these companies could provide additional manpower right away. No need for the military's recruitment and training cycle, no benefits or pensions to pay during and after the individual's employment.

The behaviour of these companies has been controversial. Thanks to a statute rammed through by Paul Bremmer when he was the "administrator" of Iraq,* employees of these organizations are not subject to Iraqi law. The problems caused by granting this immunity

---

* This was essentially a vice-regal position—Paul Bremmer's authority in Iraq was absolute, and he answered only to President George W. Bush.

came to the fore on September 16, 2007, when employees of the Blackwater company (now re-incorporated under the name of Xe) who were escorting a convoy through Nisoor Square in downtown Baghdad shot and killed seventeen Iraqi civilians. The Blackwater men claimed they thought they were under attack. They were mistaken. The incident was investigated by the FBI, which found that at least fourteen of the dead were innocent Iraqi bystanders. Despite this, none of the Blackwater employees have faced criminal charges for this incident (though a civil suit is ongoing).

A number of these companies are now active in Afghanistan, including the Canadian entry into the market, the company that employs the contractor. He has sixty-three men under his command, most of them ANA veterans who have been attracted to this job by the higher pay.

The contractor's men take care of the "perimeter defence" of the FOB. This means they have the relatively easy job of protecting the base from attack. They staff various observation posts along the FOB walls twenty-four hours a day. These are strong defensive structures, with excellent fields of fire that are constantly illuminated. Thus the tedious guard post duty is removed from the list of chores our soldiers have to perform while on the FOB. If we ever face more than harassing fire on our walls, the Canadians will join the contractor's men in repelling the attackers.

I asked the contractor the obvious question: if the Canadian Army is willing to pay these individuals more than Afghan soldiers receive, why not give the same amount of money to the Afghan government to fund the training of more soldiers? This would enhance the links between the population and the government by providing more government jobs while giving us closer control over these individuals.

The answer I got was quite reasonable. The contractor maintained that many of these individuals do not want to join the army, even for better pay, for any number of reasons. The private security company therefore gives us access to men who would otherwise be unavailable.

The presence of these men on the gates of the FOB frees up far better trained and equipped Canadian soldiers to go outside the FOB and take the fight to the Taliban.

There is no question this is useful. We do not have enough soldiers to patrol all of Zhari-Panjwayi while defending our FOBs and outposts. Either we hire this company or we sit in our FOBs and let the Taliban run riot.

So it makes sense. Nonetheless, there is something disquieting about the concept of privatizing war. Although I can't quite articulate why, I think that nations need to take responsibility for everything that happens when they decide to participate in an armed conflict. Putting some of the people armed by the state in a legal environment that is removed from military discipline doesn't seem right. I am sure these companies would claim they are not "armed by the state," but that would be a meaningless splitting of philosophical hairs. The state allows them to be armed and is their only employer.

The first Baron de Rothschild said, "When there is blood in the streets, buy property." Cynical, yes, but he was stating an eternal truth: there is money to be made during wars. In its purest expression, that money is made by men who are willing to soldier for a fee. Until their most recent incarnation as organized, for-profit companies, mercenaries always joined a national army. They fought, albeit for cash rather than for ideals, under the command of an existing military structure. What we are doing now separates the mercenary from the army he is serving.

JUNE 11 | The Things I Miss, the Things I Enjoy

Today is Michelle's fourth birthday. Although we celebrated it a few days before I left, it is still the first important family event I will miss on this rotation.

I can't help but wonder what the long-term effect of this absence will be on my daughter. I plan to cut back on my professional activities for several months after I return from this mission, to try to make up for my time away. I worry that that will not be enough.

As much as Michelle's future emotional well-being concerns me, I didn't have much time to think about it today. FOB Wilson sits astride Ring Road South, the main highway that runs the length of the northern edge of Zhari district. This road links Kandahar City with the district of Maywand (farthest west in Kandahar province) and Helmand province even farther to the west.

Supply convoys travel down this road to get to the Coalition outposts in the western part of the district and in Helmand province. These convoys are run by private Afghan companies that hire armed guards to ride shotgun on their vehicles. These guards, and the drivers they are meant to protect, provide the FOB Wilson UMS with a large proportion of its patients. The Taliban attack these convoys almost daily.

Today there were attacks on two separate convoys. Two critically injured men were sent in from the first attack. One of them had received a large piece of shrapnel in his lower left abdomen and arrived with very low blood pressure. A part of his bowel was hanging out of his body. He was barely responsive. A quick physical exam assisted by ultrasound confirmed that he had no other injuries and that there was serious bleeding in his abdomen. It is impossible to control this bleeding in the field, so it was urgent to get him evacuated to a surgical facility. My priorities were to get IV lines started to bring his blood pressure up with fluids, but only a little. If a bleeding site cannot be controlled by direct pressure, as is the case in the chest and abdomen, it is unwise to bring the blood pressure up higher than is needed for a safe transfer. We achieved this quickly; the medics here are slick at starting IVs.

Although this man was now stable in the cardiovascular sense (his blood pressure was okay), his diminished level of consciousness made it essential that I protect his airway before the medevac took place. The danger was that he would choke on his tongue or vomit into his lungs during the helicopter ride.

His intubation was delayed, however, by the arrival of the second patient. This man was alert and oriented and had normal vital signs, but he had been shot in the middle of his throat. The bullet had travelled down and to the right, exiting to the right side of his right shoulder blade. Ultrasound examination showed that there was bleeding into his chest cavity, so we prepared to place a chest tube. But it was the neck injury that needed attention first.

The danger was that one of the arteries in that part of the body had been partially cut. If this artery ruptures, a hematoma (large blood collection) can accumulate so quickly that the patient's airway is crushed. When this occurs, it is no longer possible to pass a tube from the mouth into the lungs. As much as I wanted to secure the airway of the other patient expeditiously, I intubated this man first. Once he was under general anaesthesia, I was able to put the chest tube in very easily. This drained off the blood that had been accumulating in his chest cavity, preventing it from collapsing his lung.

I then returned to the first patient. Dominic the Medic had cleaned off the extruded bowel and replaced it in the man's abdomen, then bandaged the wound. The patient's level of consciousness was still diminished, so I proceeded with the intubation I had planned for him.

We had just gotten these two patients loaded onto the medevac helicopter when another casualty reached us from the second convoy attack. He also had a gunshot wound to the chest, and ultrasound confirmed blood and air in his chest cavity. He also got a chest tube. We called for yet another helicopter, and he was away in less than twenty minutes.

My medic team performed admirably throughout this period, and I felt as well surrounded as I am in the Level 1 trauma centres I have practised in back home. This was all the more impressive because this group had not been led by an emergency specialist prior to my arrival. They had to work more quickly and more intricately than before. Master Corporal Guay, for instance, had seen chest tubes placed during her few weeks at the FOB, but never under sterile technique. She immediately understood that this additional step would help to achieve the best outcome and figured out how to assist me with the procedure.

Later in the day I called Lieutenant Colonel Ron Wojtyk, the highest-ranking doctor of the task force, to ask after my patients. Ron, who is a visionary physician, had been a student of mine on a couple of emergency ultrasound courses before we deployed. He is quite senior to me in rank, but we are close in age and careers and we have become good friends. He informed me that my patients had fared well. Two of them had required emergency surgery, but both were now on a regular ward. They will all be going home in a week or so.

Ron then asked me what I thought of the day. I replied that it had been very satisfying. Again, lots of blood and lots of life-saving procedures, everybody alive and doing well at the end. It had been pure emergency medicine, and it doesn't get any better than that.

JUNE 12 | Political Science Lesson (or, Not Much Going On)

To understand what is going on in Afghanistan, it is necessary to understand another country: Pakistan. The fates of both nations are inextricably linked.

Let's start with a bit of geography, since politics so often derives from the land. I mentioned earlier that the Taliban are almost exclusively drawn from the Pashtun tribe of southern Afghanistan. But while it is true that most Afghans living in the south are Pashtuns, it is not true that most Pashtuns are Afghans. The legacy of colonialism here, as in so many places, has split a tribe between two countries.

All through the 1800s, Great Britain and Russia vied for influence in Central Asia (roughly present-day Iran, Afghanistan, Turkmenistan, Uzbekistan, Tajikistan, Kyrgyzstan, Kazakhstan and Pakistan). Occasionally they would invade, but more often they would try to establish alliances with local warlords through bribes of money, weapons or other inducements. This went back and forth in what came to be called "the Great Game."

Warlords controlled one main city and the surrounding country-side. By the mid-1800s, the territory that would be roughly recognized as present-day Afghanistan came to be controlled by a single king-like entity, an emir. The British wanted to demarcate where Afghanistan ended and where their own colony of India began. Sir Mortimer Durand, at the time the foreign secretary of the British Indian government, mapped out the line that to this day is the border between the two countries. The only difference is that, in 1947, the Muslim part of India became Pakistan. So the Durand Line is now the border between Afghanistan and Pakistan. The problem is that the Durand Line followed physical features such as rivers or watersheds. In doing so, it divided the Pashtun tribe.

Afghanistan's government, long dominated by Pashtuns, has never recognized the Durand Line. The tribe longs to be reunited in a "Greater Pashtunistan." One could argue that Pashtunistan already exists. Pakistan has never exerted much influence or control over those of its provinces that lie next to Afghanistan. The border is a non-entity, and Pashtuns pass effortlessly in both directions.

This state of affairs served Pakistan and the United States well during the Russian occupation of Afghanistan. The Pashtun provinces of Pakistan were training grounds, rest areas and logistics bases for the mujahedeen fighters who were being armed by the CIA. The situation in Afghanistan today stems in large part from the different goals held by America and Pakistan in the war against the Russians.

The Americans wanted the Russians to hemorrhage blood and treasure. This was done out of revenge for their losses in Vietnam. Russia invaded Afghanistan less than five years after the Vietnam War had ended. America's sixty thousand dead, many of them killed by weapons supplied by Russia, still constituted a raw wound in the American psyche. It was only much later, when the Afghans began to inflict serious damage on the Red Army, that the Americans began to think of this as a proxy war they could win.

When the war was won and the last Russian soldier had left, the Americans lost interest in Afghanistan. They had won a skirmish in the Cold War. That war was ongoing, and their attention turned to where they thought the next battles would take place. No one was predicting that within two years the stresses caused by Russia's defeat here would provoke the disintegration of the Soviet Union.

Pakistan's goals were radically different. With CIA money, Pakistan was training and advising the Afghans as they prosecuted all-out war against the Russians. As Muslims, most Pakistanis had no love for the atheist communists and it suited them to help their co-religionists. The war raging to the west also served to better prepare them to confront the far more serious enemy they faced to the east: India.

Since India and Pakistan's independence, there have been three full-blown wars and countless skirmishes between these two countries. But whereas India sees Pakistan as a constant irritant, Pakistan sees India as an existential threat. A glance at the map explains why: India is gigantic. You may think of it as a Third World nation, but that would be inaccurate. It is the regional superpower. Its economy dwarfs that of Pakistan, it has five times Pakistan's population and its army is much larger and better equipped.

The Pakistani army, on its best day, could never do more than conduct raids into Indian territory. The Indian army, on the other hand, has a large number of tanks and troops massed across the border at Pakistan's midpoint. As the bomber flies or the tank drives, it is two- to three-hundred kilometres to the Afghan border. If Indian troops capture that central part of Pakistan, they will cut the country in half. The capital, Islamabad, would be cut off from the port of Karachi, the economic hub of the country. Pakistan would disintegrate.

This equation changed in 1997 when both countries became nuclear-armed (each detonated five warheads that year), but old habits die hard. Pakistan's fear of invasion remains the same, even though it can now inflict such damage on India that New Delhi would never order such an attack.

This fear dictated Pakistan's goal during the Afghans' war against the Russians and in the civil war that followed: to establish a friendly government in Afghanistan that would give Pakistan "strategic depth,"

In theory, Afghanistan would serve as a backstop for Pakistan, allowing the Pakistani army to continue to retreat westward in the face of the Indian onslaught. This would give the Pakistani army time to regroup and counterattack while leaving the Indian army at the end of a long and vulnerable supply line.

Although this has been advocated by the Pakistani military for decades, it is a lunatic concept. Afghanistan has minimal transportation infrastructure, and while the Pashtuns on either side of the border have an affinity for each other, it does not follow that the Afghans would welcome the retreating Pakistani army with open arms. The best the Pakistani army could hope for would be for a few of its members to hide in the caves of western Afghanistan. For Pakistan's generals to cling to "strategic depth" as a matter of policy shows how detached from reality they are.

Whatever the logic of the matter (or lack thereof), that was the motivation for Pakistan's support of the anti-Soviet resistance in Afghanistan. There is a further complication: "Pakistan" cannot be taken to mean a nation-state in the sense that Canadians use the term. Pakistan is not one country; it is three countries.

One Pakistan is run by the civilian government. It has institutions that look like our parties, prime minister and parliament. Although influenced by the Islamic character of most of its citizens, it is nonetheless nominally secular. Think of the United States before Kennedy was elected president. It was a huge deal, in 1960, for a Catholic to even run for this office, much less win it. And yet, the unbroken string of Protestant presidents elected before then would have described their country as having a separation between church and state. Religion was not an official government policy, but it informed people's decisions. Pakistan's civilian governments would identify with this.

Another Pakistan is run by the army. This goes beyond the regular military coups that have overthrown the civilian government. Even when it is not in power, the Pakistani army exists as a national entity unto itself. It has its own economic base: it runs thriving import-export businesses in a wide range of fields; it owns hotels and shopping malls; it runs several factories. Even more astoundingly, it conducts its own foreign policy.

The most remarkable example of this occurred in the spring of 1999. Pervez Musharraf, then the chief of the army's land forces, decided to attack India at a place called Kargil. Only a few thousand Pakistani soldiers were involved, so this was never going to be more than a raid that penetrated a few kilometres into Indian territory. Nonetheless, it was a blatant act of war, and it could have provoked India to retaliate and perhaps have led to a nuclear exchange. Musharraf decided to do this *on his own*. He did not even discuss it with the then prime minister, Nawaz Sharif,* much less any other members of the civilian government.

In Canada, our country has an army. It is beholden to our elected civilian leaders. In Pakistan, as in a lot of developing-world nations, the army has a country; the elected civilians serve only as long as the army allows them to.

Finally, there is a third Pakistan. This one is run by the spies. Their organization is called the Inter Services Intelligence, or ISI. Think of this as a combination of the CIA, the FBI and military intelligence in the United States.

The ISI is a power unto itself. The civilian government (when there is one) is not even allowed to know what the ISI's budget is. Like the army, the ISI runs a number of businesses to support its activities. And it is even more aggressive in the foreign policy arena than the army is.

During the Russian occupation of Afghanistan, the ISI controlled the CIA money that flowed to the Afghan resistance. Being largely run by Islamic fundamentalists, the ISI favoured those resistance groups who shared their theological beliefs.

---

* Pervez Musharraf went on to overthrow Nawaz Sharif in a military coup in October 1999 and to serve as the *de facto* head of state of Pakistan until August 2008.

This continued during the civil war that followed the Russian withdrawal and when the Taliban conquered the country. Despite the Taliban's behaviour while in power, Pakistan did not sever its links with the Taliban until after 9/11. Even after that, the ISI continued to arm, train and otherwise support the Taliban for many years, even as the Coalition fought them in Afghanistan.

Pakistan is the piece of the puzzle that George W. Bush never addressed. Since Afghanistan is landlocked, Coalition forces have to ship most of their heavy supplies via Pakistani airports and harbours. In exchange for this access, the Bush White House ignored the overwhelming evidence that a proportion of the Pakistani military and intelligence establishments were helping the Coalition's enemies. Instead, it kept praising Musharraf as a vigorous leader in the war against the Taliban. Musharraf would thank Bush for the compliment . . . and continue to pretend that his country was not playing both sides of the fence.

Until Pakistan is cajoled/encouraged/pressured/assisted to do its part in bringing responsible government to this area, our mission here will not have succeeded.

Addendum: The best review of the situation in Pakistan today is *Descent into Chaos,* a book by Ahmed Rashid, a Pakistani journalist who has covered Central Asia for two decades.* Rashid is critical of all sides in this mess. The difference, which he recognizes, is that his criticisms of the Coalition side will stimulate debate, which has a chance of leading to policy changes. His criticisms of the Taliban, on the other hand, have only led to death threats against him.

JUNE 13 | Combat Psychology, Combat Psychologist

The CF tries hard to identify those who will not be able to withstand the rigours of combat and to weed them out ahead of time. For the

---

* Ahmed Rashid, *Descent into Chaos: The United States and the Failure of Nation Building in Pakistan, Afghanistan and Central Asia* (New York: Viking, 2008).

soldiers who make it into combat, the CF does everything it can to support them psychologically. Here's an illustration of how far we go to make this happen.

For the past four days we have been joined in the camp by a social worker, Captain Josiane Giroux, who is posted to KAF. She has a master's degree in counselling and does a lot of the critical-incident debriefing sessions for our troops. She will spend a week at our FOB, counselling any soldier who feels the need to talk. Her timing could not have been better. She arrived the day of the ramp ceremony for Private Alexandre Peloquin, twenty-four hours before Bravo Company came back to the FOB.

A number of soldiers, including some commanders, have come to see her. This is good to see. If our troops are no longer worried about discussing their anxieties, it means that the stigma attached to these feelings is nearly gone. This bodes well for the ongoing mental health of Canadian soldiers.

It is appropriate and indeed necessary to be tough and unemotional when the bullets are flying. To be otherwise would put oneself and one's comrades at risk. After the shooting is over, many people will benefit from being able to vent their feelings. Often soldiers will seek out friends or trusted leaders to do so. The CF also provides well-trained mental health professionals to those who want to avail themselves of that service.

Things are markedly different than they were even ten years ago. It used to be that soldiers who admitted they were scared were seen as weaklings. Discussion of one's fears was subtly (and sometimes not so subtly) discouraged. Like all pendulums, this can go too far the other way. One of the men on the FOB asked to see Captain Giroux, saying that he had been ordered to talk about his feelings. He had been involved with our KIA—killed in action—and someone in the chain of command thought he was doing the right thing by shoving this soldier on the social worker. I am sure the commander's heart was in the right place, but his actions were overzealous. Some people come through a combat experience with no emotional damage whatsoever, and others are not ready to talk about their feelings. Both types of individuals should be left alone until they feel the need for help.

Captain Giroux spent some time with me discussing the relaxation and visualization techniques she uses to coax the emotionally wounded back to health. She has had good success with these techniques, but she worries about the few individuals who have not responded. I can't blame her. When my treatments fail, my patient's suffering has ended; when her treatments fail, her patient's suffering is only beginning.

JUNE 14 | EOD: Explosive Ordnance Disposal

Another day of heavy fighting all around the FOB.

The Taliban managed to pull off three attacks right after we had finished breakfast, one to the west and two to the east of our position. Two of these were ambushes of civilian convoys, and one was an attack on a police substation. ANA units and our own quick reaction force headed out to engage the enemy.

The first reports of casualties came in one hour later. There was one patient with a gunshot wound from the fighting to the west, and possibly other casualties to the east. We got ourselves revved up and ready to receive them. This involved calling all the medically trained personnel on the camp, especially the combat medics who are assigned to each platoon, to join us in the UMS. They are trained to the same level as Dominic, the Bison medic, so they are superb.

The other resources available to us in a MasCal event are the soldiers who have taken a course called Tactical Combat Casualty Care, or TCCC. They can perform basic emergency procedures and, most importantly, can help us control life-threatening bleeding. They do this with a number of different kinds of sophisticated bandages, modern tourniquets and an ingenious substance called Combat Gauze, a dressing impregnated with a substance that accelerates the formation of blood clots. Using this dressing to pack a large open wound greatly decreases the speed with which the patient loses blood. Blast injuries can also give you a tremendous amount of blood loss from diffuse oozing. Combat Gauze is invaluable in these situations.

Combat Gauze has largely replaced its predecessor, Quick Clot. This was a substance we used liberally during Roto 4. It produced an exothermic reaction when it came in contact with blood or any other source of moisture. When you sprinkled it into a wound, it got so hot it cooked the torn flesh. This sealed off the bleeding vessels.

Sounds like a wonder drug, eh? It turns out to be, like so many things doctors have tried over the centuries, a beautiful theory that gets killed by an ugly fact. Since Quick Clot would burn itself into the tissues, it was often necessary to "debride" (cut away) more tissue than would otherwise have been the case. Combat Gauze has the advantages of Quick Clot without the drawbacks.

We also put the word out for two of the senior non-commissioned officers (NCOs) to join us. These two men handle the flow of information from me to the KAF Tactical Operation Centre, or TOC, which marshalls the medevac choppers and provides a summary of the incoming patients' injuries to the receiving physicians. There is no physician-to-physician contact.

This may strike those familiar with Canadian medicine as aberrant, but in this setting it works well. Battlefield injuries, though devastating to the victim, are straightforward to manage. There's a hole in the front and a hole in the back? The part that has to be fixed is in between the two holes. The leg is ripped off? Try to save as much of it as you can. The thorough description of the patient's history and physical exam that is so crucial in civilian emergency medicine is not necessary here. In a MasCal, it would be an inappropriate use of my time—I have to focus on treating and stabilizing patients.

Having gotten ourselves prepared for a possible MasCal, we ended up receiving only a single casualty, a truck driver from one of the ambushed convoys. He had been shot from the driver's side while seated. A bullet had passed through the front of his thigh and creased his abdomen. This was another one of those incidents, so common in war, that show how much survival sometimes depends on the tiniest things. Had the bullet struck him a fraction of a second later, it would have struck him at the level of the femoral artery and then ripped into his intestines. Either one of these injuries would have had the potential to kill him before he reached the UMS. As it was, all he needed were some intravenous antibiotics and a couple of bandages. We transferred him to KAF, but as a Category B (no surgery or other care needed for at least four hours).

We had finished cleaning up the UMS after the above incident when the UMS medic came by my desk and taped a "coms lockdown" sticker on my phone: all communications except those essential to ongoing operations were to cease until further notice. I looked up at the medic, and he held up two fingers. My heart sank. We go into coms lockdown whenever a Canadian is killed. This prevents the news of the death from leaking back to Canada. Cell phones and e-mail have made the world a very small place.

There is a right way and a wrong way to learn that your loved one has been killed in combat. The right way is for senior representatives of the CF to come to your home and tell you in person. The wrong way is to hear it on the news. The CF does everything it can to make sure this always happens the right way, and so far its success rate is 100 per cent.

I walked over to the encrypted communications device that allows us to watch the flow of information within the battle group. Two men killed in action: one Afghan and one Canadian.

Corporal Martin Dubé was a combat engineer who had specialized in EOD, explosive ordnance disposal. Although dominated by army engineers, this group also includes navy and air force personnel. These are clearance divers (who go after explosives underwater) and aviation technicians (who, among other unpleasant tasks, disarm bombs that fail to release from planes).

These individuals have the most stressful job imaginable: ridding Afghanistan of explosive devices. The task is almost incomprehensibly difficult. Our enemies' main weapons are mines and other explosive-laden booby traps. Coalition forces use specialized vehicles, mine detectors and other equipment in "counter-IED" tasks. At the sharp end of the stick, we have experts like Corporal Dubé who are willing to take these things apart by hand.

Taliban mines are only part of the problem. Thirty years of war have left a phenomenal number of unexploded bombs and shells all over the countryside. Some of these explosives have been so corroded by the elements that they are harmless, but many of them are still capable of exploding if they are disturbed or handled the wrong way. Finally, there are the remnants of the numerous minefields that were scattered indiscriminately by the Russians during their occupation in the 1980s.* These devices not only impede our ability to go after the Taliban, they also inflict limb-destroying and life-ending injuries on civilians who stumble onto them.

We expend a significant amount of time and resources to rid the country of this plague. Our prime targets are the newly laid mines of the Taliban. Corporal Dubé was attempting to deactivate one when it detonated. Everything seemed to be going well, then there was a flash and a roar, and Martin was gone.

---

* Some of these minefields were made up of brightly coloured pieces of plastic, often in the shape of a bird or small animal. They were meant to resemble children's toys. It was difficult for the Afghans to convince their children not to pick them up. The small explosive charge on these weapons would not kill the child outright, but it was more than enough to blow off a hand or mutilate a face. It was a barbaric but effective way of driving people off their land, to make it more difficult for the resistance to continue. This is the kind of thing the Afghans have been going through for a generation—something to keep in mind when you hear about how difficult it is for Afghans to trust outsiders.

Try to imagine what his job entailed. Someone has placed a large amount of explosives in an attempt to harm Coalition soldiers and innocent civilians. That person has also rigged the explosives with additional charges so that the apparatus will explode if someone attempts to disarm it. There may also be other mines on the approach to the one that has been detected. Any one of these mines contains enough high explosive to tear a human being apart. Now imagine walking up to the device and dismantling it.

Of the many toxic byproducts of war, mines are one of the worst. The Geneva Conventions state that minefields must be well marked and fenced off. The devices must be detectable by conventional mine detectors. Most importantly, they must self-destruct or self-deactivate once their military objective has been achieved.

The majority of the mines laid in conflicts around the world were not placed according to these rules. Every year brings a tragic and predictable crop of farmers and peasants who have lost limbs or lives to these echoes of war.

People like Corporal Dubé have taken on the monumental task of ridding the world of these silent, lurking killers. For a soldier's wages, they take on more risk in a single morning than most of us do in a lifetime. If combat infantrymen have ice water running through their veins, combat engineers must run on liquid nitrogen ($-196°$C).

Corporal Dubé was not based at our FOB, and his body was helicoptered to KAF. I wanted to learn more about him, but there was no time to do so. We were about to be hit by two enemies, one natural and one human, and we had to prepare for both.

First, we heard the wind pick up dramatically. I went outside and was confronted with the first full-blown sandstorm I've seen since serving in Afghanistan. As is evident from the following photograph, you can see this thing coming from a distance. So we had some warning, which we put to good use. We ran around securing whatever looked like it might fly off our tents and barracks, and closing whatever openings might allow the sand into our structures.

Sandstorm coming

Look at the picture again. Can you see that there is as much dark stuff coming down from the sky as is rising up from the ground? Believe it or not, in this desert region, that is rain. After we were pelted by the wind and the sand, we got drenched by a powerful downpour.

We were still dusting ourselves and drying off when I received word that the casualties from the incidents east of here were coming to our FOB. Once again, I gathered the team to the UMS. All told, I had a couple of dozen people on hand to help me. The warning had come early enough that I was able to assign specific tasks to each individual in order to improve our organization when the casualties arrived.

Then we waited. And waited. And waited. No casualties, no further reports. More than half an hour went by before we got a call telling us that the truck carrying the casualties had arrived at the gate. The driver had taken his time because they were all dead.

The dead men were civilians who had agreed to drive trucks carrying supplies for the Afghan government and Coalition forces. It is likely that they were not motivated by political convictions; they were simply trying to feed their families. And they had paid for this with their lives.

Addendum, date unspecified: I have had the opportunity to meet the rest of Corporal Dubé's team. I will not tell you where we met, nor will I provide any photographs of them. Even these tiny hints could be used by our enemies to some advantage.

What I can tell you is that they are among the bravest and most professional soldiers you could ever meet. There is no braggadocio; these men are far past that. Discussions with them demonstrate only a cool, calm competence.

The EOD team is engaged in a very intimate war. There are probably no more than a few skilled IED men in all of Zhari-Panjwayi. When one of them rigs an IED with secondary devices designed to detonate when the primary IED is moved, he is deliberately targeting the EOD men. Similarly, the more of these IEDs the EOD men detect, disable and dissect, the more they learn about the bomb maker. This makes it easier to hunt him down and kill him.

EOD experts always refer to bombs as "devices," a dispassionate term that matches the nature of these soldiers. Watching them take an IED apart and construct various gizmos for their next mission is like watching a skillful surgeon at work. Every move is deliberate, every action well thought out, and the "bomb techs" know exactly where they are going before they begin. It is a cerebral war for them, totally different from the primal firefights of the infantry. It is still a fight to the death.

I asked these men what drew them to a career that has so much to recommend against it, and what prompted most of them to return to Afghanistan for a second tour. They all answered with variations on the same theme. They are soldiers first and foremost. IEDs are the most lethal weapon our enemies have to use against us. More than anything, they want to defeat these devices to protect their brothers in arms.

The day started on a sombre note, with a memorial service for Corporal Dubé. Major Tim Arsenault, the senior officer at FOB Wilson, spoke briefly but well. You could tell that he was still quite upset about the loss of his own soldier, Private Peloquin, seven days ago.

The rest of the day was quiet. The main event was getting a chance to speak to the individual I want to talk about today. War zones are populated by more than their fair share of colourful characters. By far the most colourful I have met on both my tours so far is Louie Palu.

55

You have probably never heard of Louie, but you have almost certainly seen at least a few examples of his art. He is the most prolific photojournalist to work in Afghanistan. He was the "Canadian Photojournalist of the Year" in 2008, and his pictures have appeared in all our major newspapers.

Louie is about halfway through his *fourth* three-month tour in Afghanistan. Twelve months in Afghanistan may not sound like that much—many of our soldiers are on their third seven-month tour and are approaching twenty months in the country—but the two are not comparable. Our troops go through regular cycles of operations and downtime. Louie goes out of his way to attach himself to a unit about to get into a fight, then leaves them when they go back to their base to rest.

He has been with us for the duration of the recent operation and is now heading off to hang out with the U.S. Marines. The Marines asked him to come along with them, on an operation they have

Louie Palu, war correspondent

The Taliban soldier I treated in 2007

(© Louie Palu/ZUMA Press, reprinted with permission)

declined to describe. He has only been told to show up at KAF tomorrow and to report to the flight line at midnight. Is there anything about this that does not scream *"Bad Idea"*?

I talked to him for about an hour, and we discovered the most amazing connections between us. During the first combat operation I participated in during Roto 4, I treated a Taliban prisoner who had been shot in the chest. It turns out that Louie was with the guys who shot him. He had helped to carry the wounded man back to my UMS.

I had seen a photograph of our medics treating the wounded Taliban soldier on the CBC website a few days after the operation. It was Louie who took the photo. I showed him a video of our resuscitation of this prisoner, and Louie recognized him.

As you can see from his portrait on the previous page, Louie has a feline look to his face. Whether he looked like that before he used up eight of his nine lives in this place, I do not know. It is most fitting he appears like this now. This guy has been in more firefights than any soldier I know. So far, not a scratch.

Louie was kind enough to let me use a few of his remarkable photographs for this book. The first appears on the previous page.

JUNE 16 | Zero Sweat

Canadian soldiers serving in Afghanistan carry at least one personal firearm. For most FOB soldiers, this is the C7 5.56 mm rifle, the standard infantry weapon of the CF. Specialized soldiers, such as machine gunners, tank crewmen and snipers, will carry other weapons that are matched to their particular tasks. Many of us, myself included, carry a second weapon called a sidearm. This is a Browning 9 mm pistol.

The members of the task force can be divided into two groups, based on whether their weapons will be used for offence or defence. The infantry, the front-line soldiers, are the archetypal examples of the first group. They use their weapons to attack. I would fall into the second group. The only time I should ever have to fire my weapon is if things have gone terribly wrong and I have to defend myself against a direct personal attack. The Geneva Conventions prohibit health-services types like me from using "area" weapons, weapons that can inflict damage on a large area. This would include grenades, rocket launchers, flame-throwers and the like. Under the Conventions' rules, I am allowed to kill the person who is attempting to kill me, but I have to do this using a "point" weapon, one that can only hit a precise spot.

Given the low likelihood that I will ever have to fire a weapon to defend myself, the CF does not expend much energy in giving me one with which I am comfortable and familiar. Rather, I am issued a rifle and a pistol at Camp Mirage from the firearm equivalent of the bulk bin at the local grocery store. The weapons are in good working order, but they need to be "zeroed."

Zeroing involves adjusting the sights so that the weapon is adapted to the person using it. Everyone holds a rifle a little differently: our arms are different lengths, our eyes are in different places. A rifle will therefore not hit the same point when held by different people. The sights can be set to compensate for this.

I got around to this important task today. One of the platoons was running some combat firing drills, so I asked to go along with them.

I spent an hour on the range not only zeroing my weapon but also going through some of the drills with the boys. I caught a break: the last person who used my rifle must have had a body type similar to mine, because I only needed to make a tiny adjustment to the right, and my rounds started landing dead on target. I was pleased to see that, once zeroed, I was able to shoot as well if not better than the youngsters on the firing line with me. I have always been a pretty good shot, and I had practised my marksmanship a fair bit before I left.

The combat firing drills, on the other hand, were another story. The sergeant running the show had us firing in a number of awkward and uncomfortable ways, to simulate positions in which we might end up after coming under enemy fire and hitting the deck. It was exhausting. I kept up with the youngsters . . . but only barely.

JUNE 17 | Downregulation

"Downregulation" is the process by which a cell becomes less responsive to a stimulus to which it is repeatedly exposed. An example of downregulation is alcohol addiction.

There are receptors on the outside of our brain cells to which alcohol molecules will attach themselves. Once the molecule is attached, the receptor sends a signal to the cell. This signal causes intoxication. These receptors are constantly being created and broken down. If the cell is repeatedly stimulated by alcohol, it will start to "downregulate" the receptors, which means that fewer of them will be made. With fewer receptors, the cell is less sensitive to the alcohol molecules. That's why chronic alcoholics need to drink far more than normal people to get drunk. Their brain cells no longer respond to the lower level of stimulation.

You can downregulate in other ways. Let me give you some examples.

When I got here, having my pistol on my hip was quite annoying—a big hunk of uncomfortable metal was pulling on my belt and weighing down my leg. This morning, I looked down and was almost surprised to see that my pistol was in its proper place. I no longer feel it there. Call that physical downregulation.

This afternoon, the Taliban attacked an Afghan National Police (ANP) strong point right beside the FOB. I was in the UMS after lunch when it started: three large explosions followed by a heavy volume of automatic weapons fire. The ANP counter-attacked, the Canadians drove armoured vehicles up to the perimeter and our mortars started firing bombs that were aimed to land a short distance from the FOB walls.

I stepped outside the UMS for a minute to listen to the shooting. I noticed it was much closer than it ever had been before. Then I went back in the UMS and continued reading my book.

It might seem bizarre to go back to one's diversions when several heavily armed men intent on killing you are firing at you from a few hundred metres away. But there is shooting every day around our FOB. The Canadian and Afghan combat troopers do the job of pushing the Taliban back. They did that effectively today, as they have on all previous occasions. If there are no reports of incoming wounded, there is nothing for the medical team to do. So we tune the sound out and go on with whatever we were doing. Call that emotional downregulation.

The most extraordinary example of emotional downregulation occurred outside the walls of the FOB. When the attack started, a farmer had been working in his field a few hundred metres away. As the ANP surged out of their strong point to attack the Taliban, he raised his head for a minute or two to watch the direction in which the attack was going. Then, satisfied that the shooting was going to pass at least a football field away from him, he went back to tilling his field. He continued even when one of our mortar bombs misfired, exploding close to where he was and scaring the crap out of a couple of his sheep (who were otherwise unharmed).

You can get used to almost anything. This man continues to tend to his crops while a full-scale firefight goes on a few dozen metres away. It is sad to think of what his life has been like, to make him so unflappable.

JUNE 18 | CDS: Chief of the Defence Staff

General Walter Natynczyk is the top soldier in the CF—he is the chief of the defence staff, or CDS. He takes a keen interest in the welfare of the soldiers serving in Afghanistan and visits the troops here every few months. He is back in Afghanistan now and was scheduled to come to our FOB today. At our regular morning briefing, the detachment commanders were ordered to assemble their people at 1300 in a large open area near the command post. The general likes to have what he calls "town hall" meetings, where anyone can ask him questions.

At 1145 I went to get some lunch, returning to the UMS about twenty minutes later. There were still at least forty minutes remaining before the general was scheduled to arrive. Wanting to be at my best, I went outside to brush my teeth, then stepped into our latrine to pee.

A few minutes later I stepped out of the latrine, toothbrush in one hand and zipper in the other, to find myself face-to-face with General Natynczyk. He already had his hand extended and Major Arsenault was introducing me, so there was no getting out of it. I tucked my toothbrush into my back pocket, took the general's hand in my unwashed one and shook it.

We spoke for a minute or so. He was surprised there was an M.D. on the FOB, and even more surprised to hear that I was doing it for a second tour. I explained my combat arms background and he replied that going from the infantry to being a FOB doc constituted "retirement failure." (Not bad for an off-the-cuff comment!) He then thanked me for my service and moved off with the major. The boys in the UMS had seen my move with the toothbrush and were all chuckling as I came back inside.

At 1245, we headed off to join the rest of the soldiers. The general joined us (almost) punctually,* asked us to huddle up and addressed us in French. As a French Canadian, I could tell that this language did not come easily to him—he must have worked quite hard to develop the facility he has. My fellow francophones and I appreciated his effort.

Whenever the CDS comes to visit a unit, he gives out CDS coins, large coins inscribed with his personal seal. They are presented to individuals who have distinguished themselves in performing their duties. I was pleased to see one of these coins awarded to Master Corporal Nick Raymond, one of the Bravo Company combat medics. Nick has dived into every casualty situation we have had since I've been here and was one of the two medics who responded to Private Peloquin. Everyone commented afterwards about how calm and competent Nick had been through this horrible event. His award was well deserved.

The general then moved off to a table that the combat team leaders had set up to show various pieces of equipment that they thought could be improved upon. They also had some gear that other nations are using which they felt was better than what we had. The general took in all these comments attentively.

Unfortunately, the items the medical team wanted him to see were not on the table but right beside it: two medic packs, one issued by the

---

* I have to give the general his due here. The word is that a group of soldiers had been assembled to speak to him at KAF yesterday. For some reason, these soldiers spent nearly an hour waiting in the sun while the general listened to yet another briefing. When he finally joined them and learned how long they had been waiting, the general tore a strip off the officer in charge of his schedule.

Nick pitches the pack to General Natynczyk

CF, and the other the one that many of our medics use. The regulation pack has one large pouch. Many of our medics, with their own funds, have bought a pack that has a large number of modular pouches inside it. When dealing with a casualty in the field, they open this pack up and instantly have a well-organized treatment area at their disposal. They can also close it just as quickly if they have to move out in a hurry.

Master Corporal Raymond was standing by to explain all this, but it was not obvious that the packs were part of the display. The general walked right by them and moved on to his next meeting. Nick did not feel comfortable enough to call out to him to come back.

I was made aware of this several minutes later. In a serious breach of protocol, I chased after the general, blew past some senior officer who tried to block me and told him my guys had something to show him. I added that it would be much appreciated if he would take a couple of minutes to come and talk to them. Although his helicopter was orbiting the FOB at the time, he came to the UMS and listened to Nick explain the advantages of this pack.

I made sure the general understood the most impressive thing about this pack: Nick had bought it with his own money so that he would be able to take better care of his guys. The pack in question costs $600; a medic makes about $3,000 a month.

Addendum, September 15: Going home in a few days. I have now met almost all the combat medics of Roto 7. *Every one* of them has bought the same pack.

JUNE 19 | Unsure About the *Shura*

A quiet day. There was a bit of combat activity up and down the main highway, but only one hit generated any casualties: a rocket strike that set a vehicle aflame. The four occupants, Afghan civilians employed as truck drivers for Coalition convoys, were burnt beyond recognition.

As things seemed to have wound down in the early afternoon, I took the opportunity to check out the weekly security *shura* (council meeting). This was attended by the Zhari district leader (a position somewhere between city mayor and provincial premier), the local chief of police, and representatives of the ANA and intelligence services. The Canadians at the meeting included the mentors we have assigned to the ANA and police, and those soldiers involved in development projects in the district.

The Afghans spoke first, giving an update on their activities over the past week. The highlight was the killing of a local Taliban leader, described by the district leader as a "beast." Given the standards of bestiality among the Taliban, I am happy not to know what he did to deserve that title. Everyone agreed the world was a better place for his having left it.

The Canadians then passed their points, mostly administrative advice about how to obtain various items. The Afghans had recently asked for a lot of gear, particularly communication devices. There is an eternal tension in these situations. The Afghans would like the Canadians to obtain the equipment for them. The Canadians insist that the Afghans use their own resupply system so that the system becomes more efficient. We are going to leave one day, and when we do we want the Afghans to have a functional system that is familiar

The *shura*

to them. This is something one encounters regularly when working in the developing world.

The more intriguing aspect of the *shura* was the performance of the translator. I have done a lot of translating, and I pride myself on my ability to provide simultaneous translation for speakers in all three of my languages. I like to watch good translators in action, but that was not the case here. Our guy was so minimally functional in English that I questioned not only his translation of what the Afghans were saying but also his understanding of what we were saying, which needed to be translated into Pashto. And yet the civilian and military leaders of Zhari district were counting on him to talk to each other.

Watching this process was disquieting. We knew as far back as 2006 that we were going to be in Kandahar province for a long time. That would have been the time to bring over a bunch of ESL teachers to KAF for four to six months to train a large number of superior interpreters. Given the importance of ensuring that allies in a war understand each other, this would seem to be a no-brainer.

This affects my work as well. I often tell medical trainees, "History beats physical exam. History and physical beats labs and imaging." This means that talking to patients gives you more information than you get from examining them. Talking to them *and* examining them gives you more information than you get from blood tests and from radiological procedures such as X-rays, CT scans and MRIS. Even with all our sophisticated tests, most of our diagnoses are arrived at by talking to the patient.

For trauma care, my minimal Pashto is all I need. However, I also treat a few Afghan civilians or soldiers every day for non-traumatic ailments. If I can't be sure of what the patient has said because the interpreter is incomprehensible, my diagnostic ability is limited. While some of our interpreters are quite good, the group includes some whose skills are clearly not up to the tasks required of them. I get the feeling that our generals do not appreciate how dysfunctional the translation service can be out here at times.

Very unusually, the day was not medically over at sundown. Our night vision equipment gives us such an overwhelming advantage in the dark that the Taliban rarely attack between dusk and dawn. FOB Wilson has not had a single trauma patient arrive after supper since this rotation began in mid-March. The case we had tonight involved another Afghan-Canadian communication breakdown, but of a more humorous nature than the one at the *shura*.

There is a medic attached to the ANA unit based here. If he is on the FOB when we have casualties, he comes over to help us out. He doesn't speak a word of English, but you can't help but like this guy. He is always smiling and eager to learn. I integrate him into the team whenever he shows up.

Tonight, as he has done on a number of occasions, he popped his head in the UMS door. He stood there with his usual big smile as I greeted him from my desk. He looked at me. I looked at him. I waited for him to clarify what he wanted, but he just stood there holding the door open. At least half a minute went by before Dominic the Medic walked over to the door and looked outside.

"Hey," says Dominic, "there's a stretcher out here."

"Uh-huh," says I, thinking that he meant the ANA medic had brought an old stretcher that he would like us to repair or replace.

Major Tim Arsenault, combat team commander

Canadians will have served in Afghanistan. Fewer than forty will have been combat team commanders.

To say that the soldiers chosen for these positions are exceptional would be a gross understatement. Major Arsenault's cv includes paratrooper training, Ranger training (a specialized commando-type course run by the Americans, along the lines of what you may have seen in the movie *G.I. Jane*), a deployment as a platoon commander in Bosnia, a stint as an infantry instructor at the Combat Training Centre in New Brunswick, and other taskings that are considered plum postings for young infantry officers. Only a few dozen soldiers in our army have Major Arsenault's skills as a combat leader.

Many civilians reading this will have a vision of combat soldiers that is grounded in Hollywood movies. The last paragraph may have conjured up images of Sylvester Stallone or Arnold Schwarzenegger in their prime. Although some of our similarly trained officers would fit the bill, Major Arsenault runs counter to type. He has a warm and engaging personality, he is invariably smiling and he speaks softly— loud enough to be clearly heard but not a decibel more.

We hit it off immediately, but I suspect that anyone who comes into contact with Major Arsenault feels the same way. Within moments, you know that you're in the presence of someone who is sincerely interested in you and what you have to say. You also sense that he will give you good advice, no matter what your problem might be.

In my case, that advice came with regard to my relationship with my daughter. For several days, Michelle has refused to speak to me on the phone. She is angry at me for leaving—she has been crying at night, saying that she misses me—and this is her way to retaliate. There is not much to do in these situations other than ride it out, but the pain this caused was so strong it was physical. How badly am I hurting my child?

Major Arsenault has three children himself, aged four, six and eight. His youngest daughter is the same age as mine. When I told him about Michelle's behaviour, he replied that a father was always a young girl's first love and that nothing could change that. It was the perfect thing to say, and the anxiety that had been building up dissipated.

Being a military leader, of course, does not only involve reassuring and encouraging those around you. There are also times when firm correction must be applied. Again, Major Arsenault's style might not be what you expect. A telling anecdote was shared by one of the combat team's warrant officers. He told me that the first time Major Arsenault chewed him out, it took him several minutes to realize that he was getting blasted, because the major's voice was so calm and polite.

Another story was related to me by the social worker who visited us last week. It is a cliché that soldiers like to complain about their officers. Most of this is inconsequential bitching and must be taken with a grain of salt, if not the whole shaker. But after spending a week interviewing soldiers who may have been less happy than their comrades about being here, she had not heard a single complaint about the major. Not one gripe. She found that extraordinary.

It would be a mistake to think that Major Arsenault's gentle manner implies that he accepts anything less than 100 per cent effort from his men. I had the opportunity to discuss a discipline issue with him, and he had no difficulty "closing the feedback loop." I am reminded of what Andrei Gromyko said about Mikhail Gorbachev: "He has a nice smile. But he has teeth of steel."

For the past three years Major Arsenault has been the commander of Bravo Company, Second Battalion, Royal 22nd Regiment ("The Bastards"). There is a cycle in the life of infantry units such as this. A company will be built up, function at a high level for a few years and then be broken up as veterans are assigned to different tasks. Major Arsenault took over Bravo Company right after it had gone through one of these periodic breakups. Over the next thirty months, he rebuilt the company. Then he took them to war.

The commander of "Bastard Combat Team" on the battlefield

One day, I saw him gazing into the distance in a thoughtful manner. I asked what he was looking at, thinking we would have a superficial but nonetheless pleasant conversation about the terrain. He replied that he was thinking about the next operation. It was only then that I saw he was looking at some of his men playing volleyball some distance away. We talked for a while, and he described everything he was doing to try to keep his men safe.

Major Arsenault lost a man, Private Alexandre Peloquin, twelve days ago. He agreed with me that the death of one of his men was almost inevitable. It would have been invasive to ask him how he felt about that, but I did ask him if he'd been prepared for it. Major Arsenault replied that, in spite of the foreseeable nature of the event, he had not been.

A note on a leader's weapons. Major Arsenault has been under direct enemy fire more times than he can count. I asked him how often he had used his personal weapon. He replied that he has not fired a single shot.

This is a mark of extraordinary coolness under fire. When someone is shooting at you, there is an overwhelming desire to shoot back. The act of firing your weapon gives you the feeling that you're doing something to regain control of the situation. It is psychologically satisfying and goes a long way towards reducing the fear you are feeling.

Every time Major Arsenault has been under fire, he has had to suppress this desire. Instead, he focuses on the evolution of the battle, directing his platoons and the various "supporting arms" of the combat team (artillery, tanks, engineers, bombers and attack helicopters).

Upon hearing his answer, I complimented him on his self-control. He modestly waved this off, saying, "My weapon is my radio." That's not exactly true: his weapon is his mind, the skill with which he choreographs the various elements of his combat team as they perform their intricate and lethal dance.

Speaking of his radio, I will point out that the previous photograph shows that Major Arsenault carries it himself. The thing weighs a ton, and some commanders opt to have a young soldier carry it for them. Major Arsenault may not have the Rambo attitude, but he definitely has the Rambo physique.

Addendum—Why things got worse: Major Arsenault was able to shed some light on why the security situation had deteriorated since I had last been here. During Roto 4 we had fought to establish a ring of FOBs and outposts that encircled Zhari-Panjwayi. This had spread our forces so thinly that we were tied down defending all these bases.

NATO had asked for more troops to be deployed to Kandahar province so that Coalition forces would still be able to patrol between our FOBS and outposts. No nation stepped up. When last summer's fighting season rolled around, there was nothing to prevent the Taliban from bringing more troops and equipment into the area to reassert their presence.

In what must have been a heartbreaking operation, Major Arsenault and "the Bastards" had to fight their way into an outpost we had built in 2008 . . . to dismantle it. He would like nothing better than to be able to help rebuild this country, but without security there can be no reconstruction. The priority now is to protect Kandahar City, where approximately 70 per cent of the province's population resides. To protect the city, we have to keep the Taliban bleeding and dying in the rural areas.

The combat team's mission statement speaks about "relentlessly disrupting insurgents." The major is more direct: "We go out and we get into fights."

MY FATHER
My father leads a company, but not any company
A company of soldiers who fight for humanity

When it is day time here
My father lays on his pillow his fear

When I go to dreamland at night
My father rises and faces the fight

He serves in a foreign country protecting kids
I will never meet
To make them all that they can be
He walks the land in dust and heat

When my father has to go away
His example teaches me to always pray
That the world will see a better day
And that all children will be free to play

—FLORENCE ARSENAULT, age 8, daughter of Major Tim Arsenault

Florence wrote this after her father had left for Afghanistan. She then memorized it and recited it to him over the phone one night, flawlessly. He copied it down and carries it everywhere he goes. He reads it every day.

JUNE 21 | Father's Day with Nichola's Daughters

How do modern armies kill?

Very few civilians are aware that the majority of soldiers killed in combat by modern armies for the past hundred years have been killed by cannon fire—what we call artillery. When you watch Hollywood movies, you come away with the impression that the infantry (foot soldiers) shoot each other on the battlefield. This is inaccurate. The role of the infantry is to push the enemy into a killing zone, where the artillery can do most of the damage.

The injuries produced by an artillery shell's explosion fall into three main categories. *Primary* injuries are caused by the sheer force of the blast: the shock wave can turn internal organs into mush. *Tertiary* injuries occur when a body that has been thrown through the air by the blast hits something. By far the largest number of injuries, however, are *secondary* and are produced by shrapnel, the tremendous amount of high-velocity debris thrown off by these explosions.

Considerable shrapnel is produced by the shell itself. As it explodes, the metal container of the shell disintegrates into hundreds of razor-sharp metal shards. Any one of these shards could do as much damage as a rifle bullet, if not more. Even more shrapnel comes from whatever was on the ground where the shell exploded: rocks, gravel, wood from trees, cement from buildings, metallic objects. Any of these things can be propelled at such high speeds that they can kill. Even "biological shrapnel," the bits of bone and flesh thrown off when a body is so close to the shell's detonation that it disintegrates, can be lethal.

The artillery represents the single most important weapon system in the battle group. If our troops get into trouble, the artillery can rain so much death and destruction on the enemy so quickly that it will be forced to break off the engagement. The infantry troopers here can tell many stories of the artillery saving their bacon.

Canada's main artillery piece is the M777 155 mm cannon. It can fire shells weighing dozens of kilograms to distances of thirty or even forty kilometres. In other words, the guns here at FOB Wilson can hit anything in the Canadian area of operations in Zhari-Panjwayi. The trick lies in telling them where to shoot. That is the job of the forward observation officer, the FOO (pronounced "foo").

FOOs perform the most critical and dangerous function in an artillery unit. They go forward with the infantry and tanks to observe the enemy and guide the fire of the cannons. This is a lot trickier than it sounds: think about trying to find a fox in the forest, but with shooting and explosions going on all around you.

It is also vital that they know where all the "friendlies" are. When a combat team of over 150 men and a dozen vehicles are scattered over a wide area, this can be nearly impossible. Yet it must be done perfectly, because FOOs can bring Armageddon down on the battlefield. The "kill radius" of the artillery shells they fire is fifty metres, so anybody caught in the open up to fifty metres away from an explosion is at high risk of lethal injury. To do their job, FOOs must be right on the front line. They are more likely to be killed or injured than anyone else in the artillery.

On May 17, 2006, Canada lost a FOO in Afghanistan. She had been serving with the Royal Canadian Horse Artillery. On the day Captain Nichola Goddard died, she had been accompanying a unit of the Princess Patricia's Canadian Light Infantry, the famed PPCLI. When they came under heavy fire, she drove her armoured vehicle to a point where she could engage the enemy with direct fire from her vehicle's weapons while simultaneously calling in the "indirect fire" of her artillery battery.

Inside her armoured vehicle, Captain Goddard had good protection from the weapons the Taliban were using, but her field of view was restricted to what she could see out of a few small, shatterproof windows. To do her job as well as possible, she stood with her head and torso outside the vehicle. FOOs often do this in combat

Gunner Mélanie Faucher

because it gives them better "situational awareness," despite the risks it entails. It was this commitment to her duty that cost Captain Goddard her life. When a rocket-propelled grenade (RPG) hit her vehicle, she was struck by shrapnel fragments and killed.

It was inevitable that this would happen. Although it is a fact not widely known outside of the military, women have been in the combat arms for several years now. There are even women serving with the hardest of hard men, the infantry. They perform the same duties, take the same risks and pay the same price.

Here at FOB Wilson, three women are serving with the artillery. I asked them if they would discuss their lives with me.

Gunner Mélanie Faucher has been in the army for two years. Now twenty-five years old, she can remember being fascinated by cannons from a young age (I didn't ask why). The artillery was a natural choice for her. She sees herself staying in the army for the rest of her career. If you think this makes her some kind of gun nut, you could not be more wrong. She exudes a warmth and empathy that is classically feminine. She does not limit this empathy to her comrades; she has been known

Bombardier Annick Vallières

to seek out Afghans who work on the base to help them with some of their more unpleasant tasks. She feels entirely accepted by her male companions.

Gunner Faucher is living a very modern kind of stress on this mission. Besides worrying about her own safety, she is also concerned about her significant other. He is a sergeant in the infantry, assigned to a neighbouring FOB. They try to talk or e-mail daily, and they see each other every few weeks. They are living an experience that would not have existed a decade ago and one that most couples could not comprehend.

Bombardier Annick Vallières, twenty-nine, is back for her second tour in Afghanistan, having been here during Roto 4. She was at FOB Wilson that time as well. She admits that her first tour was a little rough because some of the men were not as accepting of her as they could have been. I would advise the men serving with her now to do their best to be collegial: you are in the presence of a tough individual.

You might think I was describing a cliché: tough chick goes into the army and becomes tougher still. As with her colleague, first impressions are deceiving. Bombardier Vallières is the mother of three children, aged nine, six and five. When I asked what her prime motivation was for being in Afghanistan, she spoke primarily of them. She wanted to show them that their mother had done something very difficult and done it well. What is parenting, if not setting high standards for yourself as an example to your children?

Bombardier Vallières's future plans provided yet another twist. When I asked where she thought her career was headed, I was guessing she would spend the rest of her time in the combat arms. Again, expectations were confounded. In the not-too-distant future, she would like to get out of the combat arms and into an office job where she can let her hair down, wear makeup and dress in "really feminine clothing." She may be made of titanium, but she is still all woman.

Lieutenant Marie-Ève Labonté is a twenty-three-year-old graduate of the Royal Military College (RMC) in Kingston. Her father is in the military, and she grew up as a base brat; but whereas her joining the military was predictable, her path to the artillery was a bit circuitous. She started off in the navy, which she hated for a number of reasons. She accepted her current posting almost as a last-minute thing . . . and found that it clicked perfectly with her personality.

In her current position as a gun line officer, she records the information called in by the FOO and calculates the precise angle and elevation at which the cannons must fire to hit their target. I am grossly oversimplifying things here— the numerous calculations required

Lieutenant Marie-Ève Labonté

involve high-order mathematics, and many factors must be taken into account. I will mention only one, to make clear how intricate this task is: the shells go so far that Lieutenant Labonté must take into account the rotation of the Earth when deciding where she will shoot. A few days ago, I spent some time in the command post watching her direct a fire mission. She seemed completely at ease with her task.

I asked her the slightly sexist but nonetheless obvious question: how did she reconcile her feminine side with her job, where her orders caused the deaths of other human beings almost daily? She admitted that she was occasionally conflicted by this, but, like me, she thinks she is saving lives: Canadians in the short term and Afghans in the long term.

Speaking of Lieutenant Labonté's feminine side, it has had an unexpected positive effect. Her second-in-command is a warrant officer, an enlisted man with over twenty years' experience. The way the military organizes things, the officer in command is the stereotypical father figure, stern, cerebral and somewhat distant. The second-in-command is the mother, much more aware of what's going on in everybody's life than the father. Paradoxically, many of the men under her command have approached Lieutenant Labonté with personal issues that they have chosen not to share with their warrant officer. This somewhat discombobulated her second-in-command, but her troops have benefited from it.

Lieutenant Labonté had finished the first phase of her artillery officer training when Nichola Goddard was killed. Captain Goddard was legendary, initially at RMC and later in her artillery unit, for her affability and competence. Lieutenant Labonté is still visibly affected when she discusses Captain Goddard. When she did so with me, we were standing outside in 40°C heat. Yet she got goosebumps.

As the father of a young girl, I can't help but look at these proud, strong, competent, honourable women and hope that my daughter turns out like them.

Major Arsenault led the combat team out for a quick operation last night, leaving only a support staff behind. When this happens, our morning meeting is cancelled. I was looking forward to sleeping in, a hope that was dashed at 0700: the UMS medic (a somewhat immature young man who has replaced the reliable Master Corporal Guay) burst into my quarters to tell me that several ANA soldiers had been wounded by a suicide bomber. With the combat team away, there was only one other medically trained individual on the FOB. All the medics and TCCCs were with their combat units. I put out calls for all the other subunits still on the FOB to send me whomever they could spare and ended up with about a dozen people all told.

I spent some time talking to the individuals who had never done any kind of medical work before, asking them to focus on plugging whatever holes they came across. If we were to be overwhelmed with casualties, simple pressure bandages could go a long way towards saving as many lives as possible.

One of the first patients to arrive had a fair amount of blood on his upper thigh and lower abdomen on the left side. We brought him into the UMS and I attended to him first. He had a small puncture in his groin that had already stopped bleeding. I ordered his wound to be bandaged and went to the overflow tent to attend to the others. Three of the four patients there had minor wounds; the fourth had arrived on a stretcher complaining only of shoulder pain. There was no blood on the front of his shirt. His vital signs were stable, but he seemed a little drowsy. As I walked by, the UMS medic told me that he thought the shoulder might be dislocated. I put my hands on both shoulders and quickly determined that no dislocation had taken place. I then examined the patient's back and found a tiny puncture wound in his right chest, a couple of millimetres wide and no more than a centimetre long.

The UMS medic had made the classic beginner mistake of examining only the front of the patient. The shrapnel wound, though quite small, was plain to see once we had the patient sitting up with his shirt off. His drowsiness and shoulder pain now took on a much more sinister connotation. Shrapnel fragments travel at such high velocity that even tiny ones can cause massive internal damage if they hit the victim in a sensitive spot. And the chest is full of sensitive spots.*

I took the patient over to the main UMS and examined him with ultrasound. Internal bleeding had collapsed the left lung. I put in a chest tube and drained 1,200 millilitres of blood, securing the chest tube as the medevac chopper was landing. With blood no longer crushing his left lung, the patient's breathing and level of consciousness improved. It was not necessary to intubate him.

This process took a little over an hour, from first warning to last patient departure. All the while, we were serenaded by the longest and most intense fire mission any of the artillerymen can remember. They fired nearly two hundred rounds of 155 mm ammunition—another record—in support of the combat team's operation, all before lunch. This led to a temporary change in Bravo Company's nickname from "Bastard" to "Boom."

By midafternoon, the combat team had returned to the FOB. They

---

* The UMS medic would go on to make the same mistake a week later, assessing a patient by looking only at the front of the body and then telling me, "He's fine. He's got nothing." The patient was lying on a stretcher and seemed uncomfortable, so I ran my hands along his back. This is called a "wet check" and is used to look for any external bleeding. The "wet check" was positive: my hands were covered in blood when I pulled them away. When I looked at the patient's back, I noted two large shrapnel wounds. For the UMS medic to make this mistake once was bad enough. It was inexcusable for him to make it twice. I had spoken to him quietly after the first incident. Now, I had no choice but to discipline him, speaking to him rather harshly and documenting the incident for my superiors. As I have commented on many times before, the training the medics receive makes them almost universally superb. But "almost" is not "always" and commanders must recognize when a corrective needs to be applied. Errors like this can kill, and that is unacceptable.

had been in constant contact with the Taliban, meaning that they had been in gunfights all day. Several Taliban, as many as twenty, were killed. None of our guys had so much as a scratch.

JUNE 23 | God Counts the Tears of Women

I had two patient encounters today that, had they happened in Canada, would be among the most mundane. Here, they were extraordinary.

Although we cannot begin to respond to all the health needs of the local population, we make exceptions for children, particularly if they appear to be suffering from something straightforward such as a laceration or broken bone. Around midmorning, I was told there were two children at the main gate who needed care. One of them had a facial laceration; the other was reported as being "unwell."

The child with the laceration, a four-year-old girl, had been hit by a man riding a motorcycle. She had a deep gash on her right forehead that went all the way to her skull. She was accompanied by her twelve-year-old brother and was distressed at being surrounded by unfamiliar faces speaking an unfamiliar language.

What now? Giving this child an injection of local anaesthetic would have hurt her. Also, local anaesthetics only block the sensation of pain. The patient can still feel movement. That is why children who have received local anaesthesia continue to be upset: they can feel the doctor's instruments moving their skin around, and they think the pain of the initial needle is about to return. This child had been through enough already. I decided to repair her face under ketamine sedation.

Ketamine is a wonderful drug that allows emergency physicians to put patients into a sleep state equal to general anaesthesia, with one major difference. Under general anaesthesia, patients must be put on a ventilator, which will breathe for them. With ketamine, patients continue to breathe on their own. Equally important, their gag reflex remains intact. Should saliva, blood or vomit somehow end up in their throat, they will still be able to cough the material out rather than aspirating it into their lungs.

The only problem with giving ketamine is that the patient has to be observed for two to three hours afterwards, and this would tie up one of my stretchers for some time. I checked to see if there was any combat activity going on that we knew of, but everything seemed quiet. So I went for it. Within two minutes, the child was out and I was able to proceed with the tricky repair of her ragged cut. With the child immobile thanks to the ketamine, this procedure went very well: I was done in less than ten minutes. We then bandaged her and bundled her into a blanket on one of our stretchers.

The surreal part of this patient encounter came a couple of hours later, when the child was awake, alert and ready for discharge. She had been brought in from her village by the police, from one of their outposts three kilometres away. She was now going back the same way, travelling in an unarmoured pickup truck with police markings: an easy, high-priority target for the Taliban. I had thought that the children had walked in from a nearby compound. It made me sick to think of the risk we were taking with this child to get her home.

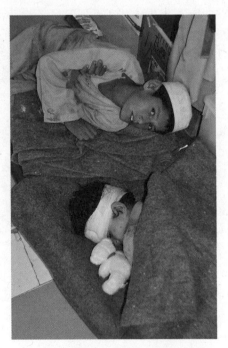

Sleeping off ketamine with new teddy bear, and big brother watching over

While only the method of discharge was aberrant in the above scenario, the other patient encounter was incredible right from the beginning. The patient was another four-year-old, a boy this time. He was accompanied by his two siblings and his mother. And no one else.

This was extremely strange.

Since Roto 7 began, FOB Wilson has treated a few dozen Afghan civilians wounded by the war. Not one of them has been a woman. In one instance, an intercity bus either overturned or was attacked with rockets (the story was never clarified) and more than a dozen males were brought to FOB Wilson for treatment, but not a single woman. All the women who were injured were taken to Kandahar City so that they could be seen by a female doctor. Even if the delay this imposed did not lead to loss of life or limb, it was medically unsound. Pashtunwali trumps medical expediency.

To have a woman not only show up at the FOB, but to do so unescorted by a male relative was a staggering departure from local norms. The local culture encourages people to try to kill individuals who merely look at their women. Even photojournalist Louie Palu, who has seen more of Afghan culture than even two-tour veterans, had never seen anything like this.

The mother was clearly motivated by concern for her child. Nonetheless, she had to be very uncomfortable, so I tried to minimize her

A woman alone

unease as much as possible. I approached her as respectfully as I could, removing my hat and sunglasses and kneeling on the ground. I took a slow and careful history, spending extra time so that the interpreter got my questions absolutely right.

The mother told me an unusual story: her son had been unwell for three years, was not gaining weight or growing, and was always listless and asking to be picked up. I asked several more questions but could not pin down any constellation of symptoms that suggested a particular diagnosis. The mother went on to say that she had seen several doctors in Kandahar City, all of whom had told her that her son needed an operation on his heart or chest. She stated that she was unable to afford the surgery.

I then examined the child. He showed signs of mild chronic malnutrition, as is the case for many children here, but was otherwise normal. His height and weight put him right between his one-year-old and six-year-old siblings. In other words, he seemed to be growing normally, at least in terms of his familial context. As well, he struggled against me while I examined him and quickly ran to his mother when I let him go. There was no lethargy whatsoever.

The benign history and physical, in the light of a complaint of three years of "unwellness," seemed to indicate that nothing serious was going on. I thought long and hard about what to say. I did not want to appear to blow off the mother's concerns, nor did I want to disparage the Afghan doctors she claimed to have visited. I decided to tell her that what her child had would go away on its own, and that he would be a healthy boy in a year or two.

Then what had been astounding became mind-boggling. The woman lifted one side of her burka, exposing her left breast, and began breast-feeding the youngest child. She then reached out and touched the male interpreter on the knee to emphasize a point she was making.

Unless you have personally observed the hyper-conservative nature of even regular Afghans in this part of the country, it is difficult to grasp the import of that last paragraph. For pure shock value, this woman's actions were the equivalent of walking in on your grandmother while she is having sex with a stranger . . . in public.

Here in rural Kandahar, another consideration made this woman's actions even more astounding. What she did was not only shocking to local sensibilities, it was also a direct contravention of the rules of God, according to the Taliban. She could well be killed by them should they discover what she has done. When the Taliban were in power, they would beat women if a flash of ankle was visible beneath the burka.

I was still reeling from what I was seeing when the other shoe dropped. The woman asked if she could have money to help take care of the child. Now I understood what was happening. The only way this woman would have been able to come to the FOB on her own would be for her to be alone in the world. Somewhere in the twenty-one months between the conception of her one-year-old and now, she had lost the rest of her family, or what was left of it. She no longer had a husband, a father, uncles or brothers, since one of them would surely have accompanied her. She was as marginalized an individual as it is possible to be on this planet. The story about the child needing heart surgery was an attempt to tug at our heartstrings even more—not that it was necessary.

This put me in a difficult spot. We cannot start giving money to beggars who come to the FOB gate. This would guarantee a non-stop lineup of people seeking the same thing every day. But not to help someone like this would have required me to stifle my emotions more than I am able. In front of the other soldiers, I toed the party line and told everyone we could not help this woman. Afterwards, I caught up to her right before she left the FOB and slipped her a U.S. twenty-dollar bill.

BEGGARS IN THE DEVELOPING WORLD

In the 1982 movie *The Year of Living Dangerously,* Mel Gibson plays Guy, a reporter who is introduced to the slums of Jakarta by Billy, an Indonesian journalist. Billy (a male character played by Linda Hunt in a

A victim of war

and became fast friends. He holds the record for most time in Afghanistan by any Canadian military physician, having spent a total of over a year at KAF since 2006. He even spent a month at an American FOB that had a surgical capability, becoming the only Canadian military surgeon to have done time "outside the wire." Max shared my concern and asked for Naquibullah to be transferred to KAF for further evaluation. This is standard. Any civilian wounded by Coalition forces will receive the best care we are able to provide. We will also pay monetary compensation for these incidents.

It took two hours to arrange the transfer to KAF. With the help of a very good interpreter, I took advantage of the delay to speak at length with Naquibullah's father, Mr. Rahkman. I know what you're thinking: how honest was this man going to be when we were treating his wounded son? What were the chances that he would honestly tell us what he thought?

It turns out that the chances were pretty good. Mr. Rahkman did criticize the Taliban severely, and said that he was happy we were here to help get rid of them. Even if we discount those words as flattery, the other things he said had the ring of truth. Although he maintained a calm and pleasant demeanour throughout our time together, he was blunt in telling us the things he did not like about us.

His complaint centred on his recent losses. Mr. Rahkman accepted that what had happened was an accident, but he was still very angry at us. He was also very critical of various branches of the Afghan government, particularly the police, who he felt were corrupt.

What struck me most about an exchange like this one was that it occurred at all. Mr. Rahkman was in a room full of armed Canadians, and yet he did not show any hesitation in criticizing his government and its allies. For a democratic society to be able to function, it is essential for the population to feel that they can voice their criticisms openly. Free societies are secure enough that their governments can take a few shots (figuratively). Things were very different under the Taliban.

AFTERNOON

This afternoon, a dead Talib* was brought to the main gate of the FOB by the ANP. For some reason, I was asked to examine the man and declare him dead. I had never been asked to do this before. I wondered whether the Canadians at the gate were also in unfamiliar territory and had reacted as non-medical people often do in these situations: call the doctor.

The Talib had been discovered while attempting to plant an IED. An alert ANA soldier spotted him and shot him once through the head, killing him. The body was in the back of a police pickup truck, along with the evidence of his crime: a 155 mm artillery shell, some wiring and a detonating device. You could tell at a glance that the man was dead, but I went through the motions of placing my stethoscope

---

* Taliban is the plural. Talib is the singular. It means "seeker of truth."

on his chest anyway. After the prescribed period, I announced that he had passed away.

The memorable part of the event came next. An Afghan policeman from the detachment based at our FOB had been kidnapped by the Taliban yesterday and executed. The Taliban and the ANP were now engaged in negotiations to arrange for the bodies of their respective soldiers to be exchanged.

There is an individual in the district who acts as a middleman in these situations. I wondered how on earth anyone would get started in such a business.

Addendum, June 27: The body exchange has taken place. Around midnight last night, the "body exchanger" came to collect the dead Talib. With the heat of the past three days, he had started to rot and stank to high heaven. I assume the police have gotten their man back as well, in a similar state.

Muslims try to bury their dead before sundown of the day they die, so it was notable that both sides were willing to neglect that covenant to be able to get their man back.

Every body goes home.

JUNE 25 | Unfriendly Fire, Part 2: Barali

Ninety-four per cent. In nearly every field, that would be a pretty good number.

Barali was the one-year-old brother of Naquibullah. He had also been caught by the blast of the artillery shell that wounded his older brother. He had been seen by my predecessor at FOB Wilson, who had noted a small laceration to a leg. There were no other apparent injuries.

Before he returned home, his oxygen saturation was checked and found to be 94 per cent. The rest of his vital signs were normal, and he seemed comfortable. Two days later he coughed up a blood clot. Then he died.

Oxygen saturation measures the percentage of red blood cells that are carrying oxygen. Anything that impedes the ability of the lungs to transfer oxygen to the blood stream will be detected by a decrease in the oxygen saturation. Normal oxygen saturation varies between 95 and 100 per cent. In other words, this child had only the subtlest indication that there might be anything wrong.

Given the history of blood clots being coughed up, it is likely that Barali had a condition called "blast lung." The shock wave of the explosion caused a multitude of tiny rips. These rips started to bleed into the lung tissue. Barali drowned in his own blood.

His father was seen today by officers of our provincial reconstruction team. Given the proximity of our artillery strike to his home, there is little doubt that our actions at least partially contributed to Barali's death. Compensation has been authorized.

What do you say to the man whose child has been killed by the actions of your army? How can we put a price on his loss? There are no good sides to the story, but there are two important points to make about the people we are fighting.

The Taliban place their bombs in areas where civilian casualties are almost guaranteed. When this occurs, their position is that it was glorious for the civilians to die for their holy cause. No compensation is paid.

And what do they do when our side harms civilians? The boy's father told us that some Taliban soldiers came by his dwelling after his child had died.

He says they laughed.

Addendum, June 29: His father brought Naquibullah back for another follow-up visit today. Max had not wanted to change anything in terms of the treatments I had prescribed, so we set him up with enough supplies for two weeks of dressing changes. Max will see him again after that.

Before leaving, Naquibullah's father complained that word of the compensation he was to receive for the death of his son had leaked out and been broadcast on a local radio station. He fears this will attract the attention of the Taliban. I asked the translator how bad that could get. He answered: "Very bad." I took that to mean "Fatal."

The money that Naquibullah's father will receive will be in the order of five thousand dollars. He has told us that he wants to use this money to move to a safer place (read: closer to the FOB). Now he has to make a choice. Accept the money and be seen as a traitor by the Taliban, with potentially lethal consequences; or stay in the middle of an active combat zone, one that has already killed one of his children.

JUNE 26 | Divine Wind in Kandahar

We captured a suicide bomber today. I'm not going to discuss how we figured out who he was, where we captured him and what is happening to him now. But the phenomenon of suicide bombing is worth examining in greater detail.

The military histories of the Western world have occasional examples of men who, in the heat of battle, have chosen a course of action that condemned them to death. The majority of these actions occurred when individuals sacrificed themselves to save one or more comrades. A soldier will dive onto a live hand grenade to protect other soldiers in the same trench. A pilot will give his parachute to another crew member, then keep his burning plane flying straight and level long enough for his buddy to bail out. A sailor will close a watertight door to prevent a submarine from sinking, even though he will be trapped in the flooded compartment.

The Western mind can comprehend this, but it cannot accept suicide as a tactic to achieve a limited military objective. You might wonder how we could ever defeat an enemy willing to do such a thing. To answer that question, we must first understand the motivation of the suicide bomber.

Many suicide bombers are not driven by deep philosophical or political convictions. On the contrary, a large number of these individuals are mentally handicapped people who do not realize what they are about to do. Many others are pressured into this role, often to pay off a family debt of some sort. These people are being used as weapons by utterly callous individuals. The only way we can stop them is to kill or capture the men who manipulate or coerce them.

The suicide bombers we need to understand are those who are of normal intellectual capacity and who are convinced of the rightness of their actions. The best explanation for this was articulated by Lawrence Wright, who wrote *The Looming Tower*, the best work on the origins, evolution and philosophy of Islamic extremism.* In a presentation he made in Toronto, Wright explained the appeal of martyrdom.

Consider what the life of a young man is like in a country such as Saudi Arabia, where all aspects of social life are controlled by Islamic fundamentalists. What outlets are there for these individuals?

The economy is barren. The total economic production of the entire Middle East is less than that of Mexico. If you take oil out of the equation, it is less than the Nokia phone company. There are few productive activities one can engage in.

Social interactions are even more limited. There is very little in the way of theatre, music or arts. Worst of all is the way that women have been removed from public life. There are none of the moderating influences that women exert on society, and none of the social interactions that occur when both sexes must share the public arena. For many of these young men life is spent living at home, with interruptions for trips to the mosque. It is a life devoid of challenge, of any possibility of expressing oneself, of any chance of making a mark on the world.

Then along comes al Qaeda. Now, these young men can change history. All they have to do . . . is die.†

---

* Lawrence Wright, *The Looming Tower: Al Qaeda and the Road to 9/11* (New York: Knopf, 2006).

† Even in societies run by Islamic fundamentalists, the appeal of martyrdom drops off sharply after one reaches maturity. Osama bin Laden said that "only fifteen- to twenty-five-year-olds are useful for Jihad" (by which he meant suicide missions). Once you have a family, the consequences of suicide are much more severe. Once you have children, you have a stake in the future.

explosion has taken place a safe distance from our convoy, the media could not care less. Superb soldiering is not nearly as newsworthy as the times soldiers kill in error. The latter gets a lot of media coverage, even though it represents a tiny fraction of the times Coalition troops open fire on civilian vehicles.

Being a stickler for grammatical accuracy, I will point out that you only hear about suicide-homicide bombers. You do not hear about the times suicide bombers really are . . . suicide bombers. In the interests of "journalistic balance," I offer one such example from a few days ago.

The first photograph on the previous page shows the remains of a motorcycle after a suicide bomber detonated himself on it.

We only found shreds of this guy. The bomber had driven his motorcycle behind the ANA vehicle shown in the second photograph on the previous page. The vehicle was shredded by shrapnel. There was no place on the vehicle that anyone could have survived.

When the suicide bomber detonated himself, the truck was empty, making him only a suicide bomber, without the homicide he had been hoping to achieve. He traded his life for a Ford Ranger.

JUNE 27 | The Elements, Part 1: Water

Let's start with a literary installment, the first verse of "Gunga Din," by Rudyard Kipling. This poem describes the desperate thirst of a wounded man lying in the heat. The location of the action could well be Afghanistan, since Britain fought a war in this area around the time Kipling was here:

> You may talk o' gin and beer
> When you're quartered safe out 'ere
> An' you're sent to penny-fights an' Aldershot it;
> But when it comes to slaughter
> You will do your work on water,
> An' you'll lick the bloomin' boots of 'im that's got it.

The temperature in Zhari district is reported as having been 47°C today. It felt like 57°C.

I have been in the Caribbean, Central America, Southern Africa and equatorial Indonesia, so these latitudes are familiar to me. Something about this heat is different, perhaps because we are in a desert.

At the risk of sounding like a broken Canadian record, I think the heat affects you more in a desert because . . . it's a dry heat. In other places I experienced tropical temperatures, I was either in a rain forest or close to an ocean. Here, the heat reflects off the sandy ground with such intensity that you feel it is exerting a physical pressure on you. Direct sunlight is so strong that you feel your exposed skin is being damaged from the moment you step outside.

Our water consumption is therefore a source of constant concern for commanders at all levels. Getting water from KAF to the combat troops occupies the minds of everyone. This starts with the general, who watches over the logistics of delivering over 200,000 litres of water to the FOBs every month. All this water is bottled. As is the case elsewhere in the developing world, it would be foolhardy to drink any locally found water, even that coming from a well.

At the other end of this pipeline, the corporal makes sure the private carries enough water before we head out on an operation. How much is "enough"? Combat infantrymen already carry a lot of weight: body armour, weapons, ammunition, rations and other gear. Most of them will also carry eight litres of water, contained in two large bags called a Camelbak. Counting the bags themselves, that is almost ten kilograms of additional weight to carry. When we resupply troops in the field, one helicopter's payload might be taken up by water alone.

The goal of all this drinking is to avoid dehydration. In these kinds of temperatures and with that much weight on their backs, the combat troopers can lose several litres of water a day through their skin. At a minimum, water intake must match the amount lost through sweating. If it does not, a person can fall into a condition called heat exhaustion. In its early stages, heat exhaustion is easy to correct, by removing patients from the heat and giving them a lot of water to drink. If the situation deteriorates even further—if individuals get dehydrated and continue to work hard in the heat—they can progress to a much more serious condition called heat stroke.

We sweat to cool off our bodies. People with heat stroke either drank so little or sweated so much that they are out of water completely. The physical characteristic that confirms they are suffering from heat stroke rather than heat exhaustion is that their skin is dry rather than sweaty.

This can be life-threatening. With sweat no longer being produced, the body stops cooling itself. Body temperature, which until then remains roughly normal, rises quickly. Somewhere between 40°C and 42°C, neurological dysfunction occurs: confusion, collapse and coma. Somewhere between 44°C and 46°C, the patient dies.

It is not all that difficult to fall victim to heat stroke. Highly motivated people can push themselves hard enough to do it. I had a case like this recently.

I was getting ready to go to bed when one of our combat troopers came in complaining of a single episode of vomiting, abdominal cramping and a headache. Although his blood pressure was normal, his pulse was worrisomely elevated. He looked, to use the medical term, like shit.

Given that he had vomited only once, it was unlikely that his rapid pulse was due to gastroenteritis. He claimed to have been well until an hour earlier. He had spent the day participating in the St-Jean-Baptiste celebrations.* He mentioned that he had acquired a new camera and had taken 227 pictures that day. Upon hearing that, I asked him how much water he had drunk that day. He thought about it for a few seconds and then said, "One five-hundred-millilitre bottle of water—maybe."

---

* The national celebration of Quebecers. It is equivalent to the July 1 celebration in the rest of Canada. Quebec celebrates both holidays, but St-Jean-Baptiste Day has the bigger parties.

This guy had been having so much fun that he forgot to drink for twelve hours in 50°C heat. This is more common than you might think, and it demonstrates the degree to which training is contextual. Had this trooper been in the field on a combat operation, he would have remembered to drink constantly. Soldiers who allow themselves to become dehydrated on an operation will be charged with negligence: they will be punished for not looking after themselves properly.

It is a testament to the resilience of the young to see how far this man, in his twenties, was able to drive himself. It took twenty-four hours and nine(!) litres of intravenous fluid before he began to urinate normally. He was off his feet for three more days after that.

JUNE 28 | The Follow-up

The little girl whose facial laceration I had repaired a few days ago returned for her suture removal today. Once again, she was accompanied only by her brother. I noticed she wore the same dress as she had the first time I met her, but the blood stains on it had been carefully removed. It is likely her one good set of clothes. This is something I have often seen in the developing world: individuals who are dirt-poor and living in mud and thatch hovels will meet you dressed in a good shirt and pants or a nice dress. They take exquisite care of that single good set of clothes. The poor take as much pride in their appearance as anyone else.

My patient was a little apprehensive, but no more than any small child confronted by a stranger would be. You will recall that I used ketamine to put her to sleep for the repair. One of the best qualities of this drug is that it erases the patient's memories starting a few minutes *before* the injection. Children who have a painful procedure done under ketamine don't even remember the shot that put them to sleep. They have no negative memories of the hospital and are much less frightened when they come back.

The little girl tolerated the procedure well. She was even feeling confident enough to express her desire for more of the Oreo cookies

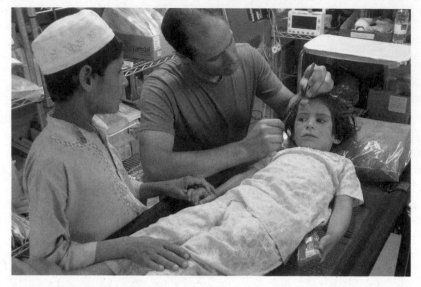

Suture removal; under Oreo sedation

that we had sent her home with last time. As you can see in the photograph above, these were provided.

JUNE 29 | Operation Tora Arwa II

The past three days have been an anxious time. The combat team has been running a major operation in Siah Choy since before first light two days ago. This is an area of intense Taliban activity southeast of here. I have been closely following their progress on our various communication networks.

This was an airmobile operation, meaning that the troops attacked by helicopter. It was one of the first times an entire combat team had been airlifted directly onto a known Taliban troop concentration. The planning and coordination involved for such an operation is monumentally complex: nearly two hundred people will land, at night, in the middle of terrain crawling with enemy soldiers. They have to be ready to fight from the moment they hit the ground. The amount of detailed information Major Arsenault had to juggle in his mind as the combat team went through its preparations and rehearsals is mind-boggling.

The operation started off on a hilarious note. Major Arsenault was on the first helicopter. He got off and had only taken a few steps when he came upon a rifle, a pistol, a radio, a canteen, some food, various maps and other Taliban documents, some night vision gear, a blanket and . . . a full set of clothing.

Our enemies are not stupid. They know we are trying hard, with some success, to figure out the locations of their main commanders and principal weapons caches. These locations are vulnerable to surprise attack by airmobile troops, and any idiot can figure out which fields are big enough for several helicopters to land on simultaneously. The Taliban place observers throughout the district to warn them of such an attack. It looks like Major Arsenault's chopper landed almost on top of one of these guys. He must have run off buck naked.

After that, things got more serious. The fighting has been fierce, and contact with the enemy has been constant. The artillery has been firing regularly, and fixed-wing aircraft and helicopters have been conducting frequent strafing and bombing runs.

Whereas the fixed-wing bombers are flown by our Coalition partners, the helicopters supporting this operation are Canadian. The combat team was flown in by our Chinooks, and strafing runs have been executed by our Griffons. The link between the Griffon gunships and the infantry is particularly strong: the door gunners are infantrymen who have taken a special course to learn how to shoot people on the ground from a moving aircraft.

Even those helicopters whose crews are made up of air force types go out of their way to help the Canadian infantry. They routinely take last-minute calls from the field and then cram their birds with whatever the combat troopers need.

One Canadian was wounded yesterday. He took a piece of shrapnel to the head. From the combat medic's description, the wound did not seem all that serious. There had been some arterial bleeding, but this was now controlled.

Towards the end of the following day, a convoy carrying one of the senior leaders of the battle group passed right over this spot. Fortunately, the Talib's courage and skill was offset by his bad timing. The trigger man detonated the IED between the first and second vehicle in the convoy. The explosion shattered the road and sent dust and debris fifty metres into the air and a hundred metres away. Incredibly, no Canadian was injured.

You might come away from this with the feeling that the Taliban are all incredibly clever. Let me show you how false this can be.

During Operation Tora Arwa II (described in yesterday's entry), the Canadian combat team was accompanied by an ANP unit that was being mentored by some American trainers. During a lull in the battle, the Afghan policemen and their mentors were resting in a field. One of the policemen got up and walked towards a nearby tree line. This was strange, because it was in the direction the Taliban were thought to be. The policeman disappeared into the trees for a couple of minutes, then walked back, taking a position on the edge of his group. No more than a minute later, an RPG (rocket-propelled grenade) was launched from the spot in the tree line that the policeman had disappeared into. It exploded more or less in the middle of the combined American and Afghan troops. This was followed by rifle and machine gun fire from several Taliban soldiers in the tree line. The Americans and ANP returned fire until the Taliban broke contact and withdrew. During the firefight, the policeman who had wandered over to the tree line was observed firing his rifle well off to the side of where the enemy was. None of our soldiers were injured during this exchange.

It is known that the Taliban have numerous infiltrators in the Afghan security services, rather more in the police than in the army. These individuals will give away the plans of patrols, attacks and ambushes that we are going to conduct. This individual appears to have wanted to take a more direct approach and tell his comrades *in person* where to shoot. It boggles the mind that he thought he would get away with this. As soon as the helicopters landed at the FOB, the spy was arrested and carted off to jail.

I suppose we should consider ourselves fortunate. There have been a couple of incidents this year in which Afghan police have opened fire on Coalition patrols. In both cases, there were American fatalities. Also in both cases, the patrol defended itself and killed the traitor, making it impossible to question him.

I have spoken to members of our intelligence services about these incidents. They feel it is likely that the identity of these individuals was somehow discovered by the Taliban. Our enemies went on to learn where their families lived. The policemen would then have been given a stark choice: open fire on the Americans, knowing full well that they would return the fire with lethal effect, or have your family murdered.

What would any of us do, if we were faced with a similar choice?

JULY 1 | Canada Day

My Canada Day celebration was delayed by the arrival of three patients, who had the good grace to arrive sequentially rather than all at the same time. As is becoming predictable, they were all either drivers or guards on the convoys that go along Ring Road South.

One of them arrived with an injury I had dealt with on my previous tour: a small bowel evisceration. Back then, an older gentleman had arrived with one loop of his intestines hanging out and I had struggled to repair his injury with inadequate instruments and medications. Today, it was a sixteen-year-old with multiple bowel loops trapped outside the body. Fortunately, I was much better equipped this time.

After ensuring that the patient had no further injuries, I put him under general anaesthesia. I washed off the bowel with copious amounts of sterile water and checked to see that there were no perforations needing repair. Then, with far better instruments than I had on Roto 4, I extended the skin wound by two centimetres. The patient was now paralyzed by my medication and his abdominal muscles could be easily stretched. This made it simple to stuff his bowel back into his abdomen.

I then washed out his abdomen with a couple of litres of sterile water, which I suctioned out. I closed the skin with a series of sutures, and we helicoptered the patient to Kandahar. What had been a one-hour, high-stress sweatfest in 2007 now took no more than six or seven minutes.

The injuries of the other two patients were, in the context of the war zone, almost trivial. One of them had shrapnel wounds in his back, and the other had a gunshot wound in his shoulder. In both cases, ultrasound ruled out any life-threatening injuries to the thorax or abdomen. Despite the visually impressive nature of the wounds, they only required simple bandaging before transfer. Both patients, though in a fair amount of pain, were stable, but the way each reacted to the pain was dramatically different.

Have you ever heard someone describing developing-world patients in general, or perhaps Afghans in particular, as being able to tolerate extraordinary amounts of pain with little or no complaint? This is utter bullshit. Although we humans can display the most remarkable variability in shape, size, physical appearance and political leanings, our nervous systems are identical. You can get used to things like walking on gravel or running in the heat, but there is no way to become accustomed to the feeling of being ripped open by shrapnel.

I have treated trauma victims on almost every continent and in a variety of cultures. I have not noted a measurable difference in any ethnic population's response to acute pain. Some *individuals* are tough, and some are wimps; the majority fall somewhere between these two limits.

As it happened, these two patients were at opposite ends of the spectrum. The one with a gunshot wound to the shoulder was stoic. When I asked him to rate his pain, he kept repeating it was manageable. I gave him some intravenous narcotics anyway, and he admitted that he felt better once that kicked in.

The other patient came in screaming and kept right on screaming, even after we had given him a generous dose of Fentanyl (a powerful synthetic variant of morphine). He then revealed something that a sizable number of the patients I have seen here have also reported: he told us he was a hashish and opium addict. This is useful information for the trauma team to have. Patients who are addicted to narcotics will need more medicine to control their pain due to the downregulation phenomenon I described in the June 17 entry. However, it is also true that addicts will sometimes exaggerate their pain to get access to narcotics.

When faced with this conundrum (Give more morphine because of downregulation? Give less because he might be lying?), it is always better to err on the side of humanity and to give the painkillers. The occasional addict cadges a dose, but everyone with genuine pain gets treated quickly and effectively.

Having said that, there is a limit to my generosity and this patient reached it. A number of things didn't fit: the first dose of Fentanyl had had no effect, the patient's pulse was not racing, he wasn't sweating at all and his facial expressions . . . didn't seem right. He kept asking for more drug, but I declined to provide it.

Whereas he might have been exaggerating his pain, he was probably being honest about his addiction. Hashish is abundant in this area. Many of our operations burn dozens of kilos of the stuff. As for narcotics, 90 per cent of the world's illicit opium comes from this country. While most of it is converted into heroin and sold in Europe and North America, a substantial portion of the harvest is siphoned off for use in Afghanistan and neighbouring Central Asian nations. The best estimates put the total number of addicts in this region between ten million and twenty million.

The reasons for this are obvious. A small proportion of the human population has a predisposition for addiction, but this does not account for the total addict population. The majority of addicts turn to psychoactive drugs for the same reason the rest of us turn to pain medication: to numb an unpleasant stimulus.

This is the case in Central Asia. Repressive governments, moribund economies and continuing strife (both within and between the countries of the region) have left the populations here anxious and bored at the same time. They turn to cheap and readily available chemical vacations as a respite from lives that are much more stressful than any we can conceive of in Canada.

The day ended with a couple of events worth reporting. First we were visited by General Jonathan Vance, the commander of the Canadian contingent. This was a low-key thing, quite different from the visit of the CDS two weeks ago. General Vance dropped in on Major Arsenault and the leaders of the combat team for less than an hour.

I wanted to learn more about his bodyguards—elite soldiers are always interesting characters—so I wandered over to talk to the men who escort the general. They are a pretty tough bunch. They are almost all on at least their second if not their third and even fourth tour. One of them was with the Canadian infantry battalion that participated in the initial attack on the Taliban in 2001.

I did not have much time to talk to these guys, but I could tell that our commander was in good hands. This morning, his convoy easily fought off Taliban ambushers firing automatic weapons and RPGs. The general himself fired off a full magazine at the enemy! I don't know if this was the first time the general had been under direct fire, but you could tell his escorts were used to this. They mentioned this morning's firefight almost as an afterthought.

The general rolled out around dinnertime and I went to catch what was, for the troops, the high point of the Canada Day celebrations: the issuing of the two beers per month that we get here. I never drink when I am on duty, but I got to enjoy the brews vicariously.

Addendum, July 19: The best part of Canada Day came three weeks later. My daughter's daycare has been very supportive of my family during my absence. They wanted Claude and Michelle to know that they were not alone in this. So they made an enormous banner, and got all the kids in Michelle's group to "sign" it with their hands. Then they had a "red shirt day" on Canada Day, to express their support for the troops, with Claude and Michelle as the guests of honour.

Walden Daycare supports the troops

JULY 2 | Sparks

I turned fifty a couple of weeks before I got to the FOB. I like to think of myself as being computer literate, but there is a generation gap between me and most of the soldiers in this respect. Computers are something I have grown familiar with over the past fifteen years, but for the twentysomethings who make up the majority of the FOB population, computers have been a natural part of their lives since birth.

It is impossible to overestimate the importance of electronic communication for this crowd. Whether it's e-mail, instant messaging or surfing the Net, these kids are permanently plugged in, so the impact on morale of any breakdown of our Internet connection would be catastrophic. It follows that one of the most valuable men on the FOB is the remarkably capable and good-natured Corporal Tom White. He is a twenty-three-year-old "signaller," one of the men responsible for everything that has to do with communications (phones, radios and the all-important Internet).

In the past few days, he has proven his worth to me several times over. In what is sure to thrill my Mac-loving friends, my PC's Internet connection broke down after I tried to upgrade Explorer. Corporal White got it running again. I will be eternally grateful to him.

From the beginning, I have called Corporal White "Sparks." But not until today did I ask him if he understood why I did this. He did not, but he had been too polite to say so. I explained that the very first radios generated their waves using spark-gap transmitters, and the sparks they gave off led to this nickname, universally given to radio operators. Corporal White went on to make me feel even older when he admitted he did not know the names of the characters in the original *Star Trek* TV series.

Addendum, September 9, at FOB *Sperwan Ghar:* My debt towards the signals people has increased. For the past several days, my personal global satellite phone has stubbornly refused to turn on. This made it difficult to keep my promise to Michelle to call her every day. It occurred to me that another Sparks might be able to help. What happened next felt like déjà vu.

Master Corporal Laszlo Pivonka fulfills the same role Corporal White did at FOB Wilson. I had run into Master Corporal Pivonka a number of times. Like his counterpart, he is always cheerful and strikes one as an all-around nice guy. The similarities with Corporal White do not end there. Master Corporal Pivonka is yet another one of those technological whiz kids who are the modern-day masters of the universe.

The parallels between these two communications gurus continued in their interactions with my equipment. Master Corporal Pivonka got a few instruments and tools, poked and prodded my phone for no more than sixty seconds and . . . *voilà!* It was working again.

I sat there, stunned by this miraculous change. I began to express my gratitude, but he cut me off with a laugh and a grin, saying, "It's my business to fix shit." When I asked him what the problem had been, he admitted that he was not sure which of the three or four things he had done had resurrected my phone. "Sometimes, when I fix shit, it starts to work by FM." And that would be? "Fucking magic," he replied.

Finally an explanation from a tech wizard that makes sense to me.

The abbreviation RIP has a negative connotation we all know. In the army, it has a second meaning, one that is more positive.

In two days I have to go to FOB Ma'Sum Ghar. The doctor who will be taking over at FOB Wilson arrived today and we conducted a RIP—a relief in place. She did a RIP In; I will do a RIP Out in two days. I got her settled into our shack and showed her around the FOB and the UMS.

Captain Valérie Lafortune had been assigned to KAF before this. She was one of the military doctors I trained in ultrasound last December. She asked if she could have a quick refresher, which I was happy to provide. Once again, good old reliable P.Y. stepped up as a model.

Captain Lafortune was pleased to be assigned here to replace me. For all the danger and the boredom, this is front-line medicine. When we spoke over the phone a few days ago to prepare her transfer, she emphasized her desire to see some trauma cases. I know that sounds morbid, but it isn't. I feel the same way. Although we wish it were

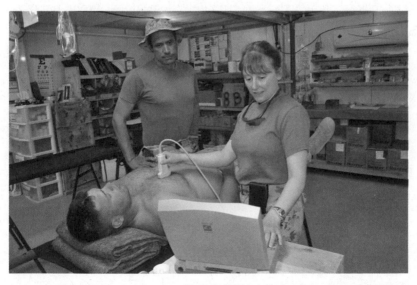

Captain Valérie Lafortune takes over at FOB Wilson

Beautifying the UMS: burning paint to bake it into the concrete

otherwise, we know bad things are going to happen to people. That being the case, we would prefer that these patients come to us. We came here because we believe in the mission, and this is how we can best support it.

Cute-as-a-button Captain Lafortune may not look the part of the hard-bitten FOB doctor, but appearances are deceptive. She is cool, collected and very competent. I was happy to leave the FOB in her hands.

She arrived as I was evacuating the day's only casualty, an Afghan convoy guard who had been shot through the upper thigh. The shooting must have taken place some hours before because his leg was covered in blood that had dried. We had a report that he had lost a considerable amount of blood at the scene, which was believable because he was displaying early signs of shock when he arrived. Fortunately, he responded to initial treatments and he will be fine.

The day ended with a remarkable display of artistic ability on the part of Corporal Nathan Nolet, one of the combat medics. He has had no formal training; his considerable experience was gained decorating overpasses. He took it upon himself to beautify the social area of the UMS. He works only with spray paint, a piece of cardboard, the top of a garbage can and a paper plate. His creation was stunning. If you have a forklift and a flatbed truck, the above masterpiece can be yours.

JULY 4 | Abbreviated Tragedy: WIA, VSA, DOW, KIA

With Captain Lafortune having taken over the UMS, I was free to take the day off. Quite a treat—I had time to read, make additional videos for Michelle and laze around. I also had time to have one last long talk with Major Arsenault, who continued to impress me with his maturity and insight. It could have been an all-around wonderful day, but it wasn't. The war came back to hurt us yesterday and today.

Our fallen are referred to as having been "killed in action," which we abbreviate as KIA. In the strictest sense of the word, this is inaccurate in a small proportion of cases.

The vast majority of Canadian soldiers killed in Afghanistan have died in explosions that ended their lives between heartbeats. They are true KIA. A minority survived for some time before expiring. We try very, very hard in these cases to stave off death, even if it seems inevitable. The motto of the KAF hospital is "If you arrive alive, you will survive." That is a promise we have been able to keep with nearly every Canadian wounded in Afghanistan. Nearly.

Canadians who are wounded are labelled as WIA: wounded in action. This gets the medevac helicopters into the air. If things go badly, WIA might get upgraded to VSA: vital signs absent. This means the wounded soldier is now in cardiac arrest. Things are grim when that happens. Soldiers are young, healthy people. If their heart stops, it is because their bodies have suffered tremendous damage and they have lost most of their blood. The chances that they will survive are slim at best. Nonetheless, the distinction between VSA and KIA is an important one. As long as we are still attempting to bring the patient back, the medevac helicopters will get to us at best possible speed in all but the worst weather. If we realize our efforts are futile and we stop trying to resuscitate the patient, they become a KIA. The evacuation then becomes a much lower priority. We may even decide to evacuate the body by road. Very rarely, a soldier survives passage through the KAF hospital only to die several days later. We learned of one such case today.

Master Corporal Charles-Philippe Michaud had been on patrol on June 23 near FOB Sperwan Ghar. He had stepped on an IED that ripped off one of his legs and badly damaged his other limbs. Initial reports were that he might end up a triple amputee. Then the reports became

with a large-calibre weapon, was well coordinated and pressed home with determination as the Taliban attempted to assault our positions at three different locations. It was broken up by an even more competent Canadian defence, and the Taliban withdrew with heavy losses. Nonetheless, when Major Arsenault spoke about the skill with which the attack was executed by the Taliban leader, it was with something approaching admiration, or at least the respect of one professional for another.

He also described how the Taliban would sprint towards the Canadian lines when our artillery would start to fall among them. The Taliban soldiers know that the closer they are to our guys, the less likely we are to bomb them, for fear of a shell hitting our own troops. So they gamble that they will be able to get under cover before the Canadian infantry can shoot them. Sometimes this tactic works, sometimes it doesn't. Even if they are not gunned down as they run towards us, they are now in a close-range fight with our troops—a fight they almost always lose.

Foolish? Irrational? Deluded? Sociopathic? Perhaps. Possibly all four. Cowards? No.

We need to accept this if we are to defeat them.

JULY 5, MORNING | Blasting Off from Wilson

Last day at FOB Wilson. It started off with a bang, literally.

I had taken care of Warrant Officer Serge Comeau, the second-in-command of the FOB's engineer detachment, when he had gotten a moderate case of heat exhaustion a few weeks ago. As a thank you, he invited me to perform a BIP, or blow in place, the controlled destruction of an enemy IED that has been detected and removed. The IED in question was the 155 mm artillery shell discussed in the June 24 entry. I enthusiastically accepted his invitation. What can I tell you? It's fun to blow shit up!

Warrant Officer Comeau, Cinquième Régiment de Génie de Combat (5th Combat Engineer Regiment), is cut from the same cloth as Major Arsenault. He is a pleasant individual who is always upbeat and a master of his trade. After the major, he is probably the most respected man on the FOB. Here's one example of why that is so.

During the recent operation in Siah Choy, Warrant Comeau helped to set up and defend a CCP, or casualty collection point. The four men who were wounded on the third day of the operation were brought to him. Before being wounded, the men had been stopped on the edge of a field. Since they were not running, they undid their helmet straps, which chafe in the heat. When they were hit—simultane-

Warrant Officer Serge Comeau, combat engineer leader

ously, from a single explosion—they fell to the ground and their helmets came off. Their comrades, in their rush to get the wounded to a safe place—the CCP—did not bother to pick up the helmets.

When the wounded arrived, there was still quite a bit of shelling going on and shrapnel fragments were landing all over the place. Warrant Comeau spontaneously removed his own helmet and placed it on one wounded man's head. That illustrates his courage, but what he did a couple of days later shows you the kind of leader he is.

He ordered every one of his men to bring a picture of a wife or a lover or of their parents and children, and then asked them to say a bit about the people in the pictures. Once everyone had finished, he asked them to reflect on how important these people were to them and how much these people wanted them to come home safely. Then he asked them to make sure they kept their helmet straps done up at all times.

Military training manuals define leadership as "the art of influencing people to do your bidding." Poor military leaders yell and scream and threaten. Average leaders give orders without explanation. The better ones explain the reasons for their decisions. With the best leaders, followers make good decisions for their own reasons. They are barely aware they are following orders.

I have one last remarkable example of Warrant Comeau's internal moral compass. At thirty-four years of age, he is quite young to have achieved the rank he holds. The CF has big plans for him—or rather, it *had* plans. Warrant Comeau has announced his intention to retire. He does not have twenty years in, so he will not qualify for a full pension. He still enjoys being a combat engineer, but he is giving it all up to be closer to his wife and young children.

JULY 5, AFTERNOON | Return to FOB Ma'Sum Ghar

It was with sadness that I bade farewell to Major Arsenault, Warrant Comeau, Dominic the Medic and the rest of the FOB Wilson team. Although it is "one FOB down, two to go" and a milestone in my progress towards going home, I have become attached to the people here and it is hard to leave them. It would be preferable for the departure to be quick. That would not be the case today.

The convoy I was booked on was delayed. After several hours it became evident that they would not arrive in time to take me to my next FOB, Ma'Sum Ghar. This would leave the FOB without medical coverage for a day or more; a lot can go wrong in that time, so I scrambled to see if I could hitch a ride with anybody else.

Going down the roads of Zhari-Panjwayi, as I have mentioned in the past, is not something one does lightly. So it was with some trepidation that I got on the only other convoy headed my way that day: an American mine-clearing unit tasked to perform a sweep of one of the Wilson-to-Ma'Sum Ghar roads. Since this unit was made up of eight vehicles, my arrival at FOB Ma'Sum Ghar had all the subtlety of a royal wedding. The man I am replacing, Petty Officer Martin Bédard, was duly impressed.

I was thrilled to see "Bed" again. He had taken my introductory ultrasound course and had been sharp and enthusiastic. He was

Looking northeast from Hilltop OP
(Photo courtesy Master Corporal Julien Ricard)

also one of the three soldiers I had trained in advanced ultrasound techniques.

It was great to be back at FOB Ma'Sum Ghar as well. It was familiar ground and aesthetically pleasing. FOB Wilson had marvellous creature comforts (though Ma'Sum Ghar comes close), but its topography left something to be desired: it was affectionately known as "FOB Flat." FOB Ma'Sum Ghar is built on a hill, which gives the UMS staff a spectacular view.

I was less pleased to learn that Ma'Sum Ghar was still Rocket Central, as it had been on Roto 4. Life here will be a lot more dangerous than it was at FOB Wilson. Everyone wears their full PPE (personal protective equipment: helmets, ballistic glasses and frag vests) anytime they are outside the protective walls of their bunker. The big hill we are on is an easy target for the Taliban rocket men. Being an eternal optimist, I chose to focus on the lower number of rockets hitting Ma'Sum Ghar (when compared with my last tour) as being a sign of progress. The other side was still lobbing more high explosive at this FOB than at any other . . . but less so. In a war zone, you cling to things like this.

Bed took me to see the UMS, which is vastly improved. Lieutenant Colonel Ron Wojtyk, my friend who is the senior doctor in the task force, told me this morning that the Ma'Sum Ghar UMS is the busiest

The treatment area of the UMS

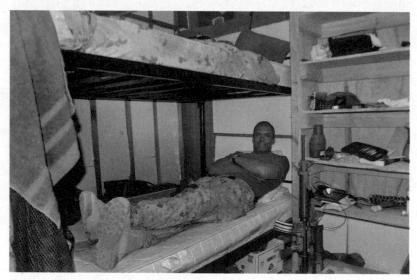

The room I share with the UMS medic

one in our area of operations. The statistics Bed showed me explained why this was so: in this intimate little war, moving a few kilometres from Wilson to Ma'Sum Ghar changes the types of wounds we see.

The injuries at FOB Wilson were mostly gunshot and shrapnel wounds from attacks on convoys on Ring Road South. As penetrating trauma goes, these wounds are relatively straightforward. The UMS here sees far more IED victims. The devastating injuries caused by these weapons are much more challenging to deal with. July will be hot in more ways than one.

An air-conditioned staff lounge is attached to the UMS. This place has everything the FOB Wilson "goodie wall" did, but here we have an area in which to sit and eat as well. To say that this is better than the old tent, when it is 50°C outside, is the understatement of the year.

The bunker we sleep in, which was one big room during Roto 4, is now subdivided into three rooms and a lounge, complete with TV. The TV is used to play video games far more than to watch the single available channel (CFTV—Canadian Forces TV). "Guitar Hero" and an amazingly realistic hockey game dominate.

Ghar means "mountain" in Pashto, and *ma'sum* means "quiet." So Ma'Sum Ghar means Quiet Mountain. This war has its ironic moments.

THE FOB MA'SUM GHAR MEDICAL GANG

The medic assigned to the UMS itself is Master Corporal Julien "Red" Ricard. Red is a veteran, having been in Kandahar Province for Roto 3. Red's older brother, Sergeant Georges Ricard, also a combat medic, was on Roto 2. They spent a week in the country at the same time, Georges leaving while Red was settling in.

Red was assigned to the provincial reconstruction team and spent the tour wandering around Zhari-Panjwayi. He travelled extensively and spent a lot of time on foot. This means that he was exposed to a considerable amount of risk.

Red made it through the tour without a scratch ... until the last week. Seven days before he was to go home, he was riding in a vehicle

The wrecked Nyala

When the rest of the soldiers in the convoy had secured the area, they withdrew back to FOB Ma'Sum Ghar. Pack up, turn around and go home. That sounds simple, doesn't it? It wasn't.

It was the middle of the night. It was pitch black outside, with no illumination coming from streetlights or nearby dwellings. A convoy of a dozen vehicles had undergone not one, but two attacks. The second attack had destroyed one of their vehicles, damaged another and wounded five of their comrades. As bad as that was, the first attack was foremost on everybody's mind because it was a "direct fire" attack. Enemy soldiers had had the convoy in their sights when they fired the RPG. They could still be lurking in the dark, waiting to fire more grenades into the now immobile and far more vulnerable convoy.

The first priority was to set up a security cordon so that the convoy would be able to defend itself if it came under attack once more. Only then could the wounded be attended to and the damage to the vehicles assessed. As it turned out, the vehicle that rear-ended the Nyala hit so hard that it was a "mobility kill" (in other words, a total writeoff).

It took four hours for the remaining vehicles and their crews to make it back to FOB Ma'Sum Ghar. Throughout this time, Red cared for the wounded. He had everybody conscious and mobile by the time they rolled into the FOB.

Red is not one of those laugh-in-the-face-of-death idiots who try to pretend that events like this do not affect them. He has no trouble telling you that the tears flowed that morning. He was given the choice of returning to KAF by road or waiting a little longer to go by helicopter. He chose the latter. Statistically, that was the safer choice, but it did not seem so a couple of hours later. Still shaking from his brush with death, Red experienced the FOB Ma'Sum Ghar specialty: a rocket attack.

In the end, waiting longer and sweating through a rocket attack made no difference. A dust storm blew up, which grounded the choppers. Red ended up going back to KAF by road anyway, in the back of a Bison ambulance. He slept all the way, not because he was fearless but because he was still very frightened. "The way my mind was working then," he says, "I thought that it would not feel as bad to be killed while I was sleeping." Like I said, it was a Bad Day.

Despite all that, Red signed up for a second tour. He has chosen a soldier's life and a medic's career. It is here that he can best follow his vocation and support his comrades. In doing do, he has demonstrated true courage: doing something that frightens him and overcoming that fear.

As the UMS medic, he is formally my second-in-command. That designation does not do him justice. The decisions that officers make are only as good as the implementation managed by the non-commissioned officers who are their partners in leadership. If an officer is doing a good job, it is often because he or she has an excellent second-in-command.

If all Red did was take my suggestions and turn them into realities, that would be enough. He goes well beyond that. He has that quality the military looks for in a future leader: he is a self-starter. Red is always looking for ways to improve the functioning of the UMS. While the rest of us are enjoying the down times, he often starts on some project or other on his own initiative. He has improved the storage space of the UMS, wired additional lighting and (my personal favourite) created a "Wall of Remembrance" where the pictures of fallen combat medics are displayed. He does all this with such quiet efficiency that I am barely aware the tasks are being done. I could not ask for a better man to have at my side.

Finally, Red is a professional-calibre photographer. Many of the images you will see from here on will be his handiwork.

We have two Bison ambulance crews here. One is attached to our quick reaction force (QRF)—the tanks and infantry tasked to respond to any emergency. The crew chief is Master Corporal Sylvain Vilandré (centre in the photo). At forty-eight, he is the only medical FOBbit (a hairy bunker inhabitant) in my age bracket. His nickname is "L'Père" ("Pops"), which leaves me nonplussed—I am two years older than he is. This is his second combat tour. He is built like a refrigerator—one of the strongest men on the FOB. This makes it even more embarrassing when he runs men twenty years younger than him into the ground. Despite hauling all that muscle around, he is in such amazing cardiovascular shape that he can go forever. He puts on a tough show on the outside, but he is so kind-hearted that he has been known to release mice caught in traps back into the wild.

Corporal Cynthia Bouthillier (left) is the medic. Twenty-two years old, she has already distinguished herself during an IED attack in Kandahar City. She did a masterful job of organizing the medical care of multiple victims. She has sought me out for extra teaching sessions on a number of topics. It is a pleasure to work with her.

Trooper Tony Houde (right), although thirty-six years old, has only been in the army for eighteen months. He is quiet and modest to a fault, but completely reliable. He helps out wherever he can when the casualties come in. He has three young children, and his oldest is going through many of the same ups and downs as my daughter. Like me, Tony worries about the effect his absences will have on her.

QRF Bison crew

Whenever possible, this crew gives clean bottled water to Afghan adults and candy to Afghan children. The locals have learned to recognize the vehicle by the teddy bear attached to one of its antennas. They invariably smile and wave, and even run after the Bison.

The second Bison ambulance crew is attached to the tank unit based here, a squadron of the Lord Strathcona's Horse. This Bison is commanded by Master Seaman Richard Turcotte (right in the following photo), a thirty-seven-year-old senior medic. It may seem odd that a sailor is running an armoured vehicle crew in a land war, but the credo of the Health Services branch is interoperability: medics from all branches can perform their duties in any environment. Master Seaman Turcotte, the father of a six-year-old girl, is also a Roto 3 veteran. He has been through some harrowing experiences but remains rock-solid.

The medic, commonly called the GIB (guy in back), is Private Daniel Labonté. At twenty-three, he has a maturity far beyond his years and the same enthusiasm for medicine that I saw in Dominic at

Strathcona Bison crew

FOB Wilson. He is always asking questions and is particularly interested in knowing how to perform emergency ultrasound examinations. He is invariably in a good mood, all the more so lately since he discovered that his wife was carrying a baby girl.

The driver, Master Corporal Jason Taylor, is a reservist from Prince Edward Island. Like many reservists you meet here, he comes closer to being a pure soldier than most regular force (full-time) troopers. No matter what combat or medical task we have assigned to him, he has accomplished it quickly and with little or no supervision. He is one of those utterly dependable individuals you sense you can count on in any situation. Because of that, I do not begrudge him his photophobia.*

---

* For the non-medical types: I am engaging here in the lowest form of humour, the pun. Photophobia is a medical term meaning that the patient finds bright lights painful. It does not mean a dislike of having your picture taken, which is the way I am using the term here.

A very bad day.

Right on the heels of the deaths of Corporal Bulger and Master Corporal Michaud came the news that one of our Griffon helicopters had crashed. This was not caused by enemy fire. Flying of any kind does not allow for much in the way of malfunction or error before catastrophic events occur; flying helicopters in combat conditions magnifies this risk. It takes a special kind of person to crew these aircraft, a person who has both courage and skill, in ample measure.

We know that two Canadians are dead, but we are unsure as to their identities. This is causing a lot of anxiety on the FOB. The pilots and flight engineers are from the helicopter squadron. We will feel the pain of their loss as we do that of any fellow soldier. But the door gunners are infantrymen, from the same regiment currently deployed here. The combat troopers are desperate to learn if one of their friends is dead.

Everyone feels a little guilty at times like this. It starts when we hear that there have been casualties on our side. We know the likelihood is that they will be Afghan, because in this civil war it is the ANA that is taking most of the casualties. If that turns out to be the case, we are relieved, although no one would ever admit it. If we learn a Coalition soldier has died, we hope he is from another country.

The guilty feeling increases when it is confirmed that one or more Canadians have died. Now we are wishing for the death of someone we know less well. We are wishing for another Canadian family to be devastated instead of ours. None of us enjoys feeling that way, but none of us can help it.

No matter who these fallen Canadians are, they will be the first to die in one of our own helicopters. It has only been since the winter of 2009 that our squadron, equipped with Griffon gunships and Chinook transports, arrived in Kandahar. They have been flying continuously ever since.

I had thought that most routine Canadian FOB-to-FOB travelling on this Roto would be done in our own helicopters. I had emphasized

129

Griffon gunship door gunner

this to Claude as a way of minimizing her worry before I left. And while some Canadians fly back and forth from the FOBs to KAF, the number of people we have travelling by convoy appears unchanged. It seems our aircraft and crews have been integrated into the overall war effort and not specifically assigned to us: our Griffon crashed at an American FOB.

So it was already a bad day, and it came to a bad ending. At last light, as I was working in the staff lounge, I heard a hissing sound I recognized. A rocket was flying overhead and was a second or two away from impact. I threw myself against the wall, waited for the detonation and then ran for the bunker. The rest of the medical team had been on the bunker's porch. When I got there, they were scrambling to get inside. We got our helmets and frag vests on and waited for the all clear.

It looks like "rocket season" is upon us.

Addendum, July 7 (morning): We now know the name of one of the dead Canadians. He is Master Corporal Patrice Audet, of the 430th

Tactical Helicopter Squadron. There is no information about his duties on the aircraft, but there are already recriminations against his branch of the service.

Our helicopter crashed on takeoff. "Experts" have been on the CBC news explaining how this was predictable because our pilots, our aircraft or our procedures are not good enough for the kind of combat operations we are flying here in Kandahar province. Apart from being extraordinarily insensitive—coming even before the bodies of our dead comrades arrive home—this criticism is Monday-morning quarterbacking at its worst.

In this heat, a helicopter's blades generate far less lift than they do in colder, denser air. This makes the aircraft harder to control and much less forgiving of even a tiny misstep at low altitude. The dust is so bad that pilots land and take off in a cloud through which they can see nothing. By themselves, these environmental factors would make for the most challenging flying conditions a helicopter pilot can face. And our pilots also contend with the enemy threat. Takeoff and landing, the trickiest manoeuvres in flying, are also the occasions when helicopters are most vulnerable to anti-aircraft fire.

In spite of these potentially lethal hazards, our air crews keep flying. In doing so, they give us an enormous edge over the Taliban: they resupply us in the most difficult terrain, they provide fire support that drives off Taliban attackers and they shuttle us around the battlefield, safe from IEDs.

Helicopters crash—even with the best pilots, flying the best machines, in the best of conditions. This is combat flying, so we should be prepared for the inevitability of incidents like this. I am sure that when this war is over our helicopters will have had an admirable safety record. I will not hesitate to get on one for the rest of my tour.

Addendum, July 7 (afternoon): The worst fears of the infantrymen here have come true. So have mine.

Corporal Martin "Jo" Joannette was a member of the Third Battalion, Royal 22nd Regiment. These are the Van Doos, the French

Canadian infantry regiment that is serving here now. A lot of people on the FOB, including me, knew Jo. Though still a minority, veterans make up an important proportion of the troops deployed on this rotation. That Jo and I met during my previous deployment is no more than a minor coincidence, but it makes writing this entry physically painful.

Jo and I were together at Sperwan Ghar, the first FOB I served at in 2007. He was the combat team commander's LAV (light armoured vehicle) driver. He went on every mission, big and small, that we ran out of that FOB. His vehicle was struck by an IED twice, had a near miss a third time, and he was under direct enemy fire numerous times. He came out of it all without a scratch. He had served another tour in Afghanistan before that. Knowing he came through so many close calls makes it somehow harder to accept that we have lost such a superlative soldier.

What I remember most about Jo was his uncanny ability to coax balky motors back to life. The internal combustion engine is something I know nearly nothing about, but Jo knew the inner workings of his armoured vehicle better than I know anatomy. He was the go-to guy for the combat team when it came to engine problems, and he was always ready to help.

In his photograph (at the back of this book), you will notice that Jo does not wear the traditional green beret of the infantry but rather the maroon beret of the airborne troops. So I close with the traditional parting wish of the paratrooper: "Light winds and soft landings, my brother."

JULY 7 | Junior

On the two-way rifle range you will not rise to the occasion. You will sink to the level of your training.

—RSM BRIAN MCKENELLEY, Second Battalion, The Irish Regiment of Canada

Corporal Nicholas "Junior" Cappelli Horth

The combat arms attracts more than its fair share of big guys. Individuals of smaller stature stand out. Corporal Nicholas Cappelli Horth (the missing hyphen is intentional) stands out, in more ways than one.

Although he is based here at FOB Ma'Sum Ghar, I had the opportunity to meet him before coming here. He is the medic assigned to the provincial reconstruction team, and these guys get around a fair bit. Whenever his team came to FOB Wilson he would pop by the UMS to look in on his medical brethren. He participated in some of the patient encounters I have described.

I know. In this photograph he does not look older than twelve, and I doubt he weighs more than fifty kilograms soaking wet. His nickname, "Junior," seems almost preordained. But he is twenty-two and one of the more impressive young men you will ever meet. The gear he carries on patrol weighs almost as much as he does, but he never falters. It must be said that he is in amazingly good shape, being a marathon runner. He is also the prototypical "good soldier." He always has a positive, can-do attitude.

His skills and attitude made him pretty much the perfect "garrison soldier." In other words, he had everything the army looks for during training: fitness, drive, teamwork and smarts. But how will the aptitudes demonstrated during training translate when under fire? That is the question on everybody's mind as a unit heads to war. For Junior, we got the answer today.

The provincial reconstruction team had been on a patrol not far from our FOB. The team was in the process of clearing a road, searching for IEDS. Junior was somewhere in the middle of the column of soldiers. An Afghan civilian on a motorcycle began to overtake them. Before he was allowed to go on, he was stopped and searched. He checked out: a villager, making his way to his fields.

The villager got back on his motorcycle and began to pass the soldiers. When he got level with Junior, a Taliban triggerman detonated a "directional" IED. The rear half of such a device is high explosive. This would not be lethal beyond a few feet. The front half consists of hundreds of metal fragments, which the high explosive will project forward at high speeds. You could think of a directional IED as a gigantic shotgun firing massive pellets.

The directional IED was a metre from the Afghan villager when it went off. Junior was two metres farther away. At such close range, a directional IED massively damages the human body. The villager had most of his mid-section blown apart. Junior was thrown to the ground, covered in blood and pieces of flesh, but the Afghan's body had created a "blast shadow." Junior's ears were ringing, but he was otherwise unhurt.

What did Junior do then? On a patrol, soldiers are assigned an "arc of responsibility," that area of the 360-degree circle around the patrol that they must watch. By the time Junior had finished rolling on the ground, he had his weapon up and facing outwards, covering his arc. In the time it took for the blast to stop acting on his body, he was back to being a fully operational combat soldier.

A patrol's first priority when it comes under fire is to defeat the enemy. Even if there are wounded soldiers who need care, the combat

medics will first help to drive back the enemy, "winning the firefight."
We are soldiers first, and Junior had reacted exactly as he had been
trained to.

Although the IED attack was not followed up with gunfire or grenades, the patrol was still in grave danger. There were signs that the Taliban had laid secondary IEDs, additional mines whose purpose is to kill
medics and others coming to assist those wounded by an initial blast.

When the patrol had secured the area, Junior rendered whatever
aid he could to the villager. Before this, he had radioed the UMS to prepare us to receive a critically wounded patient. I got the team together
and briefed them on the patient's possible injuries, and we set up our
IVs and other gear. Unfortunately, the man was long dead by the time
we got to him.

Junior reported to the UMS when the patrol returned to the FOB.
He still had his smile and his positive attitude . . . but his eyes had a
slight watery sheen, and his voice had a touch of a tremor. I took him
outside the UMS to have a word with him privately.

What do you say to someone who has come as close to dying as
it is possible to do? You start by telling him how happy you are that
he is okay. You follow that up with statements that are "normalizing."
This means that you list the possible reactions a normal human being
might have after an event like this, so that he understands that what he
is feeling is to be expected. Then you open the door for him to come
and talk to you about those reactions if they prove to be distressing.

Then you step back, give your comrade some space and hope that
he will prove to be one of the many who come through something
like this psychically intact. And not one of the few who will be damaged forever.

Addendum, July 31: I am leaving FOB Ma'Sum Ghar in a few days. I
have spoken to Junior a number of times since his close call. He seems
remarkably well. His sleep patterns got back to normal three days
after the incident and, a week ago, he had a dream in which he saw the
Afghan villager who was killed. He could not recall much about the
dream except that it had not been upsetting.

He has had a couple of other emotionally tough days, one of which I will describe in some detail later, but I think he will come through this war without any long-term emotional ill-effects.

JULY 8 | MRE: Medical Rules of Eligibility

One of today's serious casualties was unusual, as war zone casualties go, because he was suffering from blunt trauma. This is the kind you get when your body is thrown against something hard. Whereas penetrating trauma is relatively simple to manage—plug the holes, stop the bleeding, get them breathing, ship them out—blunt trauma is a much more cerebral exercise. Patients have no holes or lacerations indicating where the damage lies. They must be examined much more carefully so that no serious injuries are missed. Keep that in mind as I present today's interesting case.

As was the case at FOB Wilson, the perimeter security on the camp is the responsibility of a private company. One of their men was involved in a head-on collision with an American armoured vehicle. He was driving a pickup truck, so he was the loser in this exchange.

There was no external bleeding, and the patient was not having any difficulty breathing. He had no bruises, his vital signs were normal and ultrasound examination of the chest and abdomen were negative. He had no neurological symptoms, meaning that he had normal strength, sensation and movement in all four limbs. His only complaint was pain at the top of his head and in his cervical (neck) spine. He was alert and oriented, and he described having been projected into the roof of his vehicle.

A case like this could not be more straightforward. The accident had delivered a tremendous amount of "axial load" onto the patient's cervical spine. This is the same thing that happens when people dive into shallow water. These individuals often break their cervical spines and end up paralyzed from the neck down. The medical team must therefore immobilize the patient's spine immediately and keep it secure until X-rays or a CT scan can be done to rule out the presence of a fracture.

Pretty basic, eh? Not to some goof at KAF. The message we got back was: "We're busy. Send the patient by road."

I hit the roof. We are now doing helicopter medevacs for Canadians who need nothing more than a couple of stitches. The message I was getting was that this Afghan, with a potentially devastating injury, was not worth the same consideration. He may have been, for all intents and purposes, a mercenary, fighting for our side only for the money. That is irrelevant. He had been injured as a byproduct of the war. As a result, his care was our responsibility. Had he been a civilian or a Taliban soldier, I would have treated him the same way.

I am happy to report that this aberrant behaviour was limited to a single individual at battle group headquarters. I barked once (via a one-paragraph e-mail, dripping with sarcasm, venom and threat), and the air medevac was approved.

JULY 10 | Tac Recce: Tactical Reconnaissance

A quiet day—only a few patients, none of them critically injured.

It looked as though I would not have much to write about, but that changed shortly after lunch. Two distinguished-looking gentlemen wandered into the UMS. One of them introduced himself by saying, "We are here to replace you." I had no idea who he was so I flippantly answered, "Yeah, right! In my dreams!"

It was a poor choice of words. I was addressing Commander Robert Briggs, the head doctor of the rotation arriving in September. He was accompanied by Major Graeme Rodgman, who will be in command of the FOB medics. They were performing a "tactical reconnaissance," a direct eyeballs-on look at the combat area. As part of this recce (pronounced "wreck-ee"), they had come to Ma'Sum Ghar to check out the FOB UMS, to learn what our capabilities were and to see where their people would be deployed starting this September. I showed them the UMS and our quarters, and we discussed the medical work of the FOB.

Not wanting our guests to be bored, Master Seaman Turcotte (one of the Bison crew commanders) decided to provide us with a chance to show them how sophisticated the care in our UMS could be. So he got on top of his vehicle . . . and *fell off.*

A Bison is not a small vehicle. A fall from the top generates precisely the kind of kinetic energy necessary for one of those blunt trauma cases I described in the previous entry. To enable us to display even more of our skills, MS Turcotte helpfully landed *on his face.* This gave us a tricky facial laceration to repair as well. This was an act of selfless devotion to the job, one that we will be reminding MS Turcotte about for some time.

I got the patient sewn up quickly. Apart from the cuts on his face, he had no other apparent injuries. That left the non-apparent injuries he might have suffered in his chest or abdomen. This presented me with the opportunity to give an impromptu lesson in EDE to my two visitors, neither of whom were familiar with the technique. They were interested in the ultrasound examination, so we discussed ways they could integrate this into the practice of their physicians.

We ended the visit with a run up to the hilltop observation post. You can see most of Zhari-Panjwayi from up there. You can also see where 85 per cent or more of the Canadians who have been killed in Afghanistan met their end. Neither of my colleagues had fully appreciated that before.

I brought them back to the UMS, and we talked about a few more things before it was time for them to go. I wished them well as they headed back to KAF.

I hope they have the most boring tour imaginable.

JULY 11 | Visitors

Two notable encounters with visitors today.

MORNING: THE QUIET ONES

Every morning, right after I wake up, I run to the top of Ma'Sum Ghar a few times to get my daily exercise. It is a steep climb, and I need to breathe a bit at the top before coming back. I usually say hello to the men manning the observation post located there. Depending on the situation, they could be from the private security company or some of our own troopers. Not today.

The men looking out over the Panjwayi valley this morning were unlike any you would ordinarily see on the FOB. They had beards and longish hair. They wore no insignia of rank or unit, no name tags. Their weapons had silencers and more sophisticated scopes than the ones on a standard infantry rifle. Their body armour was custom-made and lighter than that normally issued. This represented a tradeoff: less protection in exchange for increased mobility. Their demeanour, while polite, was distant. They asked no questions and offered no information about themselves, and introductions yielded only a first name.

The Quiet Ones had come to Ma'Sum Ghar.

When a soldier joins the combat arms, he is timid. The environment is new, his instructors are terrifying, and the skills he is being asked to master are foreign. No one feels self-confident in this situation.

When a soldier finishes basic training and can now call himself an infantryman, the opposite is true. He feels like a Dangerous Man. Even if he had no self-confidence before joining the army, he has a lot now.

If the soldier receives further instruction, such as paratrooper or reconnaissance training, his self-confidence grows even more. He may even become somewhat annoying, adopting an aggressive, in-your-face attitude. I can state this with some assurance, having been that annoying guy when I graduated from the Combat Training Centre. Most soldiers mature over the course of a few years, retaining the self-confidence while shedding the bluster.

There are a few soldiers who choose to go beyond the advanced infantry training available in the regular battalions. They go on to become some of the most skillful and lethal soldiers in the world. They are our best and they take a backseat to no one, regardless of what you may have heard about the British SAS, the American Green Berets or SEALS, or the Israeli Commandos.

The paradox is that, with this additional training, the linear relationship between training and bravado is broken. Instead, the opposite occurs. You can be in a room with several of these men and still feel like you are alone. Far from bragging about their considerable accomplishments, they prefer to fade into the walls and they do so quite effectively.

I had the opportunity, a few weeks before coming back to Afghanistan, to train a number of these men in some advanced emergency medical techniques. Even in that setting, with a man who was a veteran as their teacher, they kept to their strict code of self-effacing silence.

The Quiet Ones are not assigned to any particular FOB. Rather, they wander around Afghanistan on various assignments. They will not get into major confrontations with the Taliban. They will not be involved in reconstruction work. They will not help rid the country of IEDs. What they will do is watch. Silently. And with infinite patience.

The Quiet Ones are looking for a face, one that has been identified beyond any reasonable doubt. More often than not, their patience is rewarded. The face suddenly appears in their binoculars or telescopes. Just as quickly, the face disappears. But now they know where the face is.

The culmination of all that watching is coming soon. The Quiet Ones are human, and they are no doubt feeling excited and apprehensive about what is to follow, but you could not read that on their faces. Their conversation is muted, limited to an exchange of information as the plan is developed. Their faces remain neutral.

The Quiet Ones continue to watch, until the most propitious moment. Then they move, in the same silence and with the same patience they displayed while they watched.

Then they strike.

When I was at my first FOB during Roto 4, there was a poster on the wall showing the faces of the Taliban commanders in our area of operations at the start of the rotation. Roughly half of the faces were crossed out with a red X.

Thanks to the Quiet Ones, the life expectancy for Taliban commanders in Zhari-Panjwayi is not very good.

AFTERNOON: THE PRISONER

The ANP captured a Taliban soldier last night. The circumstances of that capture are unclear to me, but the Talib was in a prisoner cage this morning. It is also unclear to me how he got out of that cage, but get out of it he did. He then attempted to flee at high speed. The ANP objected to this. An AK-47 bullet shot through the Talib's left leg settled the squabble in the police's favour.

It was a nasty wound. The bullet entered just above the calf muscle and exited in the middle of the leg, just below the kneecap. When a high-powered bullet such as this goes through a limb, it shatters the bone and causes a small explosion to occur where the bullet exits. While the entry wound was the size of the bullet (smaller than a dime), the exit wound was somewhat larger than a kiwi.

This was bad news for the patient. There are two bones in your leg: a small one on the outside that you can do without—the fibula—and a larger one on the inside—the tibia—that carries all your body's weight. The part of the tibia closest to the knee had been destroyed. When I explored the exit wound, the bone seemed to end five centimetres short of where it should have. I could not detect a pulse in the foot, indicating that the patient's blood vessels had also been damaged.

If a patient was to have a chance to keep his leg he needed surgery as soon as possible, so we called for a helicopter medevac, priority Alpha. We controlled the bleeding, bandaged the wound, splinted the leg and gave him intravenous antibiotics and pain medication. When I was done, I allowed two military intelligence types to question him.

It was interesting to watch this process. If you have visions of the interrogation sessions straight out of a James Bond movie, you could not be further off base. I had the impression I was watching the neighbourhood cops questioning a well-known and mostly harmless delinquent. The questioner was only mildly stern. He did not touch the patient, even when the patient tried to doze off. His questions were factual, and neither his words nor his tone were ever threatening. His companion took notes but said nothing.

Within thirty minutes we got word that the medevac choppers were arriving. I took a minute, as I always do in these situations, to tell the prisoner that we were Canadians and that we had taken very good care of him. I hoped that this would convince him to turn against his former Taliban mentors. Failing that, I hoped he would remember our kindness if a Canadian ever became his prisoner. Even if neither of these results ever occurs, this doesn't change my approach: I will fight this war as hard as I can, but I will fight humanely.

JULY 14 | The Elements, Part 2: Earth

The FOBS are on the front line of a war zone. Although things are better than they were during Roto 4, our existence here is still one of physical discomfort. I would be denying a key part of the soldiers' experience if I did not recognize that.

I have already described the effects of the heat. I am shielded from the worst effects of this because both the UMS and my bunker are air-conditioned. But none of us can get away from the dust, which is all-pervasive. It is a fine powder that coats everything it touches. Every footfall raises a small puff. Even in this relatively windless area, the dust seeps into the most remote recesses of our buildings. Master Corporal "Red" Ricard wages a daily battle, armed with mop and broom, to keep the floor of the UMS clean.

The dust also seems to impregnate all our belongings. Food becomes gritty before the meal can be finished. Clothing comes out of the dryer with sand trapped in the fibres. Even right after stepping out of the shower, you get the feeling that you are not completely clean.

It is in the air, however, that this phenomenon is most apparent. There was a stretch of three consecutive days last month when the dust in the air was so thick the sky looked like grey milk. There is menace in such a sky: dust is responsible for nearly all the "medevac red" periods, when our helicopters are grounded.

These are times of considerable anxiety for a FOB doc. I can do anything the patient needs for the first thirty to sixty minutes of resuscitation care. After that, the treatment options available to me are exhausted. If I have been unable to stabilize the patient, as would be the case with ongoing bleeding into the chest or abdomen, he or she needs to be in the O.R. at KAF. These patients need a blood transfusion and an operation, neither of which I can offer here. If the medevac birds are not flying, I might have to watch one of our soldiers bleed to death.

JULY 15 | Stand To

Stand to: the procedure whereby all soldiers on a base, regardless of their normal tasks, will grab a weapon and take a defensive position. Used when the base is under imminent threat of attack.

The FOB Ma'Sum Ghar combat team left for an operation at first light this morning.

It is impossible to conceal the departure of a dozen or more tanks and other armoured vehicles. The Taliban spies will have noted this. Usually, they are more concerned with where the combat team is headed. This time, it seems they focused their attention back towards the FOB.

It is unusual for the Taliban to attempt a ground attack against one of our FOBs, but it does happen. During one such attack against Ma'Sum Ghar during my last tour, the gunfight lasted so long that the soldiers on our perimeter began to run low on ammunition. The FOB commander ordered the cooks and the medical staff to reinforce them.

At today's unit commanders meeting, we were told that our intelligence had reported the FOB being observed, possibly with an eye to a ground attack. Given our reduced numbers, the FOB commander called on all of us to be more vigilant than usual and to be prepared to repel any assault.

I reflected on our previous experience and thought that we could do better this time. The cooks and medical staff, though more than willing to get into a gunfight, are initially tasked to defend the UMS. On Roto 4, it had not been clear where the commander had wanted the perimeter reinforced. I mentioned this to the FOB commander, and he agreed to come by later to give us a precise assignment.

But once an infantryman, always an infantryman. When I got back from the meeting I went for a quick walk up the hill behind the UMS to look at where I could best place Red, the remaining Bison crew (one crew went on the operation) and myself to defend our little patch of ground. As frightening as it would be to get involved in a close-range gunfight, I found that prospect far preferable to sitting in our bunker, unable to see outside and waiting for someone to come to the door.

Before the FOB commander could come to visit us, the Taliban hit us with another rocket. This one landed right on the helipad, narrowly missed one trooper, bounced up and over another trooper and then slammed into one of the concrete walls but did not detonate. Had we been running a helicopter medevac or personnel transfer at the time, it could have done a lot of damage. The EOD team went to get the rocket and placed it on the other side of the little hill located right behind the UMS. How comforting. They plan to BIP it tomorrow.

The threat of a ground attack takes everybody's anxiety up a notch. It is one thing to know that there are people here who want to kill us. It is another thing to contemplate that they might come and try it tonight.

JULY 16 | Terror

When you're wounded and left on Afghanistan's plains,
And the women come out to cut up what remains,
Jest roll to your rifle and blow out your brains
An' go to your Gawd like a soldier.
—RUDYARD KIPLING, "The Young British Soldier"

The day started badly. When Red and I came into the UMS and checked our communication devices, we saw that we were in "coms lockdown." This meant that one of our own was dead. As bad as that was, things soon got much worse.

One of our recce patrols had been deployed southeast of here onto a mountain known as Salavat Ghar to support the operation that jumped off yesterday. It is their job to explore the battlefield, to detect the enemy and report their location to the main body of our troops. The recce troopers are highly skilled and extremely fit. During a predeployment exercise I underwent prior to this mission, I was taken on a patrol by one of these men. He was so adept at camouflaging himself and was able to move through the bush so quietly that I felt I was walking with a ghost. Usually when these men go out, the Taliban have no idea they are there. Today was one of the rare exceptions to this rule.

The recce soldiers were establishing an observation post when one of them, Private Sébastien Courcy, tripped a mine. The explosion threw him off a cliff. At the same time, the patrol was under fire from a Taliban mortar. After the blast, the other members of the patrol had no idea where Private Courcy was.

That news travelled back to the FOB at lightning speed. As bad as we feel when one of us is killed, this was much, much worse. Our comrade might have been captured. It has been said that the Taliban do not take prisoners. That is inaccurate. What they do not do is allow prisoners to live. And the way they torture prisoners before killing them is nothing short of barbaric. When we heard the first reports about our missing recce trooper, we were terrified that this would be his fate.

Within an hour of the initial reports, we had more details. It was uncertain whether he had been blown off the mountain by an explosion or if he had slipped off while running, but there was no doubt that our comrade had fallen a long distance, to his death. It was nonetheless some small comfort that his body was found by Canadians, and not by the enemy.

Terror works.

If it did not, terrorists would not use it. By torturing and beheading their captives, al Qaeda and the Taliban extremists demonstrate how far they are willing to go to achieve their goals. When they threaten the local civilian population with reprisals if those civilians co-operate with us, those threats are often effective.

Occasionally, I hear a Canadian soldier complain that the Afghans are not doing enough to ward off the Taliban themselves. When I hear that, I get annoyed and I say so. For a member of a heavily armed Canadian battle group to compare himself to unarmed Afghan civilians is beyond ridiculous. Our experience of terror in Canada is limited, mostly confined to the 1963–70 bombing-and-murder campaign of the FLQ. We cannot know how we would react if we were constantly subjected to it. But the historical record is clear. When a powerful group terrorizes a population, nearly all the members of that population—regardless of ethnicity, nationality, religion or anything else—try to get along with those who are able to harm them. This is true even if it is virtually certain that the intent of those in power is to kill everyone. The key word in that last sentence is "virtually." People in these situations will cling to the slightest hope that they might survive, and they will go to unimaginable lengths to appease those who might kill them rather than commit suicide by fighting them.

But if terror can make people do unspeakable things, is it a source of real power? Only in the short run. Terrorists can cause unimaginable suffering and be very difficult to oppose, but they cut themselves off from any legitimate claim to authority. All through history, tyrants have done their best to terrorize populations. They have always fallen.

JULY 17 | Boredom

Against boredom, the gods themselves struggle in vain.
—FRIEDRICH NIETZSCHE

Reading the entries in which I describe dealing with multiple war casualties, you might get the impression that those days are busy. Nothing could be further from the truth. Even a MasCal with multiple casualties only occupies me for an hour, two at the most if we include cleanup and debrief. After that, all the casualties are either evacuated or have been treated and released. The busiest day here does not begin to approach an average shift in a large emergency department.

It would also be a mistake to assume that the presence of imminent danger, which has loomed large in the previous two days' entries, is in any way entertaining. As described in "Downregulation" (June 17), soldiers get used to this quickly. It is common to feel bored while being scared. But as boring as even my busiest day can be, one group of soldiers are a lot worse off than I am.

Individuals who have drawn shifts in the various observation posts (OPs) that ring the FOB have the worst job to which one can be assigned here. It combines the need to be constantly vigilant— a source of stress and fatigue—with the need to look at the same unchanging terrain for hours—a source of yet more stress and fatigue. If wars are 95 per cent boredom and 5 per cent terror, OP duty is 99.99 per cent boredom and 0.01 per cent "What the fuck was that?"

The graffiti one encounters in an OP reflects the mind-numbing boredom of hours spent watching the Afghan dust . . . get dustier: "I spent two weeks in this OP and nothing happened and the same will happen to you. I'm telling you it would be easier to end your life now."

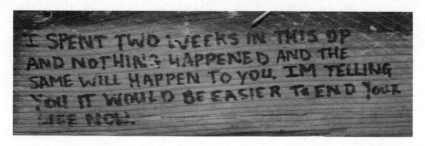

Observation post philosophy

A few feet away, we find the franco version: *"Oubliez pas vous êtes ici pour un crisse de boutte."* ("Don't forget you're gonna be here for a fuck of a long while.")

A third one says: "They should really change that military commercial so that it says: *Fight boredom. Fight bullshit. Fight each other.*" The commercial in question shows Canadian soldiers saving civilians, either on search and rescue or peacekeeping operations. The captions are: "Fight fear. Fight chaos. Fight distress."

Our army is at war, yet it produces a recruitment ad that does not mention that key detail. A little disconcerting, that.

JULY 18 | Middle of the Night Conversion

Catchy title, eh? A reference to our converting the heathens? Nope. The Coalition forces are respectful of the Islamic faith. This is about a completely different kind of conversion.

At 0230, the phone linking us to the command post rang and Red answered it: "Afghan soldier. Unconscious. ETA five minutes." Red and I bolted for the UMS. Corporal Bouthillier, the Bison medic, joined us a minute later. A minute after that, a jeep drove up. The unconscious patient was quickly moved into the UMS. Corporal Bouthillier started an IV, and Red checked the vital signs while I proceeded with my examination. When I finished, I had a patient without any detectable injuries or signs of a drug overdose but who was deeply unconscious. Stumped, I went outside to question the other Afghan soldiers.

The soldier had been on a patrol that had returned to the FOB at 0200. A half-hour later, he suddenly collapsed. They had not come under fire during the patrol, and he had seemed fine until that point. The patient had had a similar episode six months earlier and been evacuated to KAF. He had been kept there for a couple of days, but no diagnosis had been established. I went back in the UMS and carefully examined the patient again to ensure I hadn't missed any subtle signs of disease or injury. Finding none, I began to wonder if I was dealing with a "conversion reaction."

Sometimes called "hysterical conversion reaction," this is a psychological state in which stress produces a direct effect on the body: the mental feeling is "converted" into a physical symptom. This can take the form of paralysis, blindness or a number of other manifestations. The patient has very little control over a conversion reaction. It is quite different from malingering, which is the conscious attempt to fake an injury or disease.

The societal demand on Afghan men to be good fighters is extreme. To fail as a soldier is to fail at everything it means to be an Afghan man. During my previous tour, there was only one Afghan soldier who I thought might have had a conversion reaction. I was reluctant to advance the diagnosis in this case. An emergency physician should always hesitate before deciding "it's all in his head."

I then noticed that we had not checked the patient's temperature, the most commonly forgotten vital sign. Since an unconscious patient cannot co-operate with an oral temperature, I ordered Red to use the rectal thermometer. As Red touched the thermometer to the patient's anus, the buttocks clenched tightly. Seeing that, I began to relax. The patient might be unresponsive, but it was unlikely that he was sick. When Red tried again, the patient opened his eyes to look at me, then quickly shut them again.

At that point, the jig was up. While this patient may have had a conversion reaction when this all started, he was now malingering. I told the interpreter to tell him to get up and walk out. Within a couple of minutes, he did exactly that. No trip to KAF this time, bucko.

JULY 19 | Haji Baran

The title of today's entry is based in part on one of the Five Pillars of Islam. The teacher in me cannot resist telling you about all five.

The *shahadah* is a verbal expression of belief that recognizes the singular nature of God and accepts that Muhammad was God's messenger.

Zakat is compulsory charity. In Islam, you get hit for 2.5 per cent of your total income. The key question is how low your income has to

I was run over by a tank once.

In the summer of 1980, I was at the Combat Training Centre completing the process of becoming a CF infantry officer. All my training until then had been done with small groups of foot soldiers. In this last phase, we had to learn how to operate in conjunction with the other branches of the combat arms: the artillery and the tanks.

In the June 21 entry, I described the relationship between the infantry and the artillery. The infantry go out and get into a fight. When they figure out where the bad guys are, the artillery is called to blow them to ratshit. It is a long-distance affair, the parties being at either end of a radio set.

The infantry's relationship with the tanks is very different. Since World War One, tanks and infantry have always fought side-by-side on the battlefield. The affiliation is much more intimate than with the artillery.

The tanker instructors assigned to us wanted to make this point forcefully. They achieved this the first day we were with them by having us lie down in a straight line on a road and driving over us with a tank. I do not know what I learned by having dozens of tons of metal pass less than a foot from my nose while treads clanked a few feet on either side of me. I did listen attentively to everything the tankers said after that, so that they would not want to run over me again. That may have been their objective.

When civilians see a Leopard tank for the first time they cannot help but be overwhelmed by the size of the main armament. Pointing phallicly forward is a 120 mm cannon, not much smaller than the 155 mm M777 I have described earlier. This gun can shoot a massive shell several kilometres and destroy even well-protected Taliban bunkers. This massive firepower is great, but the Leopard's contribution in this war goes further. The complete story takes a bit of explanation.

Although our initial deployment to Afghanistan began in Kandahar province, this lasted less than a year. By 2003, the mission was focused on providing security to the capital, Kabul. Our soldiers were based outside the city at Camp Julien. We would conduct some combat operations, but mostly we patrolled Kabul and the surrounding area on foot and in jeeps.

In October 2003, Sergeant Robert Short and Corporal Robbie Beerenfenger were conducting one of these patrols on the outskirts of Kabul when their vehicle hit a mine. By the time they were discovered, both of them were dead. In January 2004, Corporal Jamie Murphy was killed while patrolling downtown Kabul, when a suicide bomber jumped onto the hood of his vehicle and detonated himself.*

The vehicle implicated in both these incidents was the Iltis jeep. This was a "soft skinned" vehicle, meaning that it was not armoured and offered virtually no protection against IEDs and other explosives. Following these deaths, the CF was pilloried for sending soldiers to Afghanistan without such protection.

There was some justification for this criticism. The Afghan resistance had made extensive use of IEDs and mines in the war against the Russians in the 1980s, and many Taliban fighters had benefited directly or indirectly from this experience. As for suicide bombing, it was a staple of Islamic extremism. It was predictable that our enemies would launch attacks on our patrols using high explosives delivered by a variety of means.

Pain may not be the best way to teach, but it is undeniably effective. Within months, contracts were rushed through for the purchase of small armoured vehicles called G-wagons. These were used with some success in Kabul.

Even before Canada shifted its deployment to Kandahar, however,

---

* These deaths are important in the story of Canada's involvement in the war in Afghanistan. Sergeant Short and Corporal Beerenfenger were the first Canadians killed by enemy action. Four Canadians had been killed in April 2002, but that had been at the hands of an American F-16 bomber pilot who proved to be as callous and devoid of remorse as he was incompetent. Corporal Murphy would be the last Canadian to be killed in combat for over two years, until the CF came to Kandahar to challenge the Taliban on their home turf.

the push was on to equip our forces with the LAV. The LAV is a wheeled vehicle. With even marginal roads or reasonably solid terrain, it can get around far better than a tank. Armed with a 25 mm cannon, it packs more than enough punch to defeat soldiers on foot. Its armour is thick enough to offer good protection against bullets and moderate protection against mines and other explosions. At three million dollars apiece, a LAV costs less than half what a tank costs.

With the end of the Cold War, it was unlikely that we would ever again have to face an enemy equipped with thousands of tanks, like the Soviet Union and its Warsaw Pact allies had been. The LAV was more suitable for the low-intensity conflicts in which we might become involved. We would become a lighter, more nimble force. After dominating the battlefield for a century, the tank seemed to be on its way out (in the Canadian Army, at least).

Task Force Afghanistan was equipped with LAVs by the summer of 2006. This is an important date because at the end of that summer, in September 2006, we launched Operation Medusa, Canada's largest combat operation since the end of the Korean War. Over several weeks the Canadian battle group fought its way into Zhari-Panjwayi.*Among other things, these Canadians established our first crude outposts in this area. These outposts evolved into the FOBs we have today.

---

* This was a battle group centred on a battalion of the Royal Canadian Regiment and commanded by Lieutenant Colonel Omer Lavoie. The battle group had only recently arrived in Afghanistan, taking over from the Princess Patricia's Canadian Light Infantry battle group commanded by Lieutenant Colonel Ian Hope. After having only a couple of weeks to get acclimatized, its members found themselves in the fight of their lives. Readers interested in learning more about the events leading up to Op Medusa are encouraged to read Chris Wattie's book *Contact Charlie: The Canadian Army, the Taliban and the Battle that Saved Afghanistan* (Toronto: Key Porter, 2008), which details the incredible accomplishments of Task Force Orion, the first Canadians to fight in Kandahar province in 2006.

The fighting during Op Medusa was unlike anything we have seen since. The Taliban had massed over a thousand fighters in a determined attempt to take, or at least to attack, Kandahar City. The city had been the capital of Afghanistan during their reign, and it still held a powerful attraction for them. It was the job of the Canadians to prevent this.

Canadians may recall that period, the late summer and early fall of 2006, because a dozen Canadians were killed—more than in the previous four years combined. What very few Canadians know is that Op Medusa was an overwhelming Canadian victory. Hundreds of Taliban were killed, and their access to Kandahar City was permanently denied. Apart from the infiltrators who have come singly or in pairs to plant bombs, there has been only one meaningful Taliban incursion into the city limits since then.* This was also the last time that large numbers of Taliban attempted to go toe to toe with a Canadian battle group.

The Taliban learned from their pain as well as we had. Since they could not defeat us in face-to-face encounters, they turned to IEDs. They were mirroring the actions of insurgents in Iraq, who had learned that vehicles like the LAV could be defeated with IEDs. Tanks, on the other hand, were almost impervious to these weapons.

As our losses from IEDs mounted, an urgent call went out for tanks to be deployed with our battle group. In an astounding *tour de force*, the Lord Strathcona's Horse was able to deploy a squadron of tanks to Kandahar in only six weeks.

---

* This was the very well planned and executed attack on the Sarposa jail in Kandahar City in June 2008. Taliban suicide bombers rushed the jail, destroying the gates and killing several guards when they detonated themselves. Other Taliban then entered the jail and freed several hundred of their comrades. It was a masterstroke, arguably the most successful Taliban military accomplishment of the war. But even that had to be done under cover of darkness and with a rapid retreat, or else they would have been massacred.

When the Canadian Leopards took to the field, they gave us a weapons platform that was invulnerable to anything the Taliban could throw at it. Wherever one of these beasts goes, it automatically creates a circle several kilometres in diameter within which any Taliban foolish enough to fire a weapon is very likely to die.

Another important feature of the tanks is their ability to smash through the mud brick walls that surround the compounds and line many of the roads and tracks in the area. Taliban ambushes are often launched from abandoned compounds or other areas where these walls can afford them some protection. This protection can be nullified by having a tank drive through the wall, a procedure called "breaching."

Finally, the sound of a tank attacking with its main armament is an experience that defines "shock and awe." This element is explained by Lieutenant Colonel David Grossman in his seminal book *On Combat*.[*] Grossman calls it the Bigger Bang Theory.

The equivalent of the Leopard in the American army is the Abrams. It has the same-size cannon and roughly the same dimensions. In his book, Grossman relates that battles fought in Iraq between insurgents armed with rifles and RPGs (much like the Taliban are here) lasted only a minute or two when Abrams tanks were involved. The insurgents would break contact and flee as soon as the tanks opened fire.

When the same insurgents went up against Stryker vehicles (the equivalent of our LAVs), the battles could last for hours, even though the 40 mm grenade launchers and .50-calibre machine guns on the Stryker were as lethal against insurgents on foot as the 120 mm gun of the Abrams. It seems that the sound of the tank's gun affected the insurgents on a primal level.

There are many similar occurrences throughout history. The first time muskets were used against men armed with crossbows is an

---

[*] The most recent edition of this book is David Grossman and Loren W. Christensen, *On Combat: The Psychology and Physiology of Deadly Conflict in War and in Peace*, 3rd ed. (Warrior Science Publications, 2008); the Bigger Bang Theory is described on pages 69–70.

A successful mission, a happy crew
Captain Sandy Cooper's tank is named "Stephanie," after his wife. Clockwise from left, standing: Trooper Derek ("Never-Miss") Tonn, gunner; top right: Master Corporal Darryl Hordyk, loader, tank second-in-command (a new master corporal, but he seamlessly starts directing the crew when Captain Cooper is busy talking to his commander on the radio); bottom right: Trooper Felix "I brake for IEDs" Lussier, driver; Captain Cooper.

excellent example. A man armed with a crossbow could fire a deadly projectile farther, more often and with greater accuracy than could a man armed with a musket. Nonetheless, the bowmen fled in disorder when confronted with the roar of these primitive firearms. The Leopard tank gives us a similar advantage over our enemies.

Most importantly, this firepower, breaching capability and psychological impact can be delivered with minimal risk to our troops. Leopards lead the way down the roads of the combat area and they routinely hit IEDs, but virtually all of the damage is suffered by the vehicle rather than by the men inside.

Basing our Leopards at Ma'Sum Ghar places them in the centre of our area of operations, making them readily available anytime heavy firepower and strong protection are required. They go out on operations as often as the infantry, and yesterday they returned from a five-day jaunt through Nakhonay (Operation Constrictor IV), during which they kicked some serious ass.*

JULY 21 | Michelle and Mariam

I had finished eating dinner around 1715 and my thoughts were turning to the pleasant experience I would soon have of hearing the voices of my wife and daughter. Michelle is usually full of energy in the morning, eager to tell me her plans for the day.

Mariam probably woke up the same way. She had come from Kandahar City to visit her grandfather. He lives in Bazaar-e-Panjwayi, the village beside FOB Ma'Sum Ghar. Like Michelle, Mariam would have been excited at the dawning of a new day. A trip like this would have been quite an adventure for her.

Mariam would have spent the day exploring her new surroundings. Bazaar-e-Panjwayi is a lot poorer than Kandahar City, but children do not focus on things like that. I imagine Mariam's attention was drawn more to the big mountains right beside the village. For a little girl from Kandahar City, this is "the country." It may be poor, but it is full of new sights and sounds that fascinate the young mind. No doubt she also spent a good deal of time today snuggling up to her grandfather. He may have been a fierce Pashtun in his youth, but age has mellowed him. I have no trouble seeing him doting on his granddaughter. This gives the two girls something else in common: my parents adore Michelle and love her almost as much as I do.

When one looks for hope in a place as desperate as Afghanistan, it is almost a cliché to look at the children. Will they have the wisdom

---

* I could not have written this section without the gracious and patient help of Captain Sandy Cooper, "Battle Captain" of the tank squadron, whose knowledge of the tank world in general and of the Afghan mission in particular is encyclopedic.

and the strength to do a better job than we have? Will they find a way to bring peace to this land? I hope Michelle becomes the kind of person who could contribute to this process. Mariam, tragically, will never get the chance to do so.

Around 1800 hours, one of our patrols was checking things in Bazaar-e-Panjwayi. These "presence patrols" show the enemy that we are keeping our eye on things and that there is no place we cannot go. The patrol entered the marketplace, where more people than usual were shopping and walking around.

This was neither a good thing nor a bad thing. The presence of many civilians does not guarantee that the Taliban will not detonate a mine or launch an ambush, as we have seen countless times in the past. Occasionally, the local population will get some warning of an impending Taliban attack. This makes it a very bad sign to see villagers scatter as we approach. This is called a "combat indicator," and our troops go on high alert when that happens.

Whenever our troops are out and about, they maintain a security bubble into which no civilian can penetrate without showing due cause and harmless intent. After IEDs, suicide bombers are the most lethal weapon at the Taliban's disposal. We want to make it difficult for them to get close enough to us to launch their attacks.

Taliban suicide bombers wear civilian clothing and are indistinguishable from the innocent. That is why Coalition forces have made strenuous attempts to educate the population. Signs on the roads and on our vehicles admonish civilians that they must never approach our patrols, checkpoints or convoys in a threatening manner. After eight years of war, a civilian would have to be mentally deficient not to be aware of this.

At approximately 1815, a man on a motorcycle drove towards the patrol. As he approached, the patrol made hand signals that clearly indicated the driver had to stop. The driver ignored these signals and kept driving, passing an Afghan police vehicle at the head of the patrol and getting even closer to the Canadians. This led to an "escalation of force": the patrol aimed its weapons at the motorcyclist. That did the trick, and the driver stopped at a safe distance from the patrol. He was apprehended by the Afghan police and taken away. People who approach Coalition patrols are so likely to be motivated by nefarious intent that they are inevitably questioned and, almost as inevitably, released for lack of evidence.

The patrol had gone only a few metres farther when a second man approached, also on a motorcycle. He circled the patrol four times, just outside the security bubble. He stopped and turned his motorcycle directly towards the patrol and gunned the engine several times. Then he sped forward.

The two soldiers closest to the motorcyclist had already discussed what they would do if they had to go beyond hand signals. One of them carried a C9 light machine gun and the other carried our standard C7 rifle. The C7 is capable of firing a single, well-aimed shot, whereas a single pull of the trigger on the C9 sends several bullets into a rough general area. The soldiers had therefore agreed that any warning shots would be fired by the rifleman to minimize the risk to the civilians.

This time, the hand signals and the raised weapon that followed had no effect on the driver's behaviour. The motorcyclist kept moving towards the patrol. The rifleman then fired a warning shot into the ground several metres in front of the motorcycle. The motorcyclist turned and fled.

The patrol formed into a perimeter, scanning 360 degrees for any further threats. Then it noticed a body lying on the ground. The soldiers rushed over to see if they could help, but there was nothing to be done.

The bullet had skipped off the ground and hit Mariam in the forehead. The back of her head had exploded, and most of her brain ended up on the ground beside her. She died in the blink of an eye.

"Junior" Cappelli Horth was the medic on the patrol. He bandaged Mariam's head, picked up her skull and brain matter and put them in a plastic bag, loaded her into a vehicle and rushed back to the FOB. He did not attempt CPR. This was the perfect way to deal with this horrible situation. Junior had treated the patient with dignity and professionalism. Even across cultural divides, families can see that.

The "right thing" to do, however, depends on whether one is in Canada or in the developing world. Back home, I have run a number of resuscitations on children who I knew were long gone. By the time I go to tell their parents the bad news, I can show them all the things we did to try to save their child. Parents in the West accept that even if the doctor does everything right, the resuscitation attempt might fail. They have seen enough TV shows in which that happens that it has become part of their reality. Even when it is obvious their loved one is dead, Canadians are comforted when they believe the doctor "did everything that could be done."

People in the developing world, on the other hand, are exposed to death much more often than we are. Between 10 and 20 per cent of their children die before age five, and elderly family members often

Tracer bullet ricocheting
(Photo courtesy Master Corporal Julien Ricard)

die at home. Because of this, they accept that various diseases and injuries lead inevitably to death. Conversely, they often have an unrealistic view of what modern medicine can do. The things we achieve seem so miraculous to them that they can have trouble accepting the fact that our best efforts are sometimes not enough. The futile resuscitation attempt we undertake in Canada to ease parents into the grieving process is sometimes seen in the developing world as a failure that has at least an element of physician error involved. It is wiser to forgo any such attempt if the conclusion is preordained.

That was what I had in mind when Mariam arrived at the UMS. A quick exam determined that she had no pulse, was not breathing and had fixed and midrange pupils. I loosened her bandage and felt her skull. It felt like picking up a bag of marbles. Although there was only a tiny hole in her forehead, everything behind her face was shattered.

I turned to her grandfather and told him that I was terribly sorry, but there was nothing I could do. I told him I deeply regretted his loss, but it looked like he was past that. He seemed to have already accepted the death of his granddaughter. His questions had to do with the details of getting her body back to his home. Nonetheless, I asked the interpreter to explain to him that Mariam had not suffered. I say the same thing to bereaved families I deal with in Canada. It seems to help.

When Mariam and her grandfather had gone, I turned my attention to the Canadians. I told Junior that he had done an outstanding job. He seemed okay. I spent a long time after that talking to the shooter. He is a sensitive and sophisticated man. By the time we were done talking, I think he had settled into the healthiest and most appropriate emotional reaction to this incident. He was distraught, but he recognized that his actions had been correct under the circumstances. Had he failed to defend the patrol, he might have allowed a suicide bomber to get close enough to kill several of his comrades.

The second motorcyclist, the one who caused all this, was not caught by the Afghan police. He has to have been a Taliban sympathizer, if not an active fighter. He was testing the patrol to see at what range our soldiers would fire warning shots, in an attempt to analyze its defensive procedures. In doing so, he deliberately provoked the patrol into shooting when there were numerous civilians around. He recklessly endangered those civilians and caused Mariam's death. I doubt he feels as bad about that as the shooter does.

It is now a little after 2100. I am going to call home and talk to Michelle. I will ask her what she is doing, and we will laugh together for a few minutes. Then I will try to fall asleep while thinking about her face and not the one I saw tonight.

Addendum, July 31: The press reports in Canada have been reasonable about this incident, with the exception of one news outlet in Montreal that implied we had fired several rounds at civilians without explaining the threat our troops had faced. There has been a thorough investigation, which I will write more about in a later entry. It goes without saying that the family will be compensated.

Our procedures have been reviewed, and all troops have been ordered to fire warning shots into the air from now on. This is not as effective as firing into the ground. A shot into the air generates only a loud noise, whereas a shot into the ground also produces the visual stimulus of the dust kicking up where the bullet strikes. Firing into the ground is a much more powerful deterrent. It is also awkward and time-consuming to move to a "shoot to kill" position after having fired into the air. Nonetheless, we will use this method to increase the population's safety.

Now, some context. The UN has issued a report on civilian casualties in Afghanistan over the first six months of 2009. There have been more than a thousand such deaths, over 70 per cent of them caused by the Taliban. These numbers are the opposite of what insurgencies should produce. Look at the civilian casualty rates in Sudan, El Salvador, Rhodesia and many others. Poorly armed rebel forces try to earn the trust and co-operation of the civilian population and cause few casualties among them. Entrenched powers use heavy weapons in sometimes indiscriminate ways and cause a lot of civilian casualties. Here, the proportions are completely inverted.

The report also accuses the Taliban of taking advantage of Pashtun culture, specifically *nanawati* (see the June 9 entry), to coerce civilians into giving them shelter and then attacking Coalition forces from those same dwellings. According to the report, this sometimes tricks Coalition forces into attacking the area and causing civilian casualties. This is something we are trying very hard to avoid.

Addendum, August 1: This is rich! Within twenty-four hours of the UN report coming out, the Taliban issued a statement saying they would "stop using suicide bombers to avoid harming Afghan civilians." Eight years of war and thousands of civilian deaths later.

JULY 22 | Rules of Evidence, Rules of War

We had only one war casualty today, a fifteen-year-old who took a bullet to the shoulder. His injuries were not life-threatening, the care was straightforward and the medevac helicopter came quickly. I met his father at the gate after the helicopter had left and assured him his son would be returned to him shortly and in good health.

The most important aspect of the case had nothing to do with the medicine. The boy had been brought in after FOB Zettlemeyer, an ANP outpost a kilometre north of here, had been attacked. He told us he had been catching small crabs in the Arghandab River when he was shot. The problem with his story is that he was discovered north of the outpost whereas the river is to the south, between the FOB and the outpost. For his story to be true, he would have had to have walked close to one kilometre through the bush with his gunshot shoulder. This is very difficult to believe, as this would have meant he had walked *away* from the FOB, to which he claimed to have requested to come when he was found by the ANP.

Although still a juvenile, the patient fell into the category we call FAM, a fighting-age male (the Taliban make extensive use of child soldiers). We all had a gut feeling that this guy was wrong somehow. That is not enough. He was sent to Kandahar without any restrictions on his future movements. He was not even questioned by our military intelligence people.

We have had people about whom our suspicions of Taliban affiliation were much stronger but who were also released for lack of sufficient evidence. Some soldiers are frustrated when that happens, because it is likely that these individuals will go right back to their Taliban units and be attacking us the next day. Whenever I sense that this might be the case, I tell the aggravated soldier that the ones we let go are living proof that, despite the savagery of our enemies, we continue to fight this war in a clean and honourable way.

I say the same thing when a soldier expresses frustration with our rules of engagement, the criteria we must satisfy before we open fire. The rules are different for different weapons, with the most restrictive criteria being reserved for the heaviest weapons, the ones most at risk of killing innocent bystanders. The combat troopers who are getting shot at from one family compound sometimes resent it when a commander, safe at KAF, denies them an air strike because it might damage a neighbouring compound. It speaks volumes about the discipline and professionalism of these men that they follow these rules.

JULY 23 | Investigations

I spent a good deal of time yesterday describing the circumstances of Mariam's death with a representative of the CF National Investigation Service (NIS). Any incident of this severity is investigated by NIS. Its members are senior members of the military police and serve as the detectives of that branch.

It is common for emergency physicians to have to discuss cases with police and lawyers, both in and out of court. I have had to do so several times and no longer feel any anxiety during the process. Although I had never met an NIS man before, much less been interviewed by one, this did not feel any different. Once the tape recorder was turned on, I gave my statement in one long speech. The investigator asked a few more questions and we were done. I had to go through the same process again today because of an incident that occurred this morning.

An Afghan policeman had been standing near the front gate of the FOB when one of our armoured vehicles came in. The Canadians indicated their intention to come in and turn to the left. However, it seems that the policeman did not know that tracked vehicles do not turn in the same way a wheeled vehicle does. To turn a tracked vehicle, you make one track go forward while the other one goes backward. As a result, the vehicle *pivots*, more or less in the same place. Unfortunately, the policeman did not wait for the vehicle to pass but rather walked right into its blind spot, whereupon his head was crushed between the vehicle and a wall. He was rushed to the UMS.

When he arrived, his head was covered with a sheet and he was not moving. One of the policemen accompanying him, perhaps a family relation or close friend, was distraught and screaming. He was controlled by the camp sergeant-major and removed from the premises.

I took half a second to steel myself before removing the sheet. Given the mechanism of injury and the other man's emotional state, I thought I was going to be looking at a skull that had been squashed like a grape. Somewhat to my surprise and very much to my relief, the patient started talking as soon as I exposed his head. He had multiple facial lacerations and a skull fracture of the right forehead. His right eye socket had caved in and his eye was "extruded"—it went much further forward than it should have. The optic nerve, the thing that connects the eyeball to the brain, had been stretched a considerable distance. His pupil did not react at all when a light was shined into it.

This case gave me a chance to do some on-the-spot teaching. Everyone in the UMS, medics included, was focusing on the facial wounds. These are very distracting for medical personnel because the face is such a big part of who we are as human beings. You can lose a hand or a leg and, once your prosthesis is in place, people will barely notice the difference. A mangled face, however, dramatically changes how people see you.

I therefore took a minute to show my crew that, as bad as these injuries were, none of them was life-threatening. The patient was breathing on his own, he had good air entry into both lungs and his vital signs were stable. You could see that he was protecting his airway because he was spitting up the blood that pooled in his mouth. He also appeared neurologically intact because he was moving all four limbs and was able to speak coherently. He needed maxillofacial and plastic surgery procedures, but these could be safely delayed for hours.

I like to say that these patients are "stable in their instability." So long as nothing else goes wrong, they are likely to remain stable for quite some time. It would be a terrible mistake, however, to assume that will be the case when a helicopter transfer is imminent. We therefore proceeded with a standard emergency department intubation, giving additional drugs to protect the brain as well as the usual ones to put the patient to sleep and paralyze him. We protected his cervical spine while we did this—always a good habit when the patient has a head trauma. We had barely finished securing the tube when the helicopter arrived to take him to KAF.

No more than an hour had gone by when another helicopter arrived at the FOB. This one carried a different member of the NIS, sent to investigate today's incident.

I have a number of friends who are senior police officers, and the two NIS men came across the same way my buddies do: professional, very good at their jobs, completely ethical and determined to get to the truth. Both of them are investigating incidents in which the actions of Canadians have injured Afghans. Having spoken to the men involved, I am convinced that both occurrences were tragic accidents. I am equally convinced that the investigators will only reach that conclusion themselves when they have examined all the evidence and interviewed all the witnesses. And re-interviewed them, if necessary:

the NIS man in charge of the investigation into Mariam's death called me back to confirm which side of the forehead the bullet had entered, because there was disagreement among the witnesses. This may seem trivial, but it shows how badly this guy wanted to get the story absolutely right.

JULY 24 | A Righteous Shoot?

Emergency physicians like cops. We see each other a lot in the course of our duties and we have a lot in common. Both our jobs involve some drudgery leavened by regular moments of drama. We both see people when they are at their weakest, angriest and/or most distraught. We both do shift work, that notorious killer of relationships. A lot of emergency nurses end up married to cops.

I like cops more than most people do. For the past five years, I have acted as the medical adviser for the "tactical unit" (a.k.a. SWAT team) of our police department. This relationship proved to be very useful when I re-enrolled in the CF two years ago. By the time I got back in uniform, I had already reacquired many of the infantry reflexes of my youth, thanks to the training I had done with my "tac" buddies.

Emergency physicians and policemen have something else in common: people lie to us regularly, for any number of reasons. For policemen, it only goes one way: people try to hide what they have done or what they know. For emergency physicians, the untruths cover a wider spectrum. Some people exaggerate their symptoms in the hopes of obtaining a particular treatment, commonly narcotics. Others minimize their symptoms, because they are afraid of what the diagnosis might be. Some people go either way, depending on what psychopathology is dominant in their family that particular day. And some people are just nuts.

Having to sort through all these emotions and agendas every time we are on shift gives us an ability, like cops, to "read" people. While I think I do this reasonably well, the skill is situational. It is essential to consider the patient's social and cultural milieu before drawing any conclusions. Nonetheless, my travels have taught me that there are some universal human behaviours. I may have stumbled on one more.

One of today's patients was Abdul Rahzak, a man in his forties. He had been shot three times by the ANP. One bullet went through his right ankle, shattering the tibia and leaving his foot hanging limply. One bullet went through his right hand, breaking several bones in his palm and wrist. The last bullet could have been the widow maker, but Allah was watching over Mr. Rahzak. The slug entered below his right armpit and exited halfway up his right shoulder blade, passing outside his chest cavity. Though he was in severe pain Mr. Rahzak was breathing normally, and ultrasound confirmed there was no blood or air leaking into his chest.

The medical management was almost mundane: bandage all the wounds, splint the broken bones, give pain medicine and antibiotics, wait for the chopper. Managing the circumstances in which Mr. Rahzak was wounded proved to be far more ambiguous.

For a guy who had been shot by the police, a couple of details did not add up. After dropping Mr. Rahzak off at the UMS, none of the Afghan policemen stayed behind. Somehow, an individual on whom they had used potentially lethal force half an hour ago was not even worth questioning, much less arresting.

Mr. Rahzak's behaviour in the UMS was equally unusual. The patients I have treated whom we either knew or suspected to be Taliban have all had one thing in common: they have all been afraid of me well into the patient encounter. They think we are going to torture them, because that is what the Taliban do to their prisoners. It takes a long time to convince these patients that I will treat them properly.

Mr. Rahzak behaved very differently. As soon as I identified myself in Pashto as a physician, he began to relax. When I had determined that no life-threatening injuries were present, I told him: "*Tah bah shah kaygee*" ("You're going to be all right"). Although I had not given him any pain medication, I could tell that the patient-doctor connection had been made. Mr. Rahzak looked at me with that mixture of awe and gratitude that is the emergency physician's reward when patients are convinced they will be well looked after. That struck me as un-Talibanlike.

While we were waiting for a helicopter I shared this observation with the camp's sergeant-major, Master Warrant Officer Richard Stacey of the "Strats." He is the senior non-commissioned officer on the base and a man of infinite wisdom. He was sure he had seen the patient a number of times on patrols around the FOB, and he agreed that Mr. Rahzak did not seem "wrong."

I was still wondering why Mr. Rahzak had been shot when I was called to a meeting a few hours later. Attending the meeting were Mr. Rahzak's brother, three local elders (two of them "Hajis" and the other a pharmacist) and two representatives of the police training team.

The meeting began with my report about the patient's injuries. I reassured his brother that the patient's life was not in danger, but I emphasized that the long-term function of both his right foot and right hand could be affected. Mr. Rahzak's brother asked if he could go to Kandahar to visit him, and we will try to arrange this tomorrow.

The elders spoke next. The nagging suspicion I'd had that this had not been a "righteous shoot" became much stronger. All three of the elders were emphatic: Mr. Rahzak was in no way associated with the Taliban. He was a farmer, and he had been tending his crops when he was shot. According to the elders, the police had opened fire without any provocation whatsoever.

I have to clarify something here. In looking back over the entries I have made since arriving at Ma'Sum Ghar, I see that I have not spoken much about the constant fighting that goes on outside our perimeter wire. The outposts within a few kilometres of here get attacked on a daily basis. The gunfire and explosions have become so routine that they are not even commented upon by those inside the FOB. If you stand on the hill behind the UMS and use binoculars to watch the walls of the outpost closest to us during one of these attacks, you can see the numerous puffs of dust where bullets are hitting.

The outpost closest to us, on the other side of the Arghandab River, is manned by the ANP. These men are poorly trained, poorly led and often corrupt, and they have a large number of drug addicts in their midst. To make things worse, this particular detachment of police is from a different part of the country. They are primarily Dari speakers who speak Pashto poorly.

This is a recipe for disaster. Barely competent cops spend their days cooped up in an outpost getting shot at by people they do not like and with whom they have trouble communicating. When they come out of their outpost, possibly after one of their mates has been killed or injured, they probably have blood in their eyes and dope in their veins. At that moment, they are about as far from being professional police-men as it is possible to be. It was entirely believable that they had shot Mr. Rahzak on the spur of the moment out of blind rage.

So far, so bad. But then, what I found to be the most fascinating part of the meeting began. The two Canadians with me, Leading Seaman Andy Hewlett of the Civil Military Cooperation, or CIMIC, and Constable Ferris McLean of the RCMP, engaged the Afghans in a discussion that encapsulates how we will win this war.

They began by acknowledging the strong likelihood of wrongdo-ing by the police and committed themselves to sitting down with the officers involved to get their side of the story. This might sound rou-tine in the Canadian context, but it is a revolutionary concept here. In Afghanistan, the men with the guns have always made their own rules. Anyone who could not stand up to them has had to accept their behaviour, no matter how abusive.

The idea being put forth here was radically different. This time, other men with guns, in this case Canadians, were willing to take the side of the weak and confront the police. I take it they have done this a number of times in the past, with at least some success, because the elders reacted very positively to this commitment on the part of my fellow Canadians.

Throughout the conversation, however, the Canadians empha-sized that the Afghans themselves were responsible for their own

Constable Ferris McLean, RCMP (left),
and Leading Seaman Andy Hewlett, CIMIC

future. When the elders asked that the police be transferred out and
replaced with a unit of the ANA, Leading Seaman Hewlett replied
that he understood that the army was much more honest and effective than the police, but there were not enough of them to man all the
outposts. He then stressed that much of the responsibility for improving the situation lay with the Afghans themselves. It was not enough
for the elders to complain about the police. They would have to reach
out to the police—their fellow Afghans—and try to build bridges
between the police and the community.

Constable McLean then went further and emphasized that it
was unacceptable that the outposts were being attacked every day.
Although he did not explicitly state it, he made it crystal clear that he
expected the elders to exert their influence to convince at least the
more moderate members of the insurgency to leave their area alone.
Although they did not reply directly, it was easy to tell that the elders
got his message. Constable McLean went on to offer to mediate a face-
to-face meeting between the elders and the leaders of the local police,
precisely to try to forge some links between the two groups.

As in every civil war, there are a range of motivations on both sides. Although there can never be any compromise with al Qaeda and the more extreme members of the Taliban, there exists within the Taliban movement a spectrum of political opinions. Many people on this spectrum can be convinced to renounce violence. This will be a necessary step in the ending of this war: isolating the truly evil people from those who have legitimate complaints against the government but who have chosen illegitimate means of seeking redress.

THE CIMIC

Most people have never heard of the CIMIC, but when you hear about Canadians soldiers doing reconstruction work, this is what you are hearing about. The civilian agencies, such as the Canadian International Development Agency (CIDA) and the Department of Foreign Affairs, do not send their personnel into an area as dangerous as the Panjwayi. So it is up to Leading Seaman Hewlett and the CIMIC team to manage the money we are putting into the reconstruction of this shattered area.

A good chunk of this money goes to pay claims against us from people we have hurt or owners of property we have damaged during our operations. We are guests here, and we pay for any damage to our rented accommodations. It can, however, be tricky to sort out legitimate claims from illegitimate ones. There is an enormous incentive to try to rip off the (by local standards) incredibly rich foreigners.

This goes on in all developing-world countries. Very often, the response of the Westerner is to become angry at the sometimes-blatant fraud without appreciating the human misery that motivates it. Try to think of how far you would go to improve the lives of your children if you were living in conditions such as these.

Leading Seaman Hewlett and the CIMIC team have a much more mature and constructive approach. Realizing when they arrived that a number of claims were suspicious, they changed the process whereby the claims were paid out. They involved the local Afghan leadership and tightened up the documentation process. By making the leaders accountable to their people, they killed two birds with one stone: the people get to see that not only those with connections get their claims processed, and the leadership must be aware of what is going on with the local people.

The claims process is a two-way street. A lot of information flows into the CIMIC during its interactions with the locals, some of it militarily very useful. When the procedure for making a claim was made more arduous, the amount of information being provided to the FOB Ma'Sum Ghar CIMIC decreased. Some CIMIC people concluded that the locals had been angered when the claims process got tougher and had decided to clam up. Then they realized that the amount of information being provided to the FOB Wilson CIMIC remained unchanged, even though it was using the same stricter claims criteria. It turns out the Taliban in the Panjwayi had targeted Afghans who interacted with the CIMIC. Taliban methods can be quite convincing, in the short term.

There is another aspect of the CIMIC's work that is, for Leading Seaman Hewlett, far more satisfying. This involves reviewing various submissions from the local population for projects to improve their lives. To date, they have spent about three-quarters of their money on "social" programs. These include schools, health clinics and immunization programs. The rest of the money has been spent on economic development, including enhancements in the transportation infrastructure, the creation of a farmers' market and the purchase of various pieces of machinery that the district can then lend to the farmers, among others. Programs like this give the people hope. And it is hope that keeps them away from the Taliban.

JULY 25 | HLTA

A small group of very happy soldiers left the FOB today. I thought it would be interesting to explain where they were going.

Every Canadian soldier in Afghanistan, during his or her tour of duty, goes on a three-week vacation. Any other organization would call it that: a vacation. The army, being the army, gives it a complicated name, which it then reduces to its initials.

HLTA stands for home leave travel allowance, which is the money given to the soldiers to use on their vacation. Somehow, the term for the funding morphed into the vacation itself, as in: "I am going to Thailand for my HLTA." I pointed out to a few soldiers that this means they are going to Thailand to get money, when really they are getting money to go to Thailand, but my grammatical brilliance was not appreciated.

Organizing the HLTA generates more institutional angst than any other aspect of our mission. Joe wants to go to Disneyland with his kids during his wife's holidays while Suzanne has to be the maid of honour at her sister's wedding. Both events take place at the same time, and each of these people is responsible for covering the other. You can see how this would give our commanders more than a few grey hairs.

Geographically, Afghanistan is a good place to start a vacation. With a pocket of cash and almost a month off, one can reach tourist destinations that are generally hard for Canadians to visit. Many soldiers take advantage of this opportunity to visit Europe, Africa or Asia. This last option is particularly appealing to young single male soldiers and generates a predictable number of visits to the UMS for problems of a "personal" nature, most of which respond well to high doses of antibiotics.

The HLTA is wildly popular, but I can't help but wonder about its effects on our combat effectiveness. From section to battle group, a unit's commander and its second-in-command train for well over a year to go to war together. They get to know each other intimately. Then, during the time they most need each other, they both take almost a month off. That has always struck me as a weird way to run a war.

JULY 26 | The Home Front

General Rick Hillier once asked a group of soldiers about to deploy to Afghanistan what their most important mission was. They replied that it was to defeat the Taliban, support the Afghan government, protect civilians and other things of that nature. The general disagreed. He told them that, first and foremost, they had to support their families back home.

I have taken this admonition to heart. Although it is a point of honour that I call my daughter every day, there are very few days in which I do not find a few minutes to make a separate call to my wife. With my global satellite phone and the greatly improved Internet connections of this rotation, I am able to be much more supportive of my wife and daughter's day-to-day activities than I was during my first tour. Claude and I discuss all family issues as much as we would if I were at home, and I participate in the "administration" of the family's affairs. So far, I have scheduled medical appointments for both my wife and daughter, booked flights for them, organized child care, sorted out financial issues and resolved various emergencies in our extended family. I even "babysit" long-distance, keeping Michelle entertained on the phone when Claude needs several minutes of uninterrupted time.

But today is Claude's birthday. Flowers ordered from the FOB and gifts bought before my departure notwithstanding, there is no way for me to make this day what it should be for her. Very few women (and, let's be honest, even fewer men) would tolerate a relationship like this. But for us, it works.

And for all the uncertainty the war brings to our immediate future, we have decided to take the most life-affirming and forward-facing step possible: we will adopt a second child, this one a little girl with special medical needs from Vietnam. She will be two and a half years old when we get her, which means that the effects of a prolonged stay in a developing-world orphanage will be more severe than they were for Michelle, who came into our family when she was only fifteen months old. We will have our work cut out for us.

JULY 28 | Dogs of War

The expression "dogs of war" refers to mercenaries, people who will be soldiers for whoever will pay them. I described some of them in the June 10 entry ("The Contractor"). There are a couple of guys here for whom this expression could not be more apt. Call them Luis and Alvaro.

Luis and Alvaro come from two countries in Latin America. They live at the opposite end of the FOB from me, and I was unaware of their presence here until recently. Our paths crossed while we were waiting in line for supper one day. I noticed two men wearing Canadian uniforms and speaking Spanish. I speak Spanish fluently, so I struck up a conversation with them, mostly to learn how two Latinos had ended up here.

Luis and Alvaro are the handlers of the FOB's bomb-sniffing dogs. The CF has contracted an American company to provide these services for our combat teams. The American company hired these gentlemen, who had been police dog handlers in their respective countries. Only in this globalized, semi-privatized war could you find the Canadian Army employing a U.S. company with South American subcontractors to fight in an Asian war.

There are benefits for all involved. The CF gets a bomb-sniffing capability off-the-shelf, with all the no-delay, no-training, no-pension advantages that mercenaries have. The Latin Americans get a higher wage than they could dream of getting at home ($250 USD a day, since you ask). No doubt the American middleman makes a healthy profit.

Luis and Alvaro invited me to watch one of their training sessions. They explained that training a dog to look for any substance is the same, regardless of whether the animal is being trained to look for drugs or dynamite. It was interesting, gratifying and disturbing, all at the same time.

Interesting, because it was amazing to see how quickly the dogs detected the hidden explosives. Gratifying, because seeing the love these men had for their animals provided a welcome respite from the blood and gunfire the day had otherwise been devoted to. Disturbing, because the dogs have no idea how dangerous their job is. To them it is just a game.

Addendum, August 14—A Job to Die For: Let's call this guy Pedro. He is employed by the same company as Luis and Alvaro and is based at FOB Sperwan Ghar.

The patch on his tactical vest (which I have blurred) is the flag of the African country of which he is a citizen. In his homeland, he was trained as a physician assistant and worked as one for three years. He became engaged to his girlfriend and started to consider what the future held for him. As he explained it to me, one can buy a house in his country only for cash. There is no such thing as "20 per cent down and a mortgage." At the rate he was going, he would be able to buy his house in twenty years. It was rentals or Dad's house till then. Then he saw an ad for dog handlers in Afghanistan.

Pedro and Donner (as in, "On Donner and Blitzen." Don't ask me why. And don't ask Pedro. He doesn't know either.)

The company must have been a little desperate because, although Pedro strikes you as a capable young man, he had no experience as a dog handler. Since he was willing to take the job, the company hired him and paid his salary while he went on a training course.

After this course, Pedro arrived at KAF to assume his duties. He received rudimentary firearms training, which consisted of little more than instructions on how to shoot his rifle and his pistol. He had received no military training in his country, and he received nothing resembling infantry training here. Yet he goes out with his dog on combat operations where he is expected to shoot back if the unit he is with comes under enemy fire. He has lost count of the number of times that has happened.

He has been here since March 2006. That is not a typo; he has been here almost continuously for three and a half years, looking for IEDs. He stays in Afghanistan for four to six months, then he goes home for a month. He considers himself fortunate to have found this job. So do the Filipino and the Haitian who are also on staff as dog handlers at the Canadian FOBs.

He is doing all this for the princely sum of three thousand dollars a month.* He has begun construction on his house. This will take one more year to finish. He will then return home and marry his fiancée, having jumpstarted his family life by two decades—if he survives.

JULY 29 | The Brothers

A number of Afghans work on the FOB. Some do routine maintenance and construction, and others help out in the kitchen. This evening, one of the kitchen workers invited me to their tent (ten metres up the hill from the UMS) for a cup of tea.

The Afghan workers on the FOB are supposed to seek their medical care in the neighbouring town. I was aware of this rule but never had any intention of following it. I cannot evacuate Afghans to the tertiary care hospital at KAF, but so long as the patients only need advice, a few stitches or access to some of the medications we have on the FOB, I will do my best for them. This trivial kindness seems to have endeared me to the Afghans in general and the kitchen workers in particular, hence the invitation for tea. I spent a very enjoyable evening with them, and I hope we will have the opportunity to repeat the encounter.

There are four workers in this tent, three brothers and a friend of

---

* This is less than the Latinos get. The company uses a pay formula based on the gross domestic product of the employee's home country. The theory is that all employees will enjoy a similar standard of living when they return home. That strikes me as logical and exploitive at the same time.

their family. The story of the three brothers is the story of Afghanistan's past thirty years in a microcosm: brutal hardship, liberation, economic struggle, terror, the importance of family and, perhaps, a way for the country to heal.

HARDSHIP

The brothers come from a village near Kabul. The war that had devastated their country during the ten years of the Russian occupation left this area untouched. The Russian army, though unable to pacify or even move through the countryside, had kept a grip on the area around the capital. Life there had been almost normal. That ended when the Russians withdrew in 1989.

The brothers are eighteen, twenty and twenty-three years old. The oldest one would have been three when the Russians left; the next two were born during the civil war that followed.

The groups that had been armed by the United States to fight the Russians had never been united. With their common enemy gone, these groups began fighting each other. Because of this it took them three years, until 1992, to overthrow the puppet regime the communists had left in power.

During those three years, Kabul was subjected to sporadic bombardment and street fighting. That had rarely happened in the "Russian time." As bad as that was, what came next was worse. For the next four years, from 1992 to 1996, the various factions turned on each other with a vengeance.

They tore Kabul apart. Just as hyenas will rip their prey to shreds, the warlords rocketed Kabul in a manner that was both devastating and random. Because of the inaccuracy of these weapons, very few fighters died in the bombardment. Civilian casualties were in the tens of thousands.

Things were so bad that Kabulis welcomed the Taliban when they captured the city in 1996. Although the newcomers were known for their repressive ways, anything seemed better than the anarchy and random death that had been the city's lot for so long. Almost over-night, the repression became worse than the anarchy had been. By then, it was too late to resist. The Taliban had all the guns.

LIBERATION

The brothers were in Kabul when the Coalition attacked in 2001. The eldest would have been fifteen years old, still too young to have formed a definite political opinion about what was happening in his country. The brothers remember the Taliban fleeing, and they say they were happy about that. Let's discount that as the thing any Afghan would say in the presence of foreign soldiers.

TAKING SIDES

It is a little harder to discount what the brothers did next. With the Taliban gone, they turned their attention from mere survival to the betterment of their family. One after another, they have come to work for the Canadian Army.

There is a wide range of political opinion in Afghanistan. The fanatical Taliban have equally fanatical opponents. The rest of the population is found along a spectrum between these two groups. This includes those who passively or actively support either side as well as a large number of people who want to be left alone. To work for the Coalition in any capacity clearly puts you to one side of the spectrum. So when the brothers tell me they are happy we are here and they want us to stay, I am inclined to believe them.

THE PRICE OF RESISTANCE

Working for the Canadians carries with it a very great risk. The Taliban consider what these men are doing a crime punishable by death. When they visit their families they must have a well-concocted cover story to explain where and why they are travelling, should the Taliban pull them over. They do this by, among other things, having two names: the real one they use at home and a fake one they use on the FOB.

the most patriarchal societies in the world learned to trust and respect a woman enough to learn the facts of life from her.

It is through a myriad of interactions like this that the world becomes a better place. People are changed not by politicians and demagogues. They are changed by the individuals they come into contact with, the people they can touch . . . and who touch them.

Has this contact with us altered the middle brother's view of the world? I described earlier the obvious love he had for his younger sister. I asked him if he would approve if she were to come and work for the Canadians as well. When he said no, I thought he would tell me the woman's place was still in the home. I had grossly underestimated him.

He does not want his sister to be a cook for the Canadians. He would rather see her do something that would allow her to help her fellow Afghans, while providing for herself and her family. And he says he will support her financially if she chooses to pursue that goal.

He wants her to be a doctor.

JULY 31 | The Elements, Part 3: Fire

The CF are not like any other government department.
We kill people.
— GENERAL RICK HILLIER

General Hillier was stating a self-evident truth, but it is one that bears repeating. Canadians are reticent to admit that our country is at war. We like to see ourselves as the planet's "nice guys," and wars are not nice. The corollary to this is a statement I've seen numerous times on Internet discussion boards about our Afghan mission: Canada is a peacekeeping nation. People who oppose the mission will often bring this up, as if to say that fighting wars was somehow un-Canadian.

This is ridiculous. It is true that our country has excelled at peacekeeping for the past fifty years. Partly, this is because we have behaved well on the world stage. We have often acted as honest brokers, earning respect around the globe.

But the main reason we are effective peacekeepers is that, among those countries that have been at peace since the end of the Korean War, Canada has by far the most effective army.* This means we are the best at killing people. Combatants around the world have learned the hard way not to mess with us.

Have you ever heard of the Medak Pocket? If you are like most Canadians, the answer is no. And yet, if there was any justice in the world, this name would be as familiar to every Canadian as Vimy Ridge and Juno Beach are.

In the genocidal hell that was the former Yugoslavia, we sent in "peacekeepers" when there was little peace to keep. We did our best to keep the ethnic cleansers away from the civilians. We failed to do so many times because we were hamstrung by restrictive rules of engagement: the United Nations kept our soldiers on a very short leash. The shining exception to this rule occurred in September 1993, in the area of Croatia called Medak.

Although the Serbs have far more blood on their hands than any other group in the Yugoslavian civil war, they were the victims at Medak. The Croats had launched an offensive into this area that was marked by incredible brutality towards the Serbian civilian population. It took far too long, but someone in the UN chain of command finally said "No more!"

The Canadians, in this case the Second Battalion, Princess Patricia's Canadian Light Infantry (the PPCLI), were given the task of halting the Croat advance. The orders were unambiguous: stand and fight. The Patricias proceeded to engage in the most intense gun battle Canadians had been involved in since the end of the Korean War. They faced down a superior force of Croats, killed twenty-seven of them,

---

* This is an important distinction to make. Armies that go to war from time to time get to "practise." It is a lot harder to keep your warrior edge in peacetime.

wounded many more and did not surrender an inch of ground. Four Canadians were lightly wounded by Croat artillery but stayed in the line. We kicked the Croats' asses, and they left the area.

It was too late for many Serb civilians. They had already been slaughtered. In the area of the battle, not a single survivor was found. What the Patricias did discover would mark them for the rest of their lives. Horribly burned corpses. Destroyed homes. The Croats had even shot the farm animals they had been unable to carry away.

Most eerily, our soldiers found the area littered with a large number of surgical gloves. The Croats had tried to remove their victims' bodies, but they had been too squeamish to touch the skin of those they had so readily murdered.

The Patricias' efforts did have positive results. The Croats were not expecting the UN to allow the Canadians to pummel them. When we did, they did not have enough time to remove all the evidence of their war crimes as they ran away. The proof gathered by Canadian investigators was used to prosecute Croatian war criminals in the International Criminal Tribunal for the Former Yugoslavia. The Croats' offensive—and their "ethnic cleansing"—was stopped, at least temporarily. They now knew the Canadians stood in their way and they had no desire to take us on again.

And how did the Canadian government of the day react to this display of heroism and military prowess? It became apoplectic. This came on the heels of the Somalia debacle (where a Canadian soldier had murdered a teenage civilian), and no one in Ottawa wanted to hear about Canadian soldiers killing anyone, no matter what the circumstances. They tried to bury the news as much as possible and treated the soldiers who had participated in the fighting like shit. The Patricias should have been given medals and a parade down the main street of every major city in Canada. Instead, they were hounded with questions about their actions by Ottawa-bound bureaucrats who were overreacting to the spanking the government had gotten as a result of its poor handling of the Somalia affair.

This was devastating for these men. They had gone into the darkest abyss of human monstrosity, and they had gone there on Canada's behalf. When they returned, the country did not even acknowledge their efforts. What they had seen would push people into PTSD and depression under the best conditions. Many of them fell prey to these illnesses. You can see why General Hillier called this "the decade of darkness" for the CF.

It was not until December 2002 that the members of Second Battalion, PPCLI, were finally recognized in a ceremony held in Winnipeg. Governor General Adrienne Clarkson presented the unit with the Commander-in-Chief Unit Commendation and a slew of medals were awarded to deserving individuals. We must never let such courage and sacrifice go unrecognized again.*

We must also acknowledge that our soldiers are warriors first. To claim that our status as "good peacekeepers" absolves us from the responsibility of ever going to war again is a moral cop-out. People who hold this view never wade into the ethically challenging debates to determine whether a war is moral. To do that you have to look evil in the face and decide that, painful though it may be, there are some evils that justify the use of armed force.

Protected by two oceans and the most powerful nation on earth, Canadians can go about their lives ignoring what goes on in the rest of the world. We can bury our heads in the sand and refuse to consider the plight of those who are suffering far from our shores. But if every time the subject of whether or not Canada should go to war comes up you say "We should stay out of it," that does not prove you are moral. It proves you are intellectually lazy.

I bring all this up because I have only occasionally discussed our battlefield successes. By doing so, I have mirrored the Canadian media.

---

* Readers interested in learning more about the Medak incident are encouraged to read Carol Off's book *The Ghosts of Medak Pocket: The Story of Canada's Secret War* (Toronto: Random House of Canada, 2004).

The reticence of our news outlets to talk about those times when we wipe out a whole bunch of bad guys is astounding.

Allow me to bring some balance into this story. We are killing a lot more of them than they are of us, and we have been extraordinarily successful recently. At our daily intelligence briefings, which I attend as one of the FOB unit commanders, we review the after-action reports of our combat units. For the past week, we have managed to kill between ten and twenty Taliban every day.

One hit was particularly satisfying. The Taliban brought in "judges" to administer their brutal and bizarre justice in a remote area of the district. We figured out where some of these individuals were, and killed several of them with a well-executed air strike.

This war will not be won by killing Taliban. But it can be lost if we do not hold them at bay and make it very unhealthy for them to congregate. The Canadians of Roto 7 are doing that, following in the warrior footsteps of many who have gone before us.

Addendum, same day, 2130: It seems that the Taliban have taken umbrage at my last entry and at the satisfaction I derive from the demise of so many of their members. They have spent the last half hour attacking our perimeter. I was in the staff lounge when the first rocket hit. By the time I got outside, tracer fire could be seen going from two of our observation posts towards the rocket's launch site. Shortly afterwards, a second rocket streaked in. It flew right to left across my field of vision. It looked like harmless fireworks until it impacted, less than a hundred metres away. A bright white flash, ten metres in diameter, suddenly appeared near the main entrance to the FOB. Even at that distance, I felt the blast wave in my chest.

For the next half hour, the sky was lit up with tracer rounds going back and forth while flares lit up the sky.

AUGUST 1 | The Road to Sperwan Ghar

My orders came through this morning. "Bed" Bedard comes back tomorrow and I head for my last FOB, Sperwan Ghar, in three days' time. To get there, I will go by road along Route Hyena. This is the main east-west thoroughfare in Panjwayi district. In 2007, this road was known as Route Foster and was the second-most-dangerous road in the world. We called it "IED Alley." The most stressful thing I had to do on Roto 4 was to travel along this road. Things are better now. Let me explain why.

Go back and look at the first two photographs in the June 9 entry. The top picture shows Route Hyena as it is now—paved. The top-left corner of the bottom picture shows what it was like in 2007: a dirt road. It is easy to dig in dirt, and it is easy to hide things in dirt. Those simple facts have killed a lot of Canadians.

It has been one of our priorities to pave this road and make it a lot harder for the Taliban to hide their IEDs. The project is some months behind schedule. We could have sent in our own military engineers, and they would have had the road built in a matter of weeks. Instead, we hired a local contractor and four hundred men from nearby villages to work on this project.

So we have a Third World company employing Third World workers. Things are not going to progress as fast as they would if we were in charge, for a number of reasons. But while these men are working for us, they have much less incentive to pick up a gun for the Taliban. They are also motivated to pressure the Taliban not to attack the project, and the Taliban are not immune to this pressure. The number of IEDs found on Route Foster is lower since the locals started working on it, and the number of ambushes has declined.

In Iraq, the Americans have flat-out bribed various members of the insurgency to switch sides. A large number of these individuals have motivations quite different from those of the religious fanatics of al Qaeda. These Iraqis are not thrilled that the Americans are still in the country, but they are willing to tolerate them in exchange for financial gain. In a remarkable exchange that I saw quoted in a number of different news sources, an American officer asked one of these financially motivated fighters: "Do you still want to kill me?" The fighter smiled and answered: "Yes, but not today."

It strikes me that what Canada is doing here is similar to what the Americans have done in Iraq. We are doing it less blatantly and with more socially redeeming features. How Canadian!

In this context, it is a lot easier to accept the project's slow progress. Are the workers getting a full day's pay for a half day's work? Often. Is the contractor ripping us off? Certainly. If this keeps a large number of fighting-age males gainfully employed while the children of Zhari-Panjwayi go to school, is it money well spent? Absolutely.

Making it more difficult for the Taliban to plant IEDs not only makes our life here safer, it also makes it easier for us to focus on reconstruction. Canadians hear about IEDs only when one of us dies. They do not hear about the large number of IEDs that miss us or only scratch our vehicles. But any IED blast causes major damage to the roads. This slows or halts traffic, with the inevitable economic impact that you can imagine. Because of this, a lot of our time is spent rebuilding these roads so that the Afghan people can get on with their lives. The Taliban are here to destroy. We are here to build.

Addendum, same day: This being war, the enemy will want to have their say. So as heartwarming as the previous two pages may have been, this was also the day that we received the only casualty to come from Route Hyena since I have been at FOB Ma'Sum Ghar. A private security guard stepped on an anti-personnel mine that blew off his foot. It looks like he has also lost his right eye.

As I had with the Afghan policeman whose head had been crushed by our armoured vehicle, I emphasized to my team the importance of not being distracted by visually impressive wounds, in this case a ruined face and a missing foot. The patient was alert, spoke in articulate sentences and had normal vital signs. His wounds were life-altering, not life-threatening.

Nasty things, anti-personnel mines. They do not contain much explosive; their goal is not to kill, but to maim. Wounding a man removes five soldiers from the battlefield: the casualty and the four men needed to carry him off. The wounded man then needs medical

Lucky to be alive
(Photo courtesy Master Corporal Julien Ricard)

care and rehabilitation. Dead men do not need care, and their evacuation can be delayed. These mines are as much an economic weapon as a military one.

Addendum, same day, early evening: I mentioned earlier that there are many things I love about being an emergency physician. There are only a few things I dislike. At the top of this short list I would put the fact that we rarely learn what has happened to the patients whose lives we have saved.

It was therefore a particular treat for me to be able to see in follow-up, for the first time on either of my tours, a critically injured patient who had passed through my UMS. The Afghan policeman whose head had been crushed by one of our armoured vehicles on July 23 came to the UMS after supper to have his sutures removed. His numerous facial and skull fractures had been expertly repaired by our maxillofacial surgeon at KAF. As for the eye that was hanging out of its socket, it was not blind! He was counting fingers at one metre already, and there is a good chance that his vision will continue to improve.

He said he remembered me and was grateful for the care I had provided. Emergency physicians almost never get to hear this from the semi-conscious patients for whom we do the most.

It was an ideal way to begin to wind up my stay here at FOB Ma'Sum Ghar.

AUGUST 2, MORNING | None of Your Business

We take patient confidentiality very seriously in modern Canadian medicine. When my father was hospitalized three years ago, the nurses in the intensive care unit (ICU) of my own hospital would not let me look at his chart. Like everybody else, I had to go through the treating physician or talk to my father. For some reason, the media have difficulty accepting that the same standards apply to wounded Canadian soldiers.

We lost two more men yesterday. They were combat engineers based at FOB Wilson. Like Corporal Martin Dubé (see June 14 entry), Corporal Christian Bobbitt and Sapper Mathieu Allard were killed when an IED they were defusing exploded. They never knew what hit them.

In the small world of the combat engineers these losses will be devastating: there are fewer than a hundred of them in the theatre of operations. The losses of this branch of the service exceed all others in proportional terms

I had met both of them at FOB Wilson. They were both TCCCs who had helped out with some of the casualties we treated in June. They impressed me as calm and competent individuals, even though they seemed impossibly young. We were never more than acquaintances. Partly, I regret that very much. Partly, I am relieved—the pain of their passing would have been much worse.

We also had one serious but non-fatal casualty yesterday, someone I did know well. We had seen each other daily, and I enjoyed his company.

The CF will not reveal anything about this man's injuries. I have read articles in which reporters have been critical of the CF because of this. Various media have intimated that the CF is attempting to cover up the number and severity of wounds suffered by our soldiers.

The CF has never defended itself against these accusations, so I will explain its stance here. Imagine for a moment that you were here with me. Now imagine that you have suffered a devastating, life-changing wound. When you woke up this morning, you were a young, healthy adult—your body did exactly what you wanted it to. In an instant, that has been taken away forever. Would you want to have your name and a description of your injuries on the front page of *The Globe and Mail?* Our wounded are free to participate in whatever interviews they want. It is normal that they do so only after they have had time to adjust and begin to cope with their injuries.

So I grieve for our fallen and I shudder at the thought of the pain my friend felt when he was injured, is now feeling during his multiple surgeries and will feel through his rehabilitation. I have sent him a single e-mail, telling him my thoughts are with him and letting him know that he can count on me for any assistance he might need.

Now I wait for him to answer. And if I can wait to find out how he is doing, so can the rest of the country.

Addendum, August 14: The funeral service for Corporal Bobbitt took place in Quebec City the day Warrant Officer Comeau was to leave Canada. He had been back in Canada on leave when Corporal Bobbitt died. Warrant Officer Comeau requested that his leave be extended by a single day so that he could honour his fallen comrade, a man who had fought by his side for several months. He was turned down.

That struck me and many others as completely heartless, until I learned that the engineer commander had decided that the survivors of the engineer troop* needed Warrant Comeau's leadership and compassion as soon as possible. Seen from that perspective, I agree it was the right call.

---

* The engineer equivalent of a platoon.

The sun was setting when one last chopper landed. A few minutes later, my old friend Martin "Bed" Bedard came crashing into the UMS. Our reunion was joyful, but before we could have a proper sit-down to talk about his vacation an Afghan civilian came in with shrapnel wounds to his legs. Not wasting a minute (and showing much less effect from the jet lag than I had) Bed assumed care for the patient. He was pleased to be able to show me how proficient he had become with the ultrasound machine. Given his obvious aptitude for using ultrasound, I had given him additional tips and training by phone and e-mail from FOB Wilson, and during our time together when I came to take over at Ma'Sum Ghar. One of the techniques I had taught him involved using the machine to detect shrapnel fragments buried in the patient's flesh. He used this to good effect here, locating and retrieving four shrapnel fragments. With ultrasound proving that there were no other injuries, the patient was discharged from the FOB, saving a helicopter evacuation.

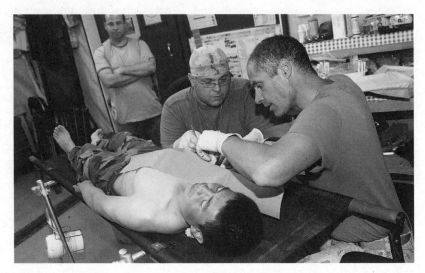

"Cut deeper!"

(Photo courtesy Master Corporal Julien Ricard)

After that, we got another chance to use ultrasound in an innovative manner. An Afghan soldier came in with what appeared to be a skin infection in his armpit. Ultrasound examination showed that there was a pocket of pus beneath the skin, but it was so deep that it could not be detected by palpation (touching the patient). On ultrasound, however, it showed up as a large black space beside the ribs.

When pockets of pus like this are present, the infection can never be cured with antibiotics alone. You have to cut into the patient and let the pus out, an operation called an "incision and drainage." Bed had done a number of these, but none of them had ever required him to cut as far as I was telling him to. Just when Bed thought he was going to pierce the patient's lung, we hit our target and a huge river of pus came streaming out. It was disgusting and satisfying, like so many things in medicine.

Bed handled himself like a pro through this. The Ma'Sum Ghar UMS will be in very good hands when I leave.

Addendum—Two Steps Forward, One Step Back: The paving project on Route Hyena I spoke of yesterday has been put on hold indefinitely. There are many reasons for this, the main ones being the ongoing Taliban threat, arguments with the contractor about money and the fact that the focus of our reconstruction efforts is shifting closer to Kandahar City. Very disappointing. But if you can't handle disappointment, best not to go to war in Afghanistan (or anywhere else).

AUGUST 3, MORNING | The Panjwayi Comprehensive Health Centre

I formally handed command of the UMS back to Petty Officer "Bed" Bedard yesterday, so today was a day off. As when Captain Lafortune had replaced me at FOB Wilson, I no longer had any direct responsibilities other than to be available in case of a MasCal event. I therefore used some of my free time to help the CIMIC people with a project that is near and dear to their hearts and in which I was happy to become involved: local health care.

The FOB UMS cannot deal with all the health care needs of the local population. The only exceptions to this are injuries caused by the war or those that present an immediate threat to life, limb or eyesight. Our primary mission is to support our warriors, and we must always be ready for a massive influx of casualties. As well, we must not undercut the nascent Afghan health care system.

This means that the villagers around FOB Ma'Sum Ghar will go to the local clinic when they are ill or injured. But the conditions in Zhari district are reproduced here in the Panjwayi: all the other clinics in the district have closed due to security threats. As in Zhari, only the one that lies within range of the machine guns of our FOB observation posts has remained open.

The CIMIC people wanted to know what the clinic's capabilities were and if there was any way we could help them, but they had not had any contact with the clinic staff. I agreed to try to help them in this regard. My first opportunity to do so came a few days ago. One of the Canadian officers mentoring the ANP had to have a brief meeting with the police chief. Out of courtesy, our officer offered to walk over to the police station, a few hundred metres from our FOB's outer walls. Since the clinic is built right beside the police station, I asked the mentor officer if I could come along: I could visit the clinic, then he could go next door and meet the police chief. We called ahead, and the director of the clinic said he would be happy to meet me.

That sounds innocent, does it not? A doctor dropping in on a colleague to have a look at his facility. Whenever I am in a foreign city, I try to visit one or more emergency departments. There is always something to be learned during such a visit. It is also a wonderfully human experience to make such a link with another person: no matter how different our respective societies, our practice of the healing arts provides an instant connection.

But while the doctor-to-doctor exchange was quickly agreed upon, putting the two of us in the same room was a major undertaking. Even in broad daylight, the risk of a Taliban attack on Canadian soldiers (or indeed on the police station itself) was so high that it was impossible

Combat patrol, well spaced

for the mentoring officer and me to simply amble over. The FOB had to put together an escort of several soldiers to take this short walk with us.

Like true professionals, the escorting soldiers left nothing to chance. They treated this like any other patrol: a map was drawn on a whiteboard showing the route we would take; the route was analyzed to estimate where ambushes were most likely to take place; an "order of march" was developed that assigned specific places in the column to each member; timings were worked out and agreed on; the evacuation plan we would use if anyone got wounded was discussed. We also came up with a plan to return me at high speed to the UMS in case the FOB received word that casualties were arriving while I was away.

The same professionalism was on display when we moved out. With only a few hand motions and fewer words, the group started down the road. The correct interval was maintained between all the patrol members: close enough so that we could concentrate our gunfire against any enemy, far enough apart that an explosion would not kill more than one of us. Approaching civilians were waved off to a safe area and, when necessary, were searched in a thorough yet respectful manner. Weapons covered each soldier's "arc of responsibility" so that there were always eyes on a 360-degree circle around the patrol.

"The Panjwai Comprehensive Health Center" (the sign at top left announces "No Weapons," in Pashto and English)

When we got to the clinic, the patrol stopped to provide security outside the building while their medic, none other than my good friend "Junior," came inside to act as my bodyguard.

I was able to meet both of the doctors working at the clinic. The older one is the director of the clinic. He has been practising for thirty years, the last ten here in Bazaar-e-Panjwayi. The younger one is in his second month of practice. I also met the pharmacist and the laboratory technician. We had a very interesting discussion about the general state of the clinic, the prevalence of various diseases and their approach to various clinical scenarios.

They also took the opportunity to ask if there was any way I could help supply them with medicines. I reiterated the standard party line that we were more than willing to assume the care of anyone

Patients and families at the entrance

wounded by the war, but that they would have to be resupplied with medicines through the Afghan ministry of health.

As I was leaving, the director asked if I would like to meet the two nurses and two midwives on staff and to visit the female ward. I appreciated his openness, but as I looked around the inner courtyard of the clinic I saw a number of Afghan men. I also noticed that while a few burka-clad women had been visible from the courtyard when I arrived, they had now all disappeared. I decided to address this head-on and asked the director if he thought there was a possibility that some of the Afghan men might object to my visiting the women's area. He agreed that this was likely. I replied that I would respectfully decline his invitation. We shook hands one last time, and I was on my way.

I rejoined the patrol and we carried on to the police station. The Canadian mentor officer held his meeting with the police chief, and less than half an hour later we were on our way back to the FOB.

Inside, Junior watches my back

I reported back to the CIMIC people and described how the clinic functioned and what it had to offer. Although the Canadian Army will not get involved in the Afghan health care system, the CIMIC people will often facilitate contacts between NGOs and various Afghan projects. When I had finished my report, they asked me if there was a project I could suggest that would have a rapid impact on the population's health but that did not involve providing medications.

I thought about this for a day or so, then went back to the CIMIC people with an idea. A predictable minority of the visits to the health centre are generated by injuries. These conditions need only minor surgery and minimal follow-up. The health centre staff already had the skills required for these procedures, but they had only a few instruments and very limited suture material.

Colleagues

People in the developing world accept that their loved ones will get sick and die of chronic illnesses such as cancer, because that is the way it has always been. These same people feel differently if their child falls and suffers a laceration: there is a strong incentive to expend a large amount of time and energy to obtain a proper repair. There is often more desire in this population for minor surgery than for medications.

The CIMIC people were enthusiastic about the suggestion, but I thought it was important to get the approval of my Afghan colleagues before we proceeded. I would therefore have to go back to the clinic. This would again require a sizable escort, this time only for me. I would have been reluctant to expose a group of Canadian soldiers to so much risk only for this visit, but the patrol commander reminded me that this was an area where our troops run regular "presence patrols" (see July 21 entry). He offered to make the objective of today's presence patrol another visit to the clinic.

We left at mid-morning and had an uneventful walk over. Once again, Junior served as my bodyguard inside the clinic. I ran my idea

My escorts on my return visit (and you thought Angelina Jolie and Stephen Harper had bodyguards!)

by the director, and he agreed it would be useful to have extra instruments and suture material. I returned to the FOB and handed in a report detailing my suggestion for the CIMIC people. I hope it helps.

AUGUST 3, EVENING | An Afghan Farewell

I mentioned earlier that my willingness to bend or even break the rules regarding treating the "local national" workers at the FOB had made me a lot of friends among the Afghans. I did not appreciate how much these small kindnesses had meant to them until this evening.

Late this afternoon, Corporal Bouthillier informed me that "the brothers" and some of the interpreters wanted to throw me a farewell party. I thought we would get together for yet another cup of Afghan tea, shake hands and say goodbye. But when I got to their tent, I was greeted by nearly all members of the Afghan staff. Even more astounding, there was a spread of Afghan food that was more impressive than anything I had seen before, including at any of the *shuras* I had attended. This could not have been easy, nor cheap, for them to put together.

We talked and ate long into the night. I wished I had spent even more time getting to know these guys. The man most responsible for the evening was Lucky, a sort of camp manager. He supervises the interpreters and the local workers who are not employed by the kitchen. He has been at the FOB for nearly three years, and he remembered me from my first tour!

At the end of the evening, Lucky shocked me even more by presenting me with two sets of traditional Afghan clothing. Again, I was boggled by the generosity of these people. I was leaving in a few hours and we will probably never see one another again, so there was no secondary gain in it for them. It was a pure expression of friendship.

As I walked back to my bunker, I reflected sadly on the difference in our futures. In a couple of months, I will be going home to a warm welcome. The best they can hope for is to live in a country with a fragile peace at some yet-to-be-determined time in the future.

These guys deserve all the help we can give them.

AUGUST 4, MORNING | Infantry. Forever.

Before my going-away party last night, I was hanging around with a group of soldiers as they planned a foot patrol for the next day. A large group was involved, and a fair bit of territory would be covered. For half the time, the patrol would be split in two. There was only one medic, Junior Capelli Horth, on the team. The risk of having a group of soldiers without a medic was obvious to everybody. One of them said, "Hey, Doc, 'Bed' Bedard, the PA, is back. He can cover the UMS now. You're ex-infantry. Why don't you come along with us?"

He had half-meant it as a joke, but in the silence that followed I could tell that everyone was thinking about the obvious advantages to the patrol of his suggestion. The kinship I felt with these men right at that moment would be impossible for someone who has not been in the combat arms to appreciate.

One other factor influenced me right then, one the other men were not aware of. The PA I was replacing at my next FOB was not going on leave immediately. Instead, he was going to be posted to KAF for two weeks. If anything were to happen to me on this patrol, the army would have two weeks to get my replacement in position.

I said I would come.

In less than twelve hours, I would be going on a Taliban hunt. Claude had predicted I would do this: go on a combat patrol. I had agreed that, under the right conditions, I would. Now it was going to happen.

I went to bed around midnight. "Bed" had reclaimed the lower bunk, and I had slept above him the previous night. That was when I discovered that my good friend snores like a sawmill. Even my top-of-the-line earplugs were no match for the thunder that blasted forth from his nasal passages. If I was to have any chance to have some shut-eye I needed to move to a different building. So I went to an overflow tent we have installed for Priority Charlie casualties.

I lay down, but I did not sleep. My mind kept playing over all the various ways my act of soldierly solidarity could go disastrously wrong, and how I would respond to each scenario:

1. *Very seriously wounded: paralysis or multiple amputations.*
   The worst. I will have failed in my promise to Claude and Michelle, not only to take care of them forever but also to return in one piece. My life will be transformed. Activity and productivity will be replaced, at least for an extended period, by pain and the frustration of rehab. I will certainly become depressed. How bad will it get? Will I get over it?

2. *Seriously wounded: single amputation or disfigurement.*
   Very bad. Depending on the location and severity of the wound, how will I get myself back into emergency medicine? What will I still be

able to do with my wife and daughter? What will I no longer be able to do? How will people see me?

3. *Wounded: hurt in a way that can be fixed but ends my tour.*
   Bad. The pain will be nothing compared with the guilt I will feel at being unable to complete my mission. I will have let the health services team down.

4. *Dead.*
   Emotionally, easier to contemplate than option 1. Better to be killed outright than to be mangled beyond recognition. Intellectually, I know that is not true. Most severely wounded soldiers are grateful to be alive, no matter how much they feared mutilation and disfigurement before.

All that kept me tossing and turning until I gave up around 0330. I got out of bed, ate some cereal and spent a minute in the incredibly bright light of the full moon, collecting my thoughts and focusing on the task at hand. I then got my gear on: helmet, ballistic glasses, frag vest, tac vest, pack with medical gear and eight litres of water, pistol, rifle, full load of ammunition. And I headed out, much earlier than I needed to. I recognized my behaviour from wars gone by: when something bad is coming your way, the worst part is the waiting. Starting, even starting early, gets the process going and reduces the anxiety you feel.

The patrol was assembling on the other side of the FOB. This turned out to be a good thing. After the first few hundred metres, I stopped and readjusted my gear. This was the first time I had worn all my "kit" over anything more than a short distance, and a few things were not as comfortable as they could be. The last thing I wanted for the next several hours was to be distracted by something chafing my skin.

When I arrived at the patrol marshalling area, the other soldiers were pulling themselves together. They had done this a hundred times or more on this tour. Their unhurried, economical movements and their calm, precise interactions with each other made it look like this was just another day at the office. Which, for them, it was. I doubt that any of them had had trouble sleeping.

At 0500 the patrol commander called us together and reviewed the plan for the patrol. Then we sat down and waited. This was to be a joint operation with the ANP. This would give the patrol more guns as we went into a dangerous area. We would also have "Afghan eyes," eyes that are more attuned to things that are out of place. But the police, far less reliable than the ANA, were late.

At 0600, the police still had not shown up. The sun was cresting the mountains behind Bazaar-e-Panjwayi. Not only were we late getting started, we would now be exposed to the sun from the start. The patrol commander was faced with an awkward choice: go forward with an undermanned patrol or waste a day. I was hoping he would pick the latter, but there was never much doubt he would go forward with the mission.

A few minutes after 0600, we moved out. I took my place in front of the rear guards, telling myself I was in the safest location. That was pure rationalization: every soldier who goes out on patrol is exposed to the same extreme risks.

The point man approached the FOB's perimeter wall . . . and all the lessons I had learned at the Combat Training Centre so long ago came flooding back.

Just before you get to the wall of the FOB, take the magazine off your rifle. The first bullet is on the right. Put the magazine back on the rifle, rack the action. Take the magazine off. The first bullet is now on the left. No misfeed, you are sure there is a bullet in the breach. Weapon on "safe." Put the magazine back on the rifle. Give the magazine a firm slap, then shake it to make sure it is securely seated. Index finger on the trigger guard. Thumb on the safety. Flick it to "fire," flick it back to "safe." Repeat.

Step outside the FOB wall. Walk slowly and deliberately. Watch your "arc," the part of the 360-degree circle that is your responsibility.

Watch your arc

Glance ahead, glance back, glance to the side. Check your spacing, not too close to any other soldier. Do not give the enemy a tempting target.

Watch your arc. Scan slowly right to left, then look quickly back to the right. Repeat. We are used to reading left to right. If you scan left to right, you can fall into a repetitive rut and become less attentive. Scanning right to left is unnatural. The slight irritation this causes keeps you alert. Scan right to left. Repeat. Watch your arc.

The patrol stops. Move off the road. Look carefully at the ground to see if it has been recently disturbed. Disturbed earth means someone may have been digging there. Digging . . . and leaving something behind. Don't think about what IEDs do to exposed legs.

Find cover. Mud walls are good; they are like concrete and will stop most rifle bullets and rocket fragments. Check behind the wall—don't ignore the obvious. Just because it is suicidal to launch an ambush from there doesn't mean the Talis won't try it.

Focus on the area right in front of you, where the threat would be greatest: the Talis have started putting directional IEDs in the trees.

Crosshairs on target

Look for wires. Then focus on the middle distance. Directional IEDS have to be detonated by someone watching the patrol. Where would the trigger-man be? Then check the far distance. Repeat the process: up close, middle distance, far distance. What could you have missed? What you don't see can kill you. Watch your arc.

The patrol is moving again. Check behind you. Make sure the rear guards, who had been facing backwards, know that we are moving out. We don't want to bunch up, but we can't be too spread out either. We have to be able to return concentrated gunfire if we are attacked.

Start walking. Check your interval. Watch your arc.

Possible threat. Someone watching us from a tree line. Rifle up. Look through the scope, check it out. It is a "fighting-age male." No obvious weapons. Just watching us. Centre the crosshairs on his chest. About three hundred metres. If I need to, I am sure I can make the shot. We have to keep moving. Note the man's position. Where will he go if he wants to engage us? Where could he be hiding weapons? Stand up. Start walking. Watch your arc.

Someone coming down the road, from behind us, on a motorcycle. The patrol stops. Same routine as before, only now you also pay attention to the rear guards. They wave the motorcyclist over to the side of the road, indicating that he should disembark and distance himself from his vehicle. One soldier searches him, then moves over to search the motorcycle. The other

A family stroll

rear guard covers him. The search uncovers nothing. The man gets waved through. Watch your arc. Watch the motorcyclist as he passes by you.

Stand up. Keep walking. Watch your arc.

After twenty minutes this routine became natural. I would not say I was any less frightened, but I was much less tense.

We continued down Route Hyena. In my more relaxed state, I was able to better appreciate the non-military aspects of what I was seeing. Three things stand out in my memory.

First, we were overtaken by a family of Afghans. They were going at a brisk pace, far faster than we were. After being searched by the rear guards, the family was waved through the patrol. They were led by a man with a child on his back. He was followed by two women, each clad in full burka. The women would be his two wives. The woman closer to him would most likely be the younger second wife. This man probably agreed more with the Taliban than with me.

While the man in the above picture led his family right by me as if I were not there, the other Afghans who crossed our patrol made eye contact with me. I would address them with the traditional Muslim greeting "Salaam aleikum" ("Peace be unto you"). They would smile and reply "Aleikum salaam" ("And peace be unto you as well"). A few of them went further and demonstrated body language that indicated pleasure at our presence. And one group of young men went much,

Holland, 1945: tulips;
Afghanistan, 2009: grapes

much further than that—into territory that may well mark them for Taliban reprisals.

There were three of them in a small truck loaded with grapes, the driver and the passenger in front and a third man in the back holding on to the produce. They were farmers headed for market. When I greeted them, the one in the back called out to the driver. The truck stopped and the man hopped out . . . and came towards me with a large bunch of grapes. I looked over at the member of the patrol closest to me. I must have had quite a shocked look because he quickly said, "It's not a problem, Doc. They're delicious. I've had them lots of times."

The man then said something in Pashto I did not understand, but he smiled even more broadly when I shook his hand and said, *"Dera manena"* ("Thank you very much"). Then he jumped back into his truck and drove off. I was only too happy to indulge in the grapes as I watched him leave. As advertised, they were delicious.

We stopped for a bit, while the patrol commander spoke to a local elder. The perimeter seemed clear and the patrol relaxed a little. I noticed we had attracted some pediatric attention. The only thing I had to give them was my grapes.

They seemed pleased with that, but mostly they seemed intensely curious about the strangers in their midst. As I always do in these situations, I focused on the little girl. Her name sounded like "Maria," and she is seven years old. It is sad to think how different her life will be from Michelle's. It is even sadder to think of what her life will be like if we do not defeat the Taliban.

Curiosity and innocence

We ended up spending nearly a half hour in this position, providing security for the spontaneous mini-*shura* the patrol commander was holding. It was harder to stand still with all that gear on than it had been to walk. I was sorry to leave the children, but I was physically relieved to get going again.

The patrol then got down to the business of the mission. There were a number of family compounds we wanted to check out. We always wait for an invitation before entering. This was somewhat illusory, the politeness of those who know they cannot be refused. Nonetheless, it did give the Afghans their dignity.

The most important element here is respecting the Afghans' *zan* (women). Under no circumstances must the search party see the women of the family. Each entry into a compound is therefore preceded by an elaborate request to please ask the *zan* to remove themselves to the women's quarters.

It is frustrating to think of what might be going on behind the compound walls while we wait outside. Anyone with something to hide has ample time to conceal potentially incriminating evidence.

Searching suspect compound

We could avoid this by crashing into every compound unannounced, but this would only guarantee that we would get some of the weapons and lose all of the people. This is a war of ideas. We have to act each time as if the Afghan we are dealing with is a potential ally, to be treated with respect, not a potential enemy, to be treated like a criminal. This holds true even if we are very suspicious that the individual's allegiances lie with our enemies.

This attitude on the part of Canadians goes a long way with most of the rural folk here in the Panjwayi. At every compound we visited on this patrol, we were greeted warmly and invited in quickly. At every one . . . except the last one we called on. The reception here was the polar opposite. The owner of the compound was totally uncooperative, not even attempting to answer our questions.

For whatever reason, he did not like us. After multiple requests to be invited into the compound were ignored, we proceeded with the

Patrol's end

search, something the Afghan security forces and their Coalition partners are legally entitled to do without a warrant.

We did not find any weapons or other "smoking gun," but we did notice a number of radios that had been taken apart. The wiring and receivers could be used for remote-controlled triggering mechanisms. We also found a large number of the plastic jugs that the IED makers stuff with homemade explosive.

This guy was obviously "wrong," but there was nothing definitive that proved he was aiding the Taliban. So we documented what we found and moved on. This compound will be watched more closely from now on. Eventually, the owner will slip up. They always do. The only questions are whether he will be killed or captured and whether he will take any of us down with him. Statistically speaking, the odds are against him.

The men of 5-1 Charlie (a well-decorated bunch, at least in the dermatological sense)

With the compound searches done, the patrol had achieved its objectives. We headed back to the FOB, arriving a little after 1000.

I was glad to have done my infantry part in this war. And I hope I never have to do anything like that again.

You have just read the description of a single, short patrol. The men in the above photograph will do this almost every day for six months. What more can I say about them?

AUGUST 4, AFTERNOON | Back to the Beginning

After returning from the patrol, I went back to my bunker, gathered up my gear, and said my farewells to Bed, Red and the Bison crews. I had greatly enjoyed my time with them and I hoped we would stay in touch. I then reported to the convoy assembly area.

Even with the road partly paved, the trip from FOB Ma'Sum Ghar to FOB Sperwan Ghar exposed me to significant risk. But everything is relative. Going on a convoy seemed like a walk in the park compared with the dangers I had faced this morning. As I sat in my vehicle I was exhausted, but elated.

We left a bit before noon. I was so baffed that I passed out before we even got to the front gate of Ma'Sum Ghar. My next memory is of someone shaking my shoulder at FOB Sperwan Ghar. As I climbed out of the vehicle, I could see that the FOB had changed quite a bit since my last visit. Canadian soldiers have worked hard to improve their living conditions here, as they have at all our FOBs.

A far greater change had taken place inside me. I first came here on November 20, 2007, arriving by helicopter after midnight. I had been in Afghanistan less than a week. I was disoriented and more than a little miserable. I was apprehensive as I wondered if I would react effectively under fire.

I soon found out: we were attacked on my fourth day here, and I had to deal with a MasCal situation. My combat reflexes reappeared and the emergency medicine machine did its thing. Over the next month, I got into the rhythm of the war and of the FOB.

This time, I am a veteran. Arriving at FOB Sperwan Ghar feels like coming back to the old family cottage. The living will be rough, the amenities will be minimal and savage animals will be lurking about.

And yet it almost feels . . . comfortable.

AUGUST 5 | They Also Serve Who Only Stand and Wait

The day started at 0200, with the arrival of an Afghan soldier at the UMS. He'd had abdominal pain for a couple of hours. He had no nausea, vomiting, diarrhea or fever, and his vital signs were normal. He indicated that the pain was around his belly button, but when I examined his abdomen he was much more tender in the right lower quadrant, the classic sign of early appendicitis. Once again, I benefited from our wonderful medevac system. One phone call and a helicopter came within minutes to whisk this man to surgery.

The physician assistant I am replacing here is Chief Petty Officer Second Class Gaétan Poulin. He jokes that he is ill at ease in his land army uniform . . . but he allowed me to take a "hero shot" as we waited

Chief Petty Officer Second
Class Gaétan Poulin

for the helicopter that would take him back to KAF. That is the photograph shown here.

Age forty-eight, CPO 2 Poulin is one of those rock-solid individuals who holds the CF together. He has had two deployments prior to this one, a relatively benign one in Cyprus in the 1980s and a horrible one in Rwanda in the aftermath of the genocide. He still talks about that experience in hushed tones and admits that it took the better part of a year after he returned home to process what he had been through and get back to normal.

He still retains the enthusiasm for our job that I have seen in the younger medics. As we discussed the practice profile of the patient load here at FOB Sperwan Ghar, he peppered me with questions about my approach to this or that clinical scenario. It was an enjoyable conversation with a fellow senior health professional of long experience.

CPO 2 Poulin is also quite modest. Since he is the last of the FOB docs I am replacing, he has spent four months on the FOB, much longer than anyone else has had to endure on this tour. I mentioned this to him, but he laughed it off and said it was no big deal. Many would disagree.

After he left I met with Corporal Sabrina Paquet, the Bison medic, to go over the UMS files. That Bison and all but one of the combat team medics are going out on an operation tomorrow, leaving me almost alone to run the UMS. As we went over the statistics, it emerged that Sperwan Ghar is the quietest of our three FOB UMSs. Corporal Paquet commented on that, saying it was still important that we be here in case anything happened. I could tell that she felt that her contribution was somehow less than that of the staff at the other two FOBs because she had not been knee-deep in blood, as we were at FOB Wilson and FOB Ma'Sum Ghar. I think it is important to correct that impression.

Napoleon said that "the moral is to the physical as three is to one." In other words, the psychological well-being of an army is three times more important than its physical state. I told Corporal Paquet that our role, as medical personnel, was only partly the medical care of the casualties. It is equally important for us to convince our warriors that we will deliver the finest medical care to them if they are wounded. First-rate medical care such as we can provide here acts as a "force multiplier," enabling soldiers to fight harder and to face more danger because they know we are here to back them up. Busy or not, we are a big part of what makes our army fight well.

Addendum: "They also serve who only stand and wait" is the last line of a poem, "On His Blindness," by John Milton. The poem is an incomprehensible paean in which Milton describes how best to serve God. During World War Two, the phrase was adopted by those who stayed in Canada to guard the nation while others went to fight in Europe and the Pacific. The service of these people who did nothing but "stand and wait" was not exciting and garnered no honours. It was often derided by the combat troops, but it was a vital service nonetheless.

AUGUST 6 | The Moderating Effect

An army is a reflection of the society from which it is drawn. Women are now ubiquitous in our army, on the FOBs and even in the combat teams, just as they can be found in all walks of civilian life.

Our ability to wage war has neither improved nor deteriorated as a result of this. Warriors are defined by the skill set they bring to the battlefield. This skill set can be mastered by a certain proportion of women, subject only to the same physical limitations that apply to men their size. And vice versa. Corporal Bouthillier (the Ma'Sum Ghar Bison medic) has shoulders and arms that are bigger and stronger than mine. She has a much easier time opening and closing the heavy armoured door on the back of her ambulance than I do.

That being said, it would be foolish to claim that sexism no longer exists in the CF. It would be accurate, however, to state that expressions of sexism are now only quietly muttered. Individuals who say such things aloud in a men-only group are often confronted by other men.

While it may not surprise you that the women in the CF train and fight side-by-side with men, I think only the youngest readers will not at least raise an eyebrow when learning that we all sleep in the same room or tent or bunker. We have no more privacy than that provided by a thin sheet hung from the ceiling, sometimes not even that.

While the constant presence of women on the front lines has in no way altered our combat efficiency, their effect has nonetheless been dramatic. Left to their own devices, guys with time on their hands degenerate pretty rapidly into a bunch of slobs who talk about nothing but sex. It is a lot of fun, but it can be a tad one-dimensional. To be honest, part of me misses the wall-to-wall porn that was an integral part of settings like a FOB twenty-five years ago. But it seems a small price to pay for the broader and more intellectual discussions that take place around me now.

Well . . . let's say it's a fair price.

AUGUST 7 | Too Quiet

With the combat team away, the FOB is empty. To use an apt, although in the current context unfortunate, expression: you could shoot a cannon through here and not hit anybody.

It is almost eerie. I am writing this after dinner, and no one has come by the UMS all day. I have dropped into the command post a couple of times to see how the operation is going. Things seem quiet on that side as well. But the day wasn't a complete write-off: I had the time to wander around and get reacquainted with the FOB.

Sperwan Ghar means "dusty mountain" (they got that right)

When I first arrived here in 2007, I looked at this big pile of sand in the middle of this flat desert and thought: *That's weird. We are below the southernmost latitude the glaciers ever reached, so there is no geological reason for this formation to exist.* One of the first things I did was climb to the top of the hill to have a look around. I even shot a video in which I described what I was seeing: the view in all cardinal directions and . . . look at that . . . trenches. Very old trenches. Trenches dug . . . in the Russian style.

There being so many more things to occupy my mind at the time, I failed to pursue the obvious connection between the Russian trenches and the geological anomaly that is Sperwan Ghar. This time, I did a bit of research and my suspicions were confirmed. The Russians created this hill by piling thousands of truckloads of sand from the nearby Registan Desert. They needed a base in this area with good lines of sight in all directions, so they built one. You have to hand it to the communists: they are not afraid of the Big Projects.

We are in the boonies here. FOB Wilson has the highway that connects it to the outside world, and FOB Ma'Sum Ghar is right beside the

Looking southwest from Hilltop OP towards the Registan Desert
(the greenery stops at the mountains and dunes in the distance)

The flags of Sperwan Ghar

bustling city of Bazaar-e-Panjwayi. FOB Sperwan Ghar, in contrast, is surrounded by desert and "rural sprawl." Although a few of the buildings nearby are family compounds and there is the occasional mosque (the call to prayers can be faintly heard), most are agricultural structures. Among these are many "grape huts," used to dry the grape harvest, thereby converting it into raisins, which are a much more portable and therefore much more valuable crop than grapes per unit of weight. When the means of transportation are at a premium (there are very few vehicles this far in the hinterland), this is a major consideration.

The military implications of this are obvious. The Taliban, by wearing civilian clothing and carrying farm implements, blend into the civilian population. They can get close to the FOB and conceal themselves in one of these nearby buildings. The FOB is within effective range of all the weapons in their arsenal at that point.

FOB Sperwan Ghar is the only one of our FOBs that has been obliged to repel a ground assault, not once but twice. These attacks have only been a serious attempt at harassment, with good reason. An attack launched by ground troops would have to cross a few hundred metres of open terrain and get through a couple of layers of barbed wire before it reached our outer walls. Given the firepower that we can lay down on that area with our direct-fire weapons (rifles, machine guns and grenade launchers), I doubt that even a force of several hundred attackers could breach our defences. I will try to focus on that and not on the way our enemies often cross over the line that separates bravery from insanity.

The FOB is home to a combat team centred on a company of the Royal Vingt-deuxième Régiment, abbreviated R22eR, the French Canadian infantry regiment more commonly known as the Van Doos. The flag in the centre of the photograph on the previous page is the flag of Afghanistan. The one on the left is the flag of the Van Doos. The symbol at the base of the Afghan flag is a stylized cobra (don't worry if it is not obvious to you; someone had to explain it to me as well). "C" company, based here, has chosen this as its emblem.

The FOB Sperwan Ghar UMS

As with all the other FOBs, the UMS has recently been upgraded. It is now housed in the modular affair shown in the above photograph. It is roomy inside and impossibly clean—that won't last!

One final anecdote.

As I was wandering around the FOB I met the ammunition technician, Corporal Audrey Gravel, who showed me around her digs. I can't show you what that looks like. The Talis would be only too happy to learn where we hide the things that go "Boom!"

She showed me the impressive arsenal we have here, which includes a generous supply of Claymore mines. These are a factory-made version of the "directional IED" described in the July 7 entry. We had Claymores when I was in the infantry. Since that time, a special safety feature has been added: a warning on the back of the mine that states:

Warning—Explosive is poisonous if eaten
Do not burn—produces toxic fumes

I can think of many non-traditional uses for a Claymore. Paper-weight, doorstop and aquarium decoration all come to mind. But no matter how desperate a situation I try to conjure up, "lunch" and "fire-wood" do not appear on my list. Product safety warnings being what they are, this admonition would have appeared *after* someone tried to do both of these things. Let us hope that it was a single person who tried to cook *and* eat the thing and that one of these methods removed him from the gene pool.

Corporal Gravel also showed me one of the echoes of wars past that infest this land: a Russian artillery shell, now more than twenty years old. This weapon and countless others like it lie strewn about the Afghan countryside, waiting to kill the innocent or to be picked up by the Taliban for use in their IEDs. We are slowly gathering these up and destroying them, but it is like cleaning the Augean stables.*

MINES

In an earlier entry I explained why I thought mines were the worst byproduct of war. Strewn indiscriminately across a large number of developing world nations, these weapons destroy lives and damage economies out of all proportion to the military benefit they provide. This destruction and damage carries on long after the end of the conflict during which the mines were laid because the minefields are almost never deactivated, or even marked, by the groups that laid them.

Canada led the way in banning these weapons. Our role was so instrumental in this process that the accord is commonly called the "Ottawa Treaty," which rolls off the tongue more easily than "Convention on the Prohibition of the Use, Stockpiling, Production and Transfer of Anti-Personnel Mines and on Their Destruction." As of May

---

* A horrifying but valuable eyewitness account of the after-effects of war is Donovan Webster's book *Aftermath: The Remnants of War: From Landmines to Chemical Warfare—The Devastating Effects of Modern Combat* (New York: Vintage, 1998).

2009, 156 countries have signed the treaty. Thirty-seven countries have not, including the People's Republic of China, Russia and the United States.

A survey done in 2006 revealed that there were 160 million anti-personnel mines in the stockpiles of all the world's armies. Armies being less than forthcoming with information like this, the true total is likely even higher. The good news is that, as of 2009, seventy-four countries have destroyed all their stocks of anti-personnel mines, totalling some forty million mines. Not a bad start.

The provisions of the Ottawa Treaty are strict. Signatories undertake "never under any circumstances to use, develop, produce, otherwise acquire, stockpile, retain or transfer to anyone, directly or indirectly, anti-personnel mines."

Never. Under any circumstances. Pretty clear, eh? So why do we have Claymore "mines" here—devices with explosive and shrapnel, designed to be placed in a precise location ahead of time and detonated there later. Are we breaking the rules?

No. We are following both the letter and the spirit of the Ottawa Treaty. Although popularly referred to as the "Mine Ban Treaty," the formal title makes it plain that only *anti-personnel* mines are prohibited. These are defined in the treaty as mines "designed to be exploded by the presence, proximity or contact of a person . . ."

These mines are the most serious problem. They make up the vast majority of the mines laid in modern conflicts, and they are the ones that will kill and maim peasants, farmers and other rural folk for decades to come.

Claymore mines are specifically excluded from the treaty. Why?

Our Claymores are placed at strategic sites all around our FOB. These sites can be seen by our OPs. They are not linked to pressure plates, trip wires or any other mechanism that would make them explode if someone walked by or even directly onto them. The Claymores can only be detonated by an intentional electrical signal sent by the FOB's defenders.

Claymores do not function as mines, but rather as a close-in defensive system for the OP, to be used if we are faced with a ground attack by foot soldiers. In other words, we use a Claymore the same way we would use a shotgun—a very large shotgun. The correct term for these devices is "defensive command detonated weapons."

We know exactly how many Claymores we have placed around the FOB and we know exactly where they are. When the time comes for us to leave the FOB, we will deactivate them and take them back with us. Nothing harmful will be left behind.*

AUGUST 8 | A Canadian Achievement

I was woken up at 0400, by yet another Afghan soldier with abdominal pain. The history and physical exam this time were much more suggestive of gastroenteritis. We kept the patient in the UMS for several hours, rehydrated him with intravenous fluids and gave him medication for the pain and nausea. By 1200 he was feeling much better and was able to go back to his barracks. The only medic remaining on the FOB, Corporal Martin Pelletier, took care of the patient from beginning to end.

That was the sum total of the visits to the UMS today, so there was not much for me to do. This makes it a good day to discuss something I have wanted to talk about for some time. I have nothing but contempt for Barack Obama's predecessor, and I totally disagree with the American invasion of Iraq. It follows that I could not agree more with the current president's decision to wind down the war in Iraq while ramping up American efforts here. I like to say that it is never too late to stop making a mistake, and I think that precisely describes what President Obama is doing in both places.

We are beginning to see the impact of his decision on the ground.

---

* For history buffs: a claymore was a heavy Scottish broadsword. Wielded by an angry Highlander stoked on single-malt scotch, it could cut a person in half.

Apart from the three main FOBs encountered in this diary, Canada has also built two smaller combat outposts. FOB Frontenac is located northeast of here, in the Shah Wali Khot district; FOB Spin Boldak is to the southeast, almost at the Pakistani border, beside a small town of the same name.

The Shah Wali Khot and Arghandab districts have always been "the other places the Canadians went." There was less combat activity in those districts, so you may well have never heard of them. They were far from the main focus of our operations in Zhari-Panjwayi, but until this roto there had been no other Coalition troops to cover them. The same could be said about Spin Boldak.

While these FOBs occasionally hosted several dozen Canadian soldiers, we never had enough long-term combat power deployed there to enable us to pacify the area. All that has changed with the increased American presence. We are therefore pulling out of these FOBs and turning them over to much larger groups of U.S. soldiers.

But whereas our withdrawal from FOB Frontenac and FOB Spin Boldak had been announced months ago, we were surprised a couple of weeks ago when it was announced that we would also be turning FOB Wilson over to our allies. Major Tim Arsenault and Bravo Company will be moving into FOB Ma'Sum Ghar. The FOB Wilson UMS staff will go back to KAF.

This makes eminent military sense. FOB Wilson is being dramatically expanded and will house a full American battalion. This is at least six times as many soldiers as we had deployed there. The Americans will concentrate on Zhari district while we focus our efforts in the Panjwayi.

This concentration of firepower will make life very difficult for the Taliban in Zhari-Panjwayi. Until now, we have been able to keep the enemy at bay. Anytime they gathered in groups of any size, we would detect them, pursue them and usually destroy them.

But we were trapped in a quandary in which counterinsurgency forces often find themselves: we could defeat the enemy on the battlefield and chase them out of any particular sector, but we did not have enough "boots on the ground" to prevent them from filtering back in once the fighting was over. Thanks to the vastly increased American presence, Zhari-Panjwayi is about to be inundated with Coalition troops.

As good as that news is, I admit that it leaves me with a twinge of worry. For three long years now, Canada has held the line in Kandahar province. In 2006, we pushed the Taliban out of what had been their homeland and denied them easy access to Kandahar City. Since then, we have kept them on the run in this, their native ground. If the Coalition is victorious in Kandahar province, it will be a victory built on that Canadian achievement. It will be a grave injustice if the histories that will be written about this war do not acknowledge that.

AUGUST 9 | Where Are They Now?

The combat team returned to the FOB early this morning. The place is bustling again and, even if it means that I have to wait in line for my meals and take my turn on the Internet, I like this better.

There was no contact with the enemy. Not a single shot was fired in anger. This is not to say that the mission was not a success. Two noteworthy events took place.

First, a mid- to high-level Taliban leader was captured. He was captured by a conjoined group of Afghan and Canadian soldiers. This particular leader had been in command of a group that had recently captured a number of Afghan soldiers. All the captured soldiers were executed near a village in the area, as a warning to the locals not to cooperate with the government. The Afghan soldiers were in the mood for some serious payback, and for a while it looked like the Taliban leader would be lynched on the spot. But the Canadians strenuously objected, and the Afghan soldiers backed off.

I have heard of other similar situations, where Canadian soldiers make it clear to their Afghan allies that we do not fight dirty wars and that we will not be a party to their fighting one either. This is again education in the purest sense: exposing individuals to different world views and trusting that, overall, groups will make wise and humane decisions.

The other important result of the operation was the discovery of a well-equipped lab for converting marijuana into hashish, along with eight hundred kilograms of the finished product. The ANA blew up the former and burned the latter. Canadian soldiers—quite wisely, I think—do not get involved in drug eradication programs. These programs mostly penalize poor farmers who are trying to feed their families. But destroying the product *after* the Taliban has bought it is almost as good as destroying an arms cache. The Taliban fund much of their war effort with drug money, so this operation made a big dent in their budget. Beyond that, the results of this operation have left an enormous question mark hanging in the air. In my first month on the FOB during Roto 4, our troops inflicted a couple of stinging defeats on the Taliban, killing over one hundred of them in two battles in December 2007. Then we launched an operation where we encountered no enemy. As I described in the July 31 entry, we hurt them badly for several days in a row at the end of the last month. Again, around a hundred enemy soldiers have been killed in under two weeks. And again, they seem to have ceded the battlefield to our forces.

Are they bringing in new recruits, tending to their wounded and regrouping? Or had they always planned to pull back at this time, to be able to hit the country hard on election day? That will be on August 20, a week and a half from now.

It is vital that these elections take place in a free and fair manner, but the chances of that happening are looking poorer every day. Despite their losses, the Taliban have done a good job of derailing the democratic process in Zhari-Panjwayi. They have murdered so many government representatives that few candidates or party workers have come here. There are not even any election posters on the walls.

Of far more concern is that I have been unable to learn where the people around FOB Sperwan Ghar will be able to vote. Some sources claim there will be a polling station a few hundred metres north of the FOB. Others insist that the people will have to go to Bazaar-e-Panjwayi (the village beside FOB Ma'Sum Ghar) to vote.

The next ten days will be tense.

AUGUST 11 | Election Perception

Just as I did at Ma'Sum Ghar, I run to the top of the hill here three or four times before breakfast to get my blood pumping. I was coming down the hill for the last time this morning when I noticed one of our patrols coming back in. We came into the barracks at the same time, and I asked the patrol leader how things had gone. There has been very little contact with the enemy lately, and the patrols had been able to get into some good conversations with the locals about the upcoming election.

I have read extensively about the tribal nature of Afghan culture, and yet I still have trouble fully grasping the power these bonds have over ordinary Afghan people. The way the local villagers perceive the election is a case in point.

When the villagers are questioned about the election, there seems to be little comprehension of what the exercise is meant to achieve. Democracy is foreign to rural Afghan culture, and the Taliban have made it difficult for the government to educate the people of Zhari-Panjwayi with regards to this. The people have therefore remained attached to what they know well. What they have told our patrols is that they are happy with their leader and that they see no need to vote.

That leader is none other than Haji Baran, the district leader. This is an appointed post, not an elected one. Haji Baran has also presented himself for election to the post of representative of the area (the equivalent of a member of Parliament). This would be like a senior manager in a city running for mayor. Nothing wrong with that; it happens in Canada all the time.

The complication comes when you learn that Haji Baran had told the CIMIC people that he was expecting very little voter turnout in the election—in the order of 10 to 20 per cent. The conflict of interest is evident. If the district turned out in force to elect a representative other than Haji Baran, there could be a real threat to his power base. I can only wonder how enthusiastically he encouraged his people to get involved in the elections. I doubt he threatened anybody, the way the Taliban did; all he would have had to do is tell his people that voting was not necessary and that he would continue to take care of them as he had always done. The people would probably be pleased with that.

They would be somewhat less pleased if they knew that, in 2008, Haji Baran was caught doing something that looked irregular with the pay of the local police. The American police mentoring team that had dropped off the funds in question took the money back. Haji Baran responded by having the building the Americans were in surrounded by gunmen loyal to him. A three-hour standoff ensued. Only the arrival of the Canadian quick reaction force convinced everybody to calm down.

Haji Baran was fired from his post after this incident. Somehow, like politicians all over the world, he has managed to insinuate himself back into the body politic. The CIMIC people tell me that he seems to have turned over a new leaf of late, but you have to wonder . . .

Regardless of his failings, however, Haji Baran supports at least the concept of democracy. And it must be recognized that being part of the local government has marked him for death. Major Patrick Robichaud, who was the combat team commander at FOB Sperwan Ghar the last time I was here, remembers the local leader well. He had to deal with him several times at regional *shuras*. In spite of Haji Baran's obvious corruption, Major Robichaud felt he genuinely wanted to protect and help the people of the area.

The Taliban, for their part, have made their opposition to the very idea of democracy perfectly clear. Their official position, as stated on their website, is that the election must be boycotted. They are enforcing this position by declaring a twenty-four-hour curfew on election day. Anyone caught outside their home during this period will be killed.

AUGUST 12 | Leadership

Through the ages, leaders have generally been physically imposing individuals. Kings were warriors who led their nations in the most direct manner possible: into battle at the head of their armies. Even today, those who have been genetically blessed with a six-foot-three muscular frame are more likely to be successful, even in fields where size and strength do not matter.

The combat team commander here at FOB Sperwan Ghar, Major Steve Jourdain, breaks this pattern. Nonetheless, he commands the same respect as Major Tim Arsenault (see the June 20 entry).

I can already perceive that there are many things Major Jourdain does well in the military sphere. He is a sound tactician. His knowledge of the weapons and equipment of his combat team is encyclopedic. He has a good appreciation of the enemy's capabilities and likely intentions. He cares deeply about his men, puts their welfare before his own and is mindful of their safety. Rather than describing his skills as a combat leader, however, I thought it would be more entertaining to show you how his leadership is displayed in a much different setting.

The combat troopers enjoy the occasional bit of gambling. The current popularity of poker in North American society is reflected here: one rarely sees anything else being played. But nowhere is it as organized as it is here at FOB Sperwan Ghar. If the combat team is not out on an operation, a dozen or more of them will congregate every night around two large poker tables for a tournament. Desperate for a new distraction, I have joined them for several evenings.

Major Jourdain is an outstanding poker player. Though soft-spoken, he is very much an alpha male. Yet somehow he manages

Major Steve Jourdain (and prospective victim)

to suppress his desire to win to give constant tips both to newcomers and to the more experienced players in the group. I fall into the former category. Major Jourdain feels that his wise words are falling on deaf ears, but I can honestly say I have never had so much fun losing money quickly as I have had over the past few nights.

Major Jourdain's leadership goes well beyond that. There is not a lot to do on the FOB. It would be easy for troopers to lose inordinate amounts of money while gambling, just to pass the time. Major Jourdain prevents this by imposing a strict $5 limit on the amount anyone can lose in a single night. Even someone as hopeless as I am cannot lose more than a day's pay over the course of the tour.

Major Jourdain's understanding of human nature is evident in the way he has structured the tournament. First, he has made the action emotionally satisfying. Your $5 entry fee buys you $12,000 worth of chips. The tough combat trooper who would feel foolish saying "I raise you 35 cents" looks quite satisfied as he tosses a green chip onto the table and says, "Raise you $1,000." Silly, but it works. Also, depending on the number of players, the games have three or four winners. Each one will go home (well, back to his room) with $10 to $40. No big winners, no big losers. No regrets, no animosity.

But there is more to the nightly poker games than creating an environment in which the troopers can have some fun without losing their shirts. Major Jourdain also uses these games to take the pulse of the company. He is always attuned to who shows up and who doesn't, what people are talking about, who seems down. He also uses these occasions to dispel (or sometimes confirm) the rumours that are an inevitable part of military life, especially on a FOB. Even when it looks like he is relaxing, he is thinking about his men and how to best look after their interests.

That's leadership.

Ten minutes into the game, the correct poker term for my position is "a chip and a chair." There goes Grandma's chemotherapy money.

Soldiers in a war zone playing poker. A stereotype, but fun!

AUGUST 13 | The Patient Mentor

While our army is mostly composed of men and women in their twenties and thirties, those in the combat arms are drawn from the younger part of that spectrum. The tasks are too physical for most older people. This is borne out by our casualties: as of today, the average age of our dead is twenty-five.

These young Canadians are much better informed about the Afghan mission than their fellow citizens are. Many of them can speak eloquently about the need to confront the Taliban. While they sometimes try to appear cynical (something the young often mistake for maturity), one can see that their motivation comes from a sincere commitment to defend human rights.

For most of them, however, this deployment is their first prolonged exposure to a foreign culture. It is also the first time they have been in contact with this level of poverty. Taken together, these elements make the Afghan villagers around here so different that most of the young troopers have a great deal of trouble relating to them.

I have noticed very little overt racism, but it is clear that most of these kids feel uncomfortable in situations of social interaction with the Afghans. Individuals like Corporal Bouthillier, the FOB Ma'Sum Ghar medic who sought out and indeed treasured her daily contacts with Afghan civilians, are rare and striking exceptions.

The Canadian soldiers who interact most with the Afghans are the ones we have assigned to train the Afghan army. These soldiers serve on Operational Mentoring and Liaison Teams (OMLTs), living and working among the Afghan soldiers. Maturity, a broad world view, strong teaching skills and experience with at least one culture other than their own would seem to be the minimum prerequisites for such a task. You would think that the people assigned to this mission would be chosen very carefully. That is not the case. Despite the vital nature of their work, the OMLTs are so small (just a few soldiers per team) that they are not high on the battle group's priority lists. Teams are sometimes put together on the fly at the last minute.

That is what happened here at Sperwan Ghar. The FOB is home to a company of ANA infantry soldiers who operate under the guidance of a Canadian OMLT team. The team commander is Captain Manuel Pelletier-Bédard.

Captain Pelletier-Bédard came to this posting by an unusual route. He has been in the army a bit more than two years. During that time, he has been posted to the Douzième Régiment Blindé du Canada (the 12th Canadian Armoured Regiment, the Québécois tank regiment). For the better part of a year, he trained on tanks and was scheduled to deploy with the Leopards at Ma'Sum Ghar. A few weeks before he was to leave for Afghanistan, the army decided to transfer him to the infantry. The infantry made him a mentor.

So far, this has all the makings of a spectacular and uniquely military screwup. It turns out to have been an inspired choice. First, Captain Pelletier-Bédard proved to be a very quick study. Building on his basic combat arms training, he quickly sharpened his infantry tactics and is an effective mentor in this regard. Even the veteran infantry officers assigned here respect him and consider him one of their own. But what is far more important is that he has been able to connect with his Afghan charges. How has he been able to achieve this? "My inter-actions with Afghan civilians were what most helped me understand the Afghan soldiers," he told me.

Captain Pelletier-Bédard did not intentionally seek out more contact with the local civilians. It happened naturally because the Afghan soldiers, even the ones who are Dari-speaking northerners, will regularly interact on a social basis with the villagers they encounter. They will even share a cup of tea with these people, knowing full well that many of them support the Taliban.

Captain Manuel Pelletier-Bédard

Captain Pelletier-Bédard has benefited professionally from these interactions. He says that his contacts with Afghan civilians have enabled him to be more patient with the Afghan soldiers. It is one thing to know that most of these soldiers are illiterate and innumerate. It is quite another thing to be regularly confronted with villagers who use the word "many" to describe any number higher than two.

I asked Captain Pelletier-Bédard the obvious question: did he think his mentorees had progressed satisfactorily over the four months he had been in Afghanistan? He replied that they had progressed very little . . . because they were already competent when he got here. In a recent evaluation exercise, his company was able to function almost independently.

Captain Pelletier-Bédard has therefore not done much "M," or mentoring. Rather, he has focused on the "L" and provided liaison between the ANA and the Coalition forces. Primarily, this has meant coordinating artillery attacks and air strikes against the enemy when his troops have been in contact. But mentor or not, Captain

Pelletier-Bédard is first and foremost an officer in the CF. His responsibility towards the men he commands (or, in this case, he advises) is sacrosanct. Here's an anecdote that shows how far he is willing to go to keep faith with that creed.

Captain Pelletier-Bédard's ANA company was involved in the recent operation around Salavat Ghar. They got into heavy contact and were taking a lot of fire from two sides. An air strike was called in on Taliban positions four hundred metres away.

The bombs that were going to be dropped weigh five hundred pounds. They are highly accurate but they have a gigantic kill radius. It is essential to pull all friendly forces back a few hundred metres from the intended target. When he tried to do so, Captain Pelletier-Bédard realized that radio contact had been lost with a section of Afghan soldiers who had pressed forward to get closer to the enemy. This squad was now within one hundred metres of the Taliban positions, well beyond "danger close."

The three hundred metres of ground between Captain Pelletier-Bédard and the Afghan squad was a flat sandy field devoid of any cover. Despite this, he did not hesitate: he headed across the open area to warn his men to take cover. He could not have been going very fast. He was wearing his frag vest and tac vest, he was carrying a heavy pack on his back and a rifle in his hands. This is rather more than I was carrying on my combat patrol ten days ago. I am sure Captain Pelletier-Bédard was giving it all he had, but I doubt he achieved anything faster than a slow jog. As soon as he broke cover the insurgents focused their fire on him. As he crossed the open field, bullets were coming from his left and his right, flying by his head and kicking up dirt at his feet. Miraculously, he made it across that field unhurt and got his men behind a mud brick wall in time to shield them from the air strike.

That would have been enough for any soldier, but Captain Pelletier-Bédard was just getting warmed up. Once the air strike was over, he went running back across the same open ground. One of the soldiers he had left behind had been shot in the leg. He had to get back as quickly

Canadian soldier in action with ANA troops
(© Louie Palu/ZUMA Press, reprinted with permission)

as possible to give him first aid and to call in a medevac. There were fewer bullets flying past him on the return leg (courtesy the air strike), but he was still dancing with death every step of the way. As he made his way back, he had to cross a deep ditch. He had no recollection of having crossed it on the way over. Combat will do that to people: the brain excludes what it does not deem essential to survival.

Captain Pelletier-Bédard describes all this in much the same way I would describe an unusual case in the emergency department: momentarily intense, but nothing more than another day on the job.

AUGUST 14 | Mentorees, Part 1

I said earlier that Captain Pelletier-Bédard felt that his ANA "mentorees" had not required much guidance from him, since they were already functioning at a high level. I met two of the people most responsible for this state of affairs at lunch today. I had gone to introduce myself,

Captain Ghioz and First Lieutenant Nooragha

somewhat belatedly, to the commanders of the ANA unit based here.

The man on the left in the accompanying photograph is Captain Ghioz, the ANA company commander. Beside him is the company second-in-command, First Lieutenant Nooragha. Like many Afghans, they have a single name. Between them, they have nearly fifty years of military experience. This explains, at least in part, the competence of their soldiers.

The way they acquired their knowledge of war is remarkable. As with "the brothers" (see the July 29 entry), the story of these two men sums up the tragedy of the past generation and the hope of the next one.

These men began fighting in the late 1980s. Captain Ghioz is a member of the Tajik tribe, which dominates northern Afghanistan. He joined the mujahedeen resistance to fight the Russian occupation. During the civil war that followed, he remained loyal to his Tajik resistance group. He continued to do so after the Taliban took over. Since 2002, he has served with the ANA.

First Lieutenant Nooragha's story could not be more different. He began his military career during the Russian occupation as an instructor at the military college in Kabul in the late 1980s. Early in our conversation, he told me that Canadian mentorship compares favourably with what he experienced under the Russians. We assign an officer and two to four soldiers to a company of 150 men; the Russians had one officer advising four thousand Afghans.

When the Russians left in 1989, they left behind a puppet communist government. First Lieutenant Nooragha continued to teach at the military college, which seems logical. When the mujahedeen took Kabul in 1992, they kept him on staff. That was astounding enough; but, incredibly, the Taliban did the same thing when they came to town in 1996. First Lieutenant Nooragha laughs about this now, saying that he had to grow his beard and wear a turban. Otherwise, he had no problems training Taliban recruits.

So what did he do in 2001 when the Coalition invaded? He shaved his beard, lost the turban and reapplied for his old job. Which he got!

To recap: in fifteen years, this guy trained soldiers for the Russians, the Afghan communists, the Islamic mujahedeen, the extremist Taliban *and* the U.S.-backed Coalition. He is now in a combat infantry company. He spontaneously mentioned that he does not enjoy fighting; he would much rather be back in Kabul in a classroom. But he is loyal to whatever government is in power. They have sent him here, and so he has come.

Anyone reading this description of First Lieutenant Nooragha's employment record could conclude that he is an amoral mercenary. Having met the man and spoken to him at length, I am convinced that is not the case. He sees himself as a loyal Afghan who follows the orders of the central government. In a country as chaotic as this one, he has chosen to define this as "whoever runs things in Kabul." For much of Afghanistan's history (as in many other places in the developing world) having a group capable of running the capital is as close as the country has ever gotten to having a national government. These governments come to power by the bullet instead of the ballot, but they are the government nonetheless. I could see the logic of his position.

I asked him what he would do if the Taliban returned to power. He smiled, laughed and said that he would go back to working for them. Captain Ghioz, on the other hand, made it perfectly clear that he would not. The Taliban were his sworn enemies. He would like nothing better than to kill every last one of them himself. You get the sense that a devastating personal loss underlies the sentiment. It would have been much too forward to ask him to confirm that at our first meeting. Perhaps I will ask him before I go.

And yet . . .

Even Captain Ghioz would be ready to accept members of the Taliban into the government, provided they renounced violence. President Karzai has made this overture to the Taliban on at least three occasions. The Taliban have refused each time.

BREAKING BREAD WITH THE AFGHAN NATIONAL ARMY

The meal we shared consisted of a large dish of delicious rice. The taste suggested that it had been cooked in a kind of beef broth, and there was more than I could finish. The rice was garnished with a couple of pieces of boiled potato and a piece of mutton. This last was a big bone from which one could tear pieces of meat. There were soft drinks, bottled water and a white yogurt drink. A large piece of flatbread, similar to Indian naan bread, rounded out the feast. I asked the Afghans what they called it. They call it naan.

We sat cross-legged on the floor. Captain Ghioz ate his rice with a spoon while First Lieutenant Nooragha ate with his hands. Although it was not truly sticky rice, it was possible to make a ball of the stuff that held together reasonably well on the way to one's mouth. I chose to emulate First Lieutenant Nooragha.

As superb as the meal was, the story of its preparation was troubling. Even though we are allies, the Afghan soldiers do not eat with the Canadians. No other element influences a soldier's morale as much as the food he receives. Afghans and Canadians have grown up with different foodstuffs, and we want to provide both groups with food that is not only nutritious and tasty, but also familiar. The last thing we want to do is force the Afghans to eat side-by-side with the Canadians.

While I understand the reasons our allies eat separately from us, I cannot understand why the ANA can be provided with twenty-first-century weapons but only nineteenth-century kitchens. The building

The ANA kitchen

The ANA cook

itself is a ramshackle structure, food preparation is done right on the ground and cooking is done over a wood fire in a mud-brick fireplace.

The worst thing about the way the ANA feeds its soldiers is the daily food-buying trip to the market in Bazaar-e-Panjwayi, the city right beside FOB Ma'Sum Ghar. That's right: *daily*, and in unarmoured pickup trucks. The Afghans have no refrigeration facilities on the FOB. This forces some of them to risk their lives every morning to purchase the food the company will eat that day. Over the past three years, many Afghan soldiers have been wounded on these grocery shopping trips. Three of them have been killed.

Thankfully, things are about to improve. The Americans have already mapped out where modern kitchen facilities, including refrigeration units, will be built for the ANA. A contractor has been hired, and construction should start within a couple of weeks. But it is disturbing that this did not happen months or even years ago.

AUGUST 15, MORNING | Mentorees, Part 2

In the June 21 entry, I explained that modern armies do most of their killing with artillery. For the ANA to be able to rout the Taliban without our help, it will have to master this skill.

It is impossible, in an insurgency war such as this, to always have numerical superiority over the enemy. The insurgents strike when it suits them, and it suits them only when they are able to concentrate their forces so that they have at least parity with the government forces. Without artillery to back them up, government forces would always be in a fair fight. That is the last thing you want in a war: you always want to be in an unfair fight, one in which you have a crushing superiority.

Canada is helping the ANA develop this kind of firepower superiority: there is a battery of ANA artillery here, with Canadian mentors (a separate OMLT team from that of Captain Pelletier-Bédard's). These guys are nowhere near being ready to go into combat, but at least the process has begun.

The beginnings of leadership

I went to watch them train this morning. I chose this day because the Canadians were not going to be present, and I wanted to see what the Afghans could do on their own. The drill they were doing involved getting their cannons "into action," that is, ready to fire. In a combat situation, a gun crew must be able to bring their cannon into action in a matter of seconds. This is something gun crews will rehearse over and over again, until it is instinctive.

After the various crews had been practising for about an hour, a senior NCO arrived. He spoke to the men for a few minutes, and I could tell he was setting up some kind of competition between them. The guns were all placed into their "out of action" position (that is, ready to be moved to a new location). Another command was shouted, and all the crews rushed forward to put their guns into action as quickly as possible.

Even someone who knew nothing about artillery would have been able to appreciate that the gun crews were . . . moderately competent. Occasionally an individual would move in the wrong direction and have to be quickly redirected by the gun crew leader. But for someone with a military eye, there was something far more important to see. It is hinted at in the above photograph.

The first thing a soldier notices is consistency of dress. When I was here on Roto 4, the ANA was still dressed in a hodgepodge of different uniforms. Here, the troops are all wearing the same clothing (with some minor variability in the headdress).

There is something else, something far more important. Did you notice the shadows? The gun crew leader is facing into the sun so that his men do not have to squint as they listen to him. He is putting their welfare above his own. This is an elementary leadership technique—elementary, once you have been told about it.

It is that leadership which is the more impressive aspect of what I saw this morning. It was obvious that the gun crew leaders were confident and capable in their jobs. There was no hesitation in their voices; they spoke with assurance. Even more notably, they spoke in warm and encouraging tones. As they ran their crews through their drills, they were enthusiastic. If one of their men made a mistake, they gently corrected him.

Armies are a reflection of the society from which they are drawn. I have spent a fair amount of time studying the armies of the developing world up close. These armies reflect the struggle for survival that defines life in these countries: discipline is often harsh, even brutal. Any action, once explained, must be performed to perfection. If it is not, the troops receive some kind of punishment, often a beating.

On Roto 4, the Afghan leaders would occasionally throw rocks at their underperforming soldiers. One can imagine the long-term effects of that kind of behaviour on morale. If the ANA is going to meet and defeat the Taliban on its own, its leaders will have to learn to motivate their men the same way Major Arsenault, Major Jourdain and Warrant Officer Comeau do.

AUGUST 15, AFTERNOON | Mentorees, Part 3

The most recent entries may have given you the impression that all the teaching that goes on here is done by Canadians. Allow me to correct that misconception.

What we have to teach:
300-115= ? 454+465 = ?

Where we have to teach it

After the morning training is over, things pretty much shut down for the Afghan army. Many of the Canadian trainers struggle with this. Like many Westerners, they are accustomed to an eight-to-five work-day. The "siesta time" concept strikes many Canadians as inefficient and lazy.

Most people in the developing world see things differently. They will maximize their efforts in the morning and late afternoon/early evening to avoid the brutal midday heat. This is the case here. As soon as the troops had finished eating lunch, they all collapsed into their bunks.

The training day was far from over, however. At 1600, the Afghan soldiers remaining in the camp assembled in a burned-out building. There were tables for half of them and chairs or benches for perhaps two-thirds. For the next couple of hours, one of their senior NCOs taught them . . . addition and subtraction.

Anyone who thinks the Afghans are not doing enough to improve their lot in life should spend an hour watching the enthusiasm with which grown men participate in these classes.

For the past three days Major Jourdain has been leading the combat team on an operation into the area of Chalgowr, a village east of here. The objective of the mission was to further disrupt insurgent activity before the elections. There was rather more enemy activity than anticipated, and the combat team got into a couple of prolonged firefights. None of our people got so much as a scratch during these skirmishes, and we inflicted some lethal casualties on the Taliban.

246

As the combat team was returning to the FOB, the lead vehicle was attacked by a remote-controlled IED. The blast rocked the vehicle slightly, leaving two members of the crew with a very mild neck strain that I treated with cold packs and a couple of days of anti-inflammatories. The trigger man was not nearly so lucky. Major Jourdain, in a vehicle following close behind, figured out almost instantly where he had been hiding. He brought his personal machine gun and his vehicle's 25 mm cannon to bear and opened fire. The Taliban soldier realized he been detected and tried to make a run for it. The Canadians' gunfire knocked him down within seconds. He did not move after that.

For my part, I had been enjoying a quiet day at the FOB and looking forward to the return of the combat team when we came under rocket attack. What was unusual was that I heard four distinct explosions: two at a distance, a pause, then two more, only much closer. I recognized that this was the sound of two rockets launching, followed a second later by the sound of their impact on the FOB. This was the first time I had heard both the launch and the impact. It meant the launchers were closer to me than they had ever been before. The rockets sailed right over the UMS and crashed into the opposite side of the FOB.

I came outside to see if there was any obvious damage. A number of soldiers on the far side of the FOB were running for cover. A few others came out of the building adjacent to mine, asking what had happened. I ordered them back under cover and reported to the command post. This is just a few steps from the UMS and any news about wounded would come there first. Fortunately, there were none.

Just another day on the FOB.

It is easy to dislike people who are not like us. "The others" frighten us, sometimes for reasons we cannot even articulate. We usually respond with rejection and anger. The others do not even have to do anything overt for us to reject them. This all has to do with perception: if someone is sufficiently different, we will feel uncomfortable around them. In the August 13 entry, I described the natural tendency of young Canadian soldiers, abroad for the first time, to look upon the Afghans as "the others" and to have difficulty relating to them. I have come to an important realization about the otherness of the local Afghans, one that I will share with my fellow soldiers.

247

When discussing the situation in Afghanistan with ordinary Canadians, the concept of the "others" often comes up. Many of our countrymen perceive Afghans through the prism of our mission here in rural Kandahar. I have often heard statements that characterize all Afghans as being backwards rural folk with antediluvian attitudes towards women. These Canadians are stunned when you tell them that, before the Taliban, there were women in skirts going to medical school in Kabul and Herat.

Most of our troopers fall into the same trap. They arrive via Hercules aircraft at KAF. A few days later, they travel in a convoy of armoured vehicles to a FOB in Taliban territory. They venture out from the FOB only in large groups, armed to the teeth. The people they interact with are among the most rural, economically depressed and socially conservative in the country. Many of them actively support our enemies. Most of our troops extrapolate what they are seeing to the rest of the country. I wish they could see what I saw last night.

I had gone back to see Captain Ghioz and First Lieutenant Nooragha. When I got there, they were playing a card game that I soon determined was a variant of bridge. My incompetence at poker notwithstanding, I play a number of other card games quite well. They invited me to sit in, and I eagerly did so. I am happy to report that my partner and I cleaned up, winning a dozen hands in a row before our adversaries threw in the towel and gave up. Afterwards, they invited

Chowing down with the ANA

me for yet another fantastic meal of mutton and potato soup along with a gigantic piece of naan.

Although I had a lot of fun playing cards and eating with these men, it would take more than that to get a young Canadian to relate to them. But what was on TV would force all but the most jaded racist to recognize the sameness and the basic humanity of the Afghans. Lieutenant Nooragha engaged in a bit of channel surfing, but three programs stand out in my mind.

The first was an Indian soap opera, in which matriarchs berated idiot men, sexy guys chased after even sexier women and tough guys got into fights with each other. You did not need to understand a word of Pashto to be able to follow the plot. The emotions on display were all too human.

The second was an election ad for Hamid Karzai. The Taliban may have destroyed any chance of a normal election taking place in Zhari-Panjwayi, but they have had little effect in Kabul. This ad showed

Karzai addressing a crowd of several thousand men and women, many of the latter uncovered, who were behaving like Canadians do at a large political rally. They were cheering and waving banners, and they seemed enthusiastic about their candidate.

Ads for two other presidential candidates also appeared. The officers in the room were evenly divided between Karzai and one of the other two. Far more importantly, they are all emphatic that, no matter who wins the election, they will remain loyal to the government of the day. The seed of democracy may have fallen on stony ground here in Zhari-Panjwayi, but it seems to be taking root elsewhere in this country.

For pure social connection, however, it was the third program that floored me. It was an episode of *Gags* from the Just for Laughs organization in Montreal. For those who have not seen this, it is reminiscent of *Candid Camera*: the comedians set up an outlandish situation on a city street or in a mall and capture people's reactions. The Afghans got the jokes and laughed as hard as I did.

Yes, these people are different from us. But they are far less different than many would believe.

AUGUST 17 | Men of God

The CF employs "padres" of various denominations. These individuals serve as spiritual advisers to the troops in the broadest possible sense. They are all "cross-trained" in the other major faiths and can bring comfort to any believer. One of these men has followed me around the war zone, arriving at each FOB a little after me and staying a week or so in each one. He has roomed with the medical crew on two occasions, so I have gotten to know him fairly well and quite enjoyed his company.

Forty-six-year-old Captain Normand Cholette is the quintessential combat padre. He is calm and perpetually cheerful, and he has a unique way of connecting with the younger troopers: he plays

Captain Normand Cholette, combat padre
(Photo courtesy Master Corporal Julien Ricard)

rock-and-roll on the electric guitar better than anyone in the battle group. At FOB Wilson, he would be in the "Rock House" till well past midnight most evenings. We have had some fascinating conversations, usually about the way he reconciles his role here—to improve morale, thereby making us a more effective fighting force—with the fact that he rejects war as a political option and never carries a weapon.

Another man fulfills the same function for the Afghan infantry company posted here. He is Faisal Hak, the company mullah (the Islamic equivalent of a Catholic priest, Protestant minister or Jewish rabbi). I had the opportunity to sit down and speak to him at length today, with the help of an excellent interpreter.

First, let me give you some basic demographics. Although he looks older, he is only twenty-four years old. He is from the city of Jalalabad, in eastern Afghanistan. His wife and three children live there, in a family compound with his parents and two younger sisters. He finished his religious training a year ago and volunteered for army service.

This is the first time I have had a conversation with an Islamic religious authority of any description since arriving in Afghanistan. My first priority was not to give offence in any way (how Canadian!), so I began by asking "safe" questions about his family, his motivation for joining the army and the places he had served. I should not have worried. Faisal Hak may be a devout Muslim, but he is not afraid to engage in a serious theological debate.

He was the one who kicked things off by asking me to describe my concept of heaven and hell. I told him that I was an agnostic and that,

Faisal Hak, the company mullah

although I believed there was a supreme being, I was not sure about much else. I told him the main reason for my uncertainty was the perfect certainty shown by so many who held diametrically opposed beliefs. We batted that back and forth for a while. He said it would be better to believe in one faith, to have a chance of getting into heaven if it was the right one. I countered with the argument that perhaps an absence of belief would be less offensive to God than the wrong one. Call that one a draw.

Faisal Hak had been sent to some isolated outposts. Just getting to these outposts, much less fighting from there, is dangerous. I asked him whether his faith made him somewhat nihilistic. If he believed that God was all-powerful, did he also believe that the time and manner of his death had been preordained? And if the answer was yes, did that make it easier to go forward into danger?

The response I got was carefully nuanced. Faisal Hak said that while the time and place of his death were immutably determined by God, it was his responsibility as a sentient human being to avoid being wounded. He was therefore not to take unreasonable risks to accomplish missions.

I then asked him what he thought of the Taliban and whether they were good Muslims. He replied emphatically that they were not Muslims at all. He buttressed this argument by pointing out all the things they did that are forbidden in the Quran. These included suicide bombing, the killing of innocents, the subjugation of women and the rejection of education.

With the opening he had given me, I asked him about the situation in his own household. He answered that both his mother and his wife had received a high school education (which is more than most women get in this country) and that his two sisters were currently pursuing the same thing. His three daughters are one, two and four years old. When he stated that they would all go to school, I asked him if he would have any objections to one of them becoming a doctor. He replied that he would not.

He then asked me about my profession and about my role here. After I had finished my reply, he told me that the Quran itself could be used to cure various ailments. I fell silent, and my body language was no doubt expressive. He asked me what I thought about what he had said, and I decided to reply honestly. I told him I was not happy to hear such things because it gave people false hope.

When he remonstrated, insisting that the Quran did heal, I asked him if he had ever seen it heal a bullet wound. He allowed that that was different, but then he seized the interpreter's hand and insisted he could cure him of his warts. I took a look and saw that the interpreter had three warts on his index finger, one on his thumb and one on his middle finger. I suggested we compete: I would treat the warts on the index finger with my methods; he would treat the rest of the hand with the Quran.

Before continuing, I should mention that he had already asked me a couple of times if I wanted to become a Muslim. Both times I answered his question with another question and avoided the subject.

But faced with an expression of belief that I consider dangerous—faith healing—I decided to challenge him. I offered him a bet: if by the time I left here (in a month) the index finger was healed, he would become a Christian; if the other two warts were healed and mine were not, I would become a Muslim. He readily agreed. After more discussion, I found out why: he explained to me that it was up to God to heal the warts. If the warts did not heal, it did not prove his method had failed. It only proved that God had not *wanted* the warts to heal. Ergo, his method had not failed. Indeed, it could not fail. This made it a bet that I could, at best, tie.

I was going to keep arguing about that, but then I remembered that it is a serious crime in Afghanistan to proselytize for any faith other than Islam. What I had done could be construed as attempting to convert a Muslim to Christianity. I began to backpedal furiously. I explained that since I was *not* a Christian, I had no desire to see him become one either. I suggested we change the terms of the bet. He agreed: if my warts do better than his, one of his daughters must become a doctor. As for me, I am off the hook if I lose.

Addendum, September 10: The index finger looks great, the other warts are unchanged. Paging Dr. Hak!

AUGUST 18 | Strategy and Tactics

When Task Force Orion arrived in Kandahar in early 2006, it was given an area of operations that, in retrospect, seems unimaginably large. The combat teams ranged all the way to the Pakistani border in the south, to the Arghandab and Shah Wali Khot districts in the north and as far west as Helmand province. This is more than ten times the surface area of Zhari-Panjwayi.

Since late 2006, we have focused on Zhari-Panjwayi. Half of this, Zhari district, has now been turned over to the Americans. This was already good news, because it meant we would be concentrating far more firepower in an area the Taliban want to contest.

The battle group commander, Lieutenant Colonel Jocelyn Paul, stopped by the FOB last night to describe our campaign plan for the next year or more. What he had to say was both reassuring and disappointing.

Take another look at the map in the June 4 entry that shows our FOBs dividing Zhari-Panjwayi on a north-south axis. It is to the east that the majority of the population resides.

From here on, we will deploy our forces mainly in the eastern part of the Panjwayi. The line of FOBs, which for so long served as springboards for operations into the Taliban heartland to the west, will now serve as a shield behind which we will operate in a different manner than we have until now.

The plan is to apply the principles of counterinsurgency in the way they were meant to be applied. For the first time, Canadians have the resources to accomplish this. Our troops are going to live right in the villages with the Afghan civilians. They will patrol intensively. In other words, there will be Coalition eyes and ears everywhere between our two remaining FOBs (Ma'Sum Ghar and Sperwan Ghar) and Kandahar City.

Militarily, I think this is a wise move. We are concentrating our forces into a region that represents less than a third of the area for which we were previously responsible. The impact this will have on combat operations can be easily imagined. As for the increased contact with Afghan civilians, I can only applaud this.

Emotionally, it is pretty tough to take. It was the soldiers of my first tour, Roto 4, who fought their way into western Zhari-Panjwayi and established outposts in the far reaches of those districts. On Roto 7, the current tour, we started off with a major operation to dismantle those outposts. Some soldiers were on both operations. You can imagine how they felt.

It is even harder to accept that, while we may be protecting 90 per cent or more of the population by following this new course, we are abandoning a small number of people to Taliban domination for the foreseeable future. Knowing that many of these people are staunch Taliban supporters only slightly lessens my regret.

AUGUST 19 | Anticipation and Anxiety

The elections will be held tomorrow.

Twice in the past three days, Taliban suicide bombers have struck in the capital, Kabul, killing a dozen people and wounding well over one hundred in total. Kabul has multiple medical resources to deal with such disasters. The same is not true in my little corner of the Panjwayi.

It appears there will be a polling station at an ANA observation post a kilometre north of here. No other situation since my arrival in Afghanistan has had so much potential for disaster. If a suicide bomber attacks a polling station while a large number of civilians are gathered, I could be faced with an overwhelming number of casualties. To make things worse, two-thirds of the combat team (and almost all the combat medics) as well as my Bison ambulance crew have been posted away from the FOB on security operations for the elections. The only soldiers with medical training currently on the FOB are a medic and a handful of TCCCs.

I have called a meeting with all of them for 1645. We will review triage concepts, how we will use the various spaces available to us near the UMS and who will be assigned to specific versus general tasks.

But my worries over whatever medical catastrophe may befall us tomorrow is nothing compared with my anxiety over the fate of the Afghan nation. The Coalition countries will be watching this election very closely. Support for the mission is lukewarm in many of these states. If the election is a fiasco, opinion polls could drift even further away from staying the course.

There are any number of ways things could go badly. Taliban intimidation could produce such a low voter turnout that the winner would lack legitimacy. Reports of widespread fraud would do the same even if voter turnout was high. Finally, even a well-attended, reasonably clean election could be fatally undermined in the eyes of the West if it comes at the cost of large numbers of civilian casualties.

To top it all off, incumbent president Hamid Karzai has chosen this week to curry favour with a small group of traditionalists by enacting a law that seems to enshrine a man's right to deny his wife food if she refuses to have sex with him every four days. Proving himself every bit the able politician and insincere democrat, Karzai snuck the law through the parliamentary process while the legislators were in recess.* The law applies only to the Shia minority and it is unlikely to survive on the books for long, but the damage has been done. Even some people who are staunch supporters of the mission have e-mailed me asking if this country is worth saving.

AUGUST 20 | Election Day in Afghanada†

0630—Go to the command post to see how things are going in the district. There has been a lot of Taliban activity over the last several hours, about ten separate attacks on various Coalition outposts. So far, these have been nothing more than minor harassment attacks, including a couple of sniper rounds fired at us from the cemetery about eight hundred metres north of here.‡ I tell the duty officer I am going to go for my morning run up and down the hill anyway. Even if the shooter is still

---

* Ironically, on the day the news of this law broke, one of Karzai's main campaign stops was with a women's organization: 2,500 women, none of them in burka, were there to meet him. I wonder how that went.

† "Afghanada" is an informal name for the Canadian area of operations: Zhari-Panjwayi and, until recently, the Arghandab district. Also a CBC radio show of the same name.

‡ Having just written that, I cannot believe how completely my perception of risk has changed over the past three months. Someone has just fired two bullets at the football-field-sized area I live in, and I consider it "minor harassment."

in place, which is doubtful, I will be a moving target nearly a kilometre away at a different elevation. Only the best snipers in the world can make such a shot. If the Taliban had anybody in that class, we would know about it—the men in the guard towers would be dropping like flies.

0730—I ran to the top of the hill five times instead of my usual four. A quick shower and another stop at the command post. The bad guys put one in their own net: someone planting a bomb in Bazaar-e-Panjwayi blew himself up.

0800—I am at my desk in the UMS. I hear incoming automatic weapons fire, from much closer than I have ever heard it before. I run back to my room to get my gear. First, enhance my survivability: frag vest, ballistic glasses, helmet. Then, get ready to fight. Tactical vest with ten extra magazines for my rifle (my pistol and its extra mags are already on my belt), gun gloves. My hands shake for a moment as I pull my gloves on, then the moment passes. Outside the door, I hear one of the senior NCOs yell, in that inimitable Québécois frenglish: *"Let's go, les boys! La FOB* se fait attaquer!"* I grab my rifle, chamber a round, put the weapon on safe and run outside. I am the first one out of the building. I scan the immediate surroundings. The firing sounded so close, I was afraid a Taliban might have infiltrated the FOB. If so, we would be in a close-quarters gun battle. I surprise myself by remaining calm and controlled.

The other soldiers came boiling out of the building and fanned out to their assigned defensive positions. The hilltop observation post located the source of the enemy fire and began hammering back with heavy and medium machine gun fire. Now that I was outside, I could tell that the incoming and outgoing fire was taking place on the west side of the FOB. The UMS is close to the northeast side, and there did not seem to be anything coming from that direction. Nonetheless,

---

* There is a perfectly good abbreviation in French for FOB—BOA: *Base opérationelle avancée.* Considering we are Combat Team Cobra, you would think "BOA" would have caught on, to keep the serpentine theme going. But no.

Sergeant Dominic Labelle, one of the infantry section commanders, and I went to the perimeter wall to check things out. The other men in his section are on leave, so there was no one else available on this side of the FOB to back him up.

We observed the ground to our front for several minutes through our rifle scopes. Although the people here were only a few hundred metres away from the fire being traded between Taliban and Canadian soldiers, their "pattern of life" seemed unaffected. Women and children were walking around in all directions, farmers were tending their crops. This made it less likely that there were any Taliban on our side of the FOB. When the Taliban attack us, these people know our retaliation will inevitably follow. As we have seen, we sometimes hurt people despite our best efforts. The Taliban, for their part, regularly use civilians as human shields. If at all possible, the civilians clear out before the Taliban launch an attack from their vicinity.

The machine gunners on the hilltop continued firing for a few more minutes, stopping when the enemy had withdrawn. I returned to the UMS and carefully arranged my gear on a chair in case I needed it again.

0830—"Operation Election" is starting in earnest. Despite all the combat activity, some polling stations are opening in Zhari-Panjwayi.

0900—IED strike on Ring Road South against an ANA vehicle. No casualties, no damage. The trigger man is detected and killed.

A lot of shooting is going on but, thus far, no attacks on electoral facilities, voters, candidates or observers. The Taliban are targeting our FOBs and other outposts, but not doing any damage. No casualties on our side.

0930—One of our outposts farther west has called in artillery support. Our cannons are firing over the UMS. The building shakes with every round.

First attack reported on a polling station, a high school on the outskirts of Kandahar City. It seems to have been an RPG. Some shattered windows, one door blown off its hinges. The principal of the high school states that the voting station will reopen shortly.

Taliban mortar attack on FOB Ma'Sum Ghar falls short. A six-year-old child is wounded in his left leg. "Bed" Bedard uses his ultrasound skills to locate a shrapnel fragment. The child is evacuated to KAF.

Nearly all polling stations are open in Zhari-Panjwayi, even in areas with very strong Taliban support. Voter turnout is minimal so far.

1000—Captain Normand Cholette, the padre, brings me one of the infantry troopers. The soldier has learned that his mother is in the ICU. She had been quite ill before he left, but it is still hard to take. The soldier asks me to contact the hospital in Canada because he has received only second-hand information from his girlfriend. I reach out to one of my emergency medicine buddies, who vouches for me to the ICU staff. "Yes, he really is calling from Afghanistan."

Things are not looking good. No aggressive measures are planned and the patient will be transferred out of the ICU and into a private room within twelve hours, if she has not expired by then. I send a quick e-mail to the battle group commander, Lieutenant Colonel Paul, recommending immediate repatriation. He replies within minutes, giving his approval. I hope this lad gets back to Canada in time to talk to his mother at least once more. I am very happy that Captain Cholette will be by his side till he leaves. If anyone can give the trooper comfort at a time like this, it's him.

Ma'Sum Ghar hit by a rocket. No injuries.

1040—Four Taliban are caught in the open by one of our choppers and killed.

1110—Election employees at a polling centre in Zhari district are caught stuffing ballot boxes. They are arrested.

1130—Two of our guys are on the edge of the FOB when a couple of mortar bombs are fired at us. One of the bombs lands well short, but the other one lands right behind them. They hear the bang, turn around and see the smoke . . . and get the hell out of there. I had been checking in with the command post when they arrived. They are in control, but are almost vibrating from the tension.

Major Jourdain is unruffled. He looks like a maestro conducting an orchestra as he uses various radios and land lines to determine where the mortars were fired from and to organize retaliatory fire. He spins up our own mortars to fire a "counter-battery" mission, our artillery attacking their artillery. Our observers have triangulated the launch site of the enemy mortars. It is out in the open desert. No "collateral damage" is possible, so we will blanket the area with high explosive.

Our mortars are on the verge of firing when one of our observers calls out that . . . *what the fuck?* . . . women and children have suddenly appeared right beside the launch site we have targeted. These are open fields. There are no buildings or crops anywhere near there. Major Jourdain snatches up one of the radio handsets. "Mortars! This is the commander! Check fire! *Check fire!*" The mortars, who were about to fire, reply that they are standing down.

If anyone reading this is not convinced of the thoroughly evil nature of the Taliban, let me spell out what just happened. The Taliban forced a group of women and children, who were certainly not members of their own families, to accompany them into the desert. Then they fired at us with a mortar. The launch site of this weapon is something we can easily detect, and the Taliban know this.

For them, there was no downside. If we fired too quickly, they would lambaste us for having killed innocent women and children. If we held our fire, their gunners would get away. Major Jourdain has lived through similar events before.

1200—One of the ANA infantry units based at FOB Ma'Sum Ghar, along with their Canadian mentors, has been in contact with the enemy for half an hour. The enemy has broken off and withdrawn. At least eight Taliban have been killed, the ANA and Canadians are all right.

1230—Multiple Taliban attacks throughout Zhari-Panjwayi over the past three hours. Still no casualties on our side, and only the child mentioned earlier among the civilians.

The Taliban are throwing a lot of stuff at us. They have evidently been husbanding their heavier weapons for some time to be able to mount a major offensive today. I note that about half of the Taliban weapons fail to detonate on impact or miss their targets. This suggests that the Taliban are even using ordnance they know is no longer effective militarily. I don't think this concerns them. It is effective in scaring the population so that they do not vote. That is the Taliban's goal.

1240—Spoke too soon. A Taliban rocket in the Arghandab district has killed one child, badly wounded two others.

1250—Spoke way too soon. Two Afghan policemen have been wounded. One of them has been shot in the head. His pupil on the affected side is fixed and dilated. At best, he will be paralyzed on one side. We evacuate him to KAF.

1300—The FOB is attacked once more, again from the west. Less automatic weapons fire than last time, more RPGs. Once again, Sergeant Labelle and I head for the northeast wall. This time, there is a single woman in one of the fields. She runs into a building and disappears. Otherwise, there is nobody to be seen. As clear a "combat indicator" as you will ever see. Trouble's coming.

A stray bullet goes through the command post of the engineer troop. It passes right beside Warrant Officer Stéphane "Fuse" Pelletier, the troop warrant officer, and lands beside Lieutenant Jonathan Martineau, the troop commander. They label the entry hole with today's date and go back to work.

1315—Another successful air strike kills five Taliban in the Arghandab district.

1320—Voting is finished at the Sarposa prison in Kandahar City. The criminals locked up there have nothing to fear. They all vote.

1400—Multiple rocket and mortar attacks on various coalition locations. One of them gives an American soldier a concussion.

1430—A series of mortar rounds impact the west side of the FOB. Then, the "combat indicator" proves its worth: sustained rifle fire comes at us from right outside the FOB walls. And this time it is coming from the east, the side closest to the UMS. Sergeant Labelle and I run over to our previous positions. We peek over the Hesco Bastions . . . and four shots go right over our heads. We eat gravel. For the next several minutes, we move around, always looking over the wall from a different place. We can only look for a few seconds each time before another volley of shots sends us back down. The shooter is zeroed in on our part of the wall. As soon as our heads pop up, we have to assume the sniper has detected the movement and is lining up his gunsight on our helmets.

As long as he stays hidden and does not move, the sniper has the advantage. He knows roughly where we are going to come out, but it is extraordinarily difficult for us to detect where the sniper is firing from. There is a loud "crack" as the supersonic projectile passes over us, then the distant "thump" of the gun firing. The direction of the source can only be guessed at (within an arc of thirty degrees or so). Unless we are looking right at the sniper's location when he fires, we will not see the puff of smoke from the rifle barrel.

Faced with this, undisciplined soldiers often stick their rifles above the wall and spray bullets downrange. This is out of the question for us. If we do not have a target, we do not shoot.

After about ten minutes of this, Major Jourdain sends one of the few LAVs (light amoured vehicles) remaining on the camp to help us out. It drives into position and starts tracking its 25 mm gun across the eastern side of the FOB. No further shots are fired at us. The LAV's big gun and its invulnerability to rifle fire have turned the tables. The enemy sniper no longer has the advantage. To open fire from close range now would be suicidal.

Nothing further happens for the next hour and a half, so we assume the sniper has decided to crawl away.

1500—The number of attacks on Afghan, Canadian and other Coalition outposts in Zhari-Panjwayi is unprecedented. The Taliban are doing their best to tie us down close to our FOBs and to intimidate the voters. They are succeeding on both counts. There are several reports of Taliban soldiers threatening potential voters, and two more reports of ballot-box stuffing.

One of the children wounded in the earlier rocket attack in the Arghandab has died.

1530—A Taliban soldier fires an RPG at an American convoy departing FOB Ma'Sum Ghar. He is killed by a single shot from a Canadian Leopard tank.

1540—"Bed" Bedard is busy again! It looks like the tankers fired a bit too quickly. The recoil of that last tank shot has given one of their men a lacerated and possibly broken leg. Off he goes to the KAF.

1630—Voting to the east of our line of FOBs has been going well. To the west, it has been dismal. In Howz-e-Madad, only two people have come to vote. One was an interpreter working with Combat Team Bastard. The other was a Taliban scout, who was arrested by the ANA. I wonder who he voted for?

1800—The polling stations all closed at 1700, but it seems that the Taliban are intent on going out with a flourish. All our FOBs have been attacked again in the last hour: mortars and RPGs here, rockets at Wilson and Ma'Sum Ghar.

There was also a gigantic blast southwest of here a little after 1700. Initial reports indicated that an ANA vehicle had been nearby. We got everything ready for a MasCal: all the TCCCs came to the UMS, we laid out all the gear the way we had discussed yesterday, I assigned specific tasks to some of them (triage assistant, gear quartermaster) and Master Corporal Charles Cloutier, my last remaining medic on the FOB, organized resuscitation gear in the UMS.

I am happy to report that all the Afghan soldiers near the blast were unhurt. It turned out only to have been a good practice run for my team.

1900—The day's toll. Headquarters has released the total damage for the day in Zhari-Panjwayi:

ANA Killed: 0
ANA Wounded: 6
Police Killed: 0
Police Wounded: 2
Taliban Killed: 22
Taliban Wounded: 10?

Civilians Killed: 3
Civilians Wounded: 10
Coalition Killed: 0
Coalition Wounded: 1

IEDs found and defused: 14
IEDs detonated: 8
Total rocket/mortar attacks: 112

1915.—We get hit three more times. Make that 115 rockets.

With everything that was going on, I missed calling Michelle for the second day in a row. To make things worse, she went to sleep last night saying "I have tears in my eyes because I miss my daddy." I had sworn to myself I would call her this afternoon (her morning, before she went to daycare). I tried to call her before going to bed, but Claude and I got our wires crossed and were not able to connect.

I know this seems trivial compared with the death and destruction all around me, but I am sick at heart . . .

COMBAT

I had been in war zones before coming to Afghanistan, but always as an unarmed medic. During these missions, I had been in situations where people were trying to kill me.

Today, for the first time in my life, I was trying to kill the person who was trying to kill me. I have reflected on this experience and drawn some conclusions.

1. *Winston Churchill was only partly right (see addendum to June 29 entry).*
Although I have been "fired upon without any effect," I do not feel particularly elated. The feeling after my combat patrol on August 4 was a hundred times more powerful. Before going on that patrol, I had spent twelve hours dreading what was coming. As we left the FOB, I was as frightened as I had ever been in my life. When I came back unhurt, I had the feeling that I had escaped a horrible fate. The attacks we were subjected to today started suddenly and ended quickly. Each time, my

attention was focused on my response to the attack. I had no time to consider what would happen if I was hit. This was particularly true when I was ducking bullets at the east wall. Someone was shooting at my FOB; I wanted to stop them. All I thought about were angles, distances and hit probabilities. I considered the possibility of getting shot, but only in the sense that it was something to be avoided if I wanted to complete my mission. The speed at which events unfolded made it impossible for me to spend much time being scared. Since I was not frightened for very long today, I am not very relieved this evening. It seems that what Churchill was describing was mostly relief, a feeling of having been spared.

2. *I am a soldier.*

It would have been hugely satisfying to shoot back, even without a target, on a number of levels. When one is under fire, there is a strong urge to do something proactive—to strike back at the enemy even if the chosen method is not very effective. But that is not what disciplined soldiers do. We fire only at clearly identified targets.

My finger was always along the trigger guard, never on the trigger.

3. *I am capable of killing another human being.*

As I tried to locate the sniper, I realized that an enemy soldier was doing his best to end my life. I felt no anger towards this individual. He was doing his soldier job, and I was doing mine. But if I had been able to figure out where he was, I would have put a bullet in his brain without hesitation. I doubt I would have lost a moment's sleep over it.

Addendum—after the tour

I wrote that last sentence while still under the effects of the post-battle adrenalin rush. It is incorrect—part of the protective mechanism human beings employ to survive the combat environment. Soldiers are invariably affected by the lives they take. Had I been given the opportunity to kill my enemy that day, I know I would not have wavered. But I would have regretted it for the rest of my life.

I am very happy that I never had to pull that trigger.

Like Muslims, the Vietnamese use a lunar calendar. The celebration of the lunar New Year is a big deal in Vietnam. It is properly called *Tet Nguyen Dan* (New Year's Day), but this is commonly shortened to "Tet."

266

In 1968, that day fell on January 31. The American forces in South Vietnam at that time were in a relaxed posture. They were therefore caught off guard when the North Vietnamese and Viet Cong launched their largest offensive of the war in the early morning hours of Tet. In a masterful feat of concealment they managed to place sizable units near every major city and base in the country. These units attacked simultaneously. The Tet Offensive, as it came to be known, was the turning point of the Vietnam War, but in a way that neither of the belligerents could have predicted.

The military and political situation in South Vietnam in early 1968 has numerous parallels with the situation in Afghanistan today. The war had been raging for a generation. A land that had never known democracy was struggling to develop this system. Corruption was rife. The Americans, with a bit of help from a smattering of other countries, were attempting to help the government contain a violent insurgency. While some of the insurgents were ideologically motivated, a large number were nationalists who were often uncomfortable with the dyed-in-the-wool communists among them.

The fighting in South Vietnam before Tet was similar to what is going on in Zhari-Panjwayi. The insurgency relied heavily on booby-traps and small-unit ambushes in which they used rockets and small arms virtually identical to those used by the Taliban. The Americans, who had over half a million soldiers in the country, were supported by the most modern artillery and aircraft available.

The Tet Offensive marked a radical departure in the tactics of the communists. For more than a month, they engaged in conventional warfare with the Americans and the South Vietnamese Army. They attacked in large groups and attempted to hold whatever ground they captured. They had hoped to score major military victories and provoke a large segment of the population of South Vietnam to join them in a general uprising.

The communists got it completely wrong.

By operating in large groups and staying in one place for prolonged periods, they exposed themselves to the overwhelming firepower of the Americans. They were slaughtered. Although the claims seemed outlandish at the time, the Vietnamese have since confirmed that close to 50 per cent of the 100,000 men they sent into battle were killed. It was a catastrophic defeat.

To make things worse, there was no popular uprising against the South Vietnamese regime. If anything, a number of well-documented atrocities on the part of the communists turned the population against them. After Tet, the South Vietnamese were more united than they had ever been. As the communists retreated back to North Vietnam, they thought they had suffered a massive setback.

The Americans, although initially stunned by the scope of the communist offensive, recovered quickly. As the battle progressed, they could not believe their good fortune. The communist units repeatedly stayed in place long enough for American heavy weapons to be brought to bear. By the time the battle ended, they thought they had scored a lopsided victory.

The Americans got it completely wrong.

Over the previous four years, the United States had sent more and more soldiers to South Vietnam, each time reassuring Americans that only a little more effort was required to guarantee victory. Instead, the American people watched on their televisions as the communists showed more strength than they ever had.

What had even more impact were the numbers of American deaths in combat. These deaths spiked during the Tet Offensive. The "kill ratio" was even more in favour of the Americans than before, but that did not matter. The American people had been promised victory, but what they got was a larger number of body bags.

The effect on the American war effort was devastating. Support for the war evaporated. This had not been anticipated by the North

Vietnamese. It was only after the American public turned solidly against the war as a result of Tet that the communists began to speak of the offensive as a victory for their side. The U.S. Army was dumbfounded. It had utterly defeated the enemy, yet the world was seeing it the other way.

Within a year, a new president was elected with a mandate to bring the troops home. Four years later, there were no American combat units left in South Vietnam. Two years after that, the communists swept out of the North and invaded.

This series of events can be summed up by an exchange that occurred between two senior officers in this conflict.

American General: "You know you never defeated us on the battlefield."

Vietnamese General: "That may be so, but it is also irrelevant."

Looking at what happened in Zhari-Panjwayi yesterday, I wonder if other amateur military historians might draw the same conclusion.

If you followed the news on the various Western media outlets, you would have learned that there were a few bomb attacks in Kabul and some incidents in Kandahar City. Several other major cities received a rocket or two. One, Baglan, was attacked by Taliban ground troops who withdrew after destroying the polling stations.

But what is happening today? Nothing.

Since you hear about Afghanistan only when there is something violent going on here, you might get the impression that the violence we experienced yesterday was run-of-the-mill. But this is the most combat activity I have seen in a single day on either of my tours. And this is where the Taliban are strongest.

I think the Taliban threw their Sunday punch at us yesterday—one for which they have been saving men and munitions for a long time. Militarily, they achieved nothing while losing a moderate number of men.

So this is nowhere near what Tet was. During Tet, all of South Vietnam was aflame for a month. Yesterday, on the other hand, was a continuation of what we have lived through for the past three years. The

Canadians held the line in Zhari-Panjwayi against the worst the Taliban were able to throw at us. And their worst, concentrated in this twenty-by-forty-kilometre piece of land, failed to kill or injure a single one of us. With the majority of their combat power tied up here, the Taliban were only able to inflict pinprick attacks elsewhere.

But was our military success irrelevant?

The Taliban did succeed in terrorizing the local population and undermining the election. How will voters in the Coalition countries react to this? No doubt there will be many who will say that (a) the democratic experiment has failed in Afghanistan, and (b) we have no business requiring the Afghans to adopt such a system.

To the first point, I would answer that democracy has always taken root slowly, even in countries with good economies and no civil war. In our country, it took half a century of democratic rule before the female half of our population was allowed to vote. But the desire for democratic government seems to be hardwired into the human genome. How else can we explain its inexorable spread over the past three hundred years? Democratic experiments struggle sometimes, but they do not fail. I defy you to name a single country that has started down the road from totalitarianism, be it in the form of a theocracy or a monarchy, and moved towards democracy only to revert back.

As for the second point, I think it has a slight racist tinge. The underlying assumption is either that the majority of Afghans are sheep-like and happy to live in a non-democratic system or that they have not evolved enough for this kind of government. Is it possible that there is a people that is so different from us that they prefer *not* to be asked their opinions on matters that affect their lives? Is it possible that there is a people that is so different from us that they cannot grasp the concept of democracy?

The argument that democracy cannot take root in a country that has never known democracy is nonsense. It flies in the face of what can only be called overwhelming evidence to the contrary. *Every country* that is currently a democracy was *not* one before it was a democracy. Why do we think the Afghans will be any different?

Churchill knew what he was talking about when he said that "democracy is the worst form of government, except for all those other forms that have been tried from time to time."* But here's the best thing about democracy.

Can you name a single country whose government was elected by universal suffrage that has declared war on another country with the same system? You cannot. Because it has never happened.

It is easy for totalitarian regimes, no matter what their philosophical underpinnings, to send their people to war: once the leadership decides something, the people—the ones who do the fighting and the dying—have no say in the matter.

It is far more difficult for democracies to initiate hostilities, but they can be convinced under special circumstances. Those circumstances have always included an absence of democracy on the other side.

The world will be done with war when the planet embraces democracy. I cannot think of a better reason to encourage the spread of the democratic ideal. I cannot think of a better reason to stay here and fight those who would oppose this process.

Addendum, August 22—Data Without Context: One story about the election on CBC.ca today. The following is from that article: "turnout was weaker than the previous vote in 2004 because of fear, disenchantment and election-related violence, which killed 26 people." †

That's it? The violence "killed 26 people," period? Would it not have given that number a little context to follow it with: "The majority of those killed were Taliban. A minority were civilians killed by the Taliban. There were few deaths among the various armed services of the Afghan government. There were none at all among Coalition forces. No civilians were wounded or killed by Coalition or Afghan government forces."

---

* In his Remembrance Day House of Commons Speech, November 11, 1947.

† "Afghan Election Victory Claimed by Rivals," CBC.*ca*, August 21, 2009, www.cbc.ca/world/story/2009/08/21/afghanistan-election-results021.html?ref=rss.

In another story, this one written on election day itself, the following comment appears: "While millions went to the polls, Zekria Barakzai, a top election official, told The Associated Press he thinks 40 to 50 per cent of the country's 15 million registered voters cast ballots—a turnout that would be far lower than the 70 per cent who cast ballots for president in 2004."[*]

So . . . in a country with a shattered infrastructure and an active civil war, where a violent insurgency has threatened to murder anyone who votes, the turnout may not reach 50 per cent? I think it's time for . . . a table!

	CANADA	AFGHANISTAN
VOTER REGISTRATION	Comes in the mail.	Have to go to government office. Could get murdered for doing so.
CAMPAIGN RALLIES	They almost pay you to come.	Could be attacked by suicide bomber.
VOTING	Drive to polling station on way to/from work. Takes five or ten minutes.	Walk to polling station could take one or two hours. Could get murdered on way there. Wait for voting can be several hours. Could get executed while there.
AFTER VOTING	Whine about the guy you elected.	Finger marked with ink; gets you executed by Taliban if found before it wears off.
IF YOU DON'T VOTE	Won't miss *Seinfeld* rerun. Whine about the guy someone else elected.	Get castigated by the world as "not ready for democracy."

* "Afghan Voter Turnout Low, Officials Say," CBC.*ca*, August 20, 2009, www.cbc.ca/crossroads-afghanistan/story/2009/08/20/afghanistan-election-polling-president.html.

The Afghan election saw a voter participation rate "far lower than . . . 70 per cent," eh? That would be quite low, wouldn't it? Maybe not.

Looking at voter turnout since Confederation, the percentage of eligible Canadian voters who have voted remained above 70 per cent almost continuously for over 120 years. But the last time we managed that was 1988. Participation percentages in Canadian federal elections has been drifting down to the low 60s over the past twenty years. In the last election (2008), we dipped into the high 50s.

With everything we have going for us, and with everything the Afghans have going against them, there might end up being as little as 10 per cent difference in our participation rates.

I do not hear anyone suggesting that we're not ready for democracy.

AUGUST 22 | Ramadan

This is the first day of Ramadan, the holiest month in the Muslim lunar calendar. Over the next twenty-nine or thirty days, depending on the behaviour of the moon, Muslims must refrain from eating, drinking, sex, smoking or "anything that is in excess or ill-natured" from dawn till dusk. The fasting in particular is meant to give Muslims a chance to cleanse themselves, to appreciate what they have and to recognize that others may have less. The two most important themes seem to be connecting with family and caring for the poor.

During this month Muslims get up before dawn to eat. Even though they gorge themselves then, the grumpiness level starts to rise around midafternoon. This is alleviated by another large meal after sundown. Between lack of sleep, post-meal torpor and late-afternoon grumpiness, there are only a couple of hours each day when everyone is firing on all cylinders.

Some Muslims take their fasting so seriously that they carry around a little cup into which they spit their saliva. This prompts the obvious question: if the Taliban see themselves as good Muslims, will they take this month off to fast? Or will they accept a decrease in their operational effectiveness as their soldiers go around hungry and tired during the afternoons, when most of the fighting takes place?

The answer is no. The Taliban have given their troops a pass on this one, just as they have played fast and loose with most other parts of the Quran as well. That has been the case in years past. Summer is traditionally the "fighting season" in Afghanistan and there has been no decrease in combat activity during Ramadan for the past three years. The most intense fighting Canadians ever experienced in Zhari-Panjwayi occurred when they arrived here in 2006. The Taliban massed their troops to try to prevent Canadian troops from entering these districts. The fighting continued for several weeks, well past the date Ramadan began that year. If things remain as quiet as they have for the past two days, it will be because the Taliban shot their bolt on election day.

Ramadan ends on the first day of the next new moon. This is the holiday of *Eid ul-Fitr*, "The Festival of the Breaking of the Fast," a day-long party during which there is supposed to be a lot of eating, praying and donating to the poor. Human nature being what it is, I am willing to bet that the order I listed for those items is the order in which they are given priority.

I dropped in on the ANA officers late this afternoon, happy to see that they were none the worse for wear for their twelve foodless hours. They invited me to join them for dinner, and I readily agreed. They told me to drop by at 1900, which is the same time that they had told me to arrive every other time I had had dinner with them. On each occasion, dinner had started at 1930 or a little later. This is no different from what goes on elsewhere in developing world environments, and I have no trouble with it. Either I wait and chat with the officers until dinner starts, or I factor this in and arrive late myself.

On this day, I knew they could not start eating until after sunset, so I waited until about ten minutes after dark to wander over. As I was walking towards their barracks, it dawned on me that I was displaying, if not cultural, then at least culinary, insensitivity. This was confirmed when I arrived.

After fasting for twelve hours, no one had been in the mood to wait a minute longer for dinner. They have made sure that everything was ready to go the second the sun dipped below the horizon. By the time I got there, everyone had finished eating. This didn't stop them from welcoming me warmly and sitting me down to a large dish of some kind of vegetable I've never eaten before, supplemented by the usual huge piece of naan.

AUGUST 23 | The Warrior Princes

When I described the role of Major Tim Arsenault, the combat team commander at FOB Wilson, I spoke mostly in terms of his responsibilities. Let's look at the other side of that coin and consider the power of Major Steve Jourdain, the combat team commander here. I compared Major Jourdain earlier to the warrior kings of antiquity. This is not an exaggeration.

Just as Major Arsenault's responsibilities dwarf anything encountered in the civilian world, the destructive force Major Jourdain has at his disposal is almost beyond comprehension for someone outside the military.

There are very few officers the CF trusts this much. There is no one looking over Major Jourdain's shoulder here, and his word is law. We have to be sure that he will never abuse his position. If that were to happen, the damage he could inflict on innocent Afghan civilians, on our mission's goals and even on his own troops would be incalculable. In Major Jourdain's case, the trust is entirely merited.

So how does Major Jourdain exercise a good portion of his power? The combat team contains a large number of "supporting arms." I have already introduced several of these groups, including the engineers, tankers, artillerymen and reconnaissance soldiers. But no matter how many members of the supporting arms might be in a combat team, by far the largest group of soldiers belongs to the "arm" that is being supported: the infantry. Since more than one hundred men are in the company based at the FOB, Major Jourdain could not possibly control them all on the battlefield. Rather, he guides the three men who are most responsible for turning his orders into reality.

These are the platoon commanders, each one of whom is in charge of thirty to forty soldiers, divided into three infantry sections with ten soldiers each and a fourth "headquarters/heavy weapons"

Major Steve Jourdain, the warrior king

section. This last section contains the platoon commander, platoon second-in-command and other specialized soldiers such as radio operators and the soldiers who man the rocket launchers.

I admit that I have a fondness for the platoon commanders. When I graduated from the Infantry School of the Combat Training Centre in 1979, this is the job I did for the next three years. I learned a great deal about leadership as a platoon commander, and this was one of the key formative experiences of my life.

I was a competent platoon commander: my platoon was regularly chosen to take on the more challenging assignments, and I had good success in field exercises. But after observing the three platoon commanders of Combat Team Cobra for a few weeks, I can see that I was not in the same league as they are. The war has made them develop as commanders, but they had to have been quite sharp to begin with. I sat down with each of these extraordinary young men separately to conduct the only formal interviews I did for this book.

Captain Vincent "Vince" Lussier, like me a Franco-Ontarian, is the oldest of the three. He shares many of my beliefs about the value of the mission and has a sophisticated understanding of who we are

Captain Vincent "Vince" Lussier, commander, First Platoon

fighting and why. During our interview, he astounded me by describing the effect of Taliban rule on infant mortality—the single best measure of a population's health. This is something very few non-medical people would do.

Almost twenty-seven years old, he has been a platoon commander for three years. All that time has been spent with the same platoon. Many of the men he has taken to war were wet-behind-the-ears seventeen-year-old recruits when they joined him. He has watched them grow up not only as soldiers but also as individuals.

The affection he feels for his men is intense. He expresses this in familial terms: "I feel more like their older brother than their commander." It is a cliché to refer to an infantry platoon as a "band of brothers," but it is very apt.

Even stronger than this affection is Captain Lussier's pride in his platoon's troopers. This pride has not blinded him to their failings. On the contrary, Captain Lussier spontaneously volunteers that "the other platoons have men who are better shooters, better patrollers or better tacticians than mine." But he insists that his men have the most heart: "We may not be the best soldiers, but we are definitely the best team."

Captain Lussier told me that he moulded this team in the best but also the most tiring way possible. He was present for all their training exercises, even the physical training that he was not required to attend. During this time, he was able to assess how well various individuals worked together. If they are the best team today, it is because Captain Lussier specifically chose them for that role.

This devotion to his men has been returned to Captain Lussier in powerful ways, at both the platoon and the personal levels. As a platoon, his men accept the tasks they are assigned, no matter how dangerous or onerous. As individuals, several of them have already saved his life. He describes a poignant example of a trooper whose soldier-skills were marginal when in training back in Canada but who had guts and drive. So Captain Lussier brought him along. On one mission, the trooper placed himself with a mine detector in a position of maximum danger and discovered an IED on a path Captain Lussier was about to take. "If he had not been there that day, I'd probably be dead," Captain Lussier says. There are many similar stories in his platoon, connecting each man to several others. It is those connections that Vince tells me are what he will treasure most about his experiences here.

Lieutenant Alex Bolduc-Leblanc, twenty-four years old, was encouraged to join the army by his uncles, both of whom were infantry officers. He graduated from the Royal Military College in 2007 and joined his battalion in September that year. He was assigned to a platoon and, a few months later, began work-up training to go to Afghanistan.

Lieutenant Bolduc-Leblanc's motivation for coming to Afghanistan mirrors my own: he sees this conflict as a war of good against evil. His upbringing gave him a strong moral code and, in a way, he looked forward to being able to do his part here. His view on the strategy we must pursue to achieve victory is also similar to mine: protecting the population until they are educated and trained enough to defend themselves militarily against the Taliban and to reject their extremist ideology.

Lieutenant Bolduc-Leblanc had all the normal anxieties one would expect prior to deployment: "Would I be able to function under fire? Would I be frightened?" But if anyone was born to be a warrior, it is this guy. "Being in combat is a rush!" he says, with a bit more enthusiasm than most civilians would find proper. But he is only being honest. Combat hyperstimulated all his senses and he "felt more alive than ever before."

He has not killed anyone yet, but his men have. "Even though this is a war, that was hard on them," he told me. "I had to counsel a number of them afterwards." It is reassuring to me that Canadian soldiers do not take killing lightly. And it is comforting to know that,

Lieutenant Alex Bolduc-Leblanc,
commander, Second Platoon
(© Louie Palu/ZUMA Press, reprinted with permission)

when they have to take a human life, Lieutenant Bolduc-Leblanc is there to help them come to terms with what they have done.

Lieutenant Bolduc-Leblanc admitted that he has been "scared, really scared" three times since arriving in the Panjwayi. Those were the occasions when vehicles containing some of his men hit an IED. Each time, the vehicle disappeared in a cloud of dust. "Each time, it took a full minute for the crew commander of the vehicle to get on the radio to tell me that everyone was all right." The way Lieutenant Bolduc-Leblanc described his emotions during those three one-minute eternities was so vivid that the intensity of the anxiety he felt was physically palpable to me as a listener.

In some ways, Lieutenant Bolduc-Leblanc is still a very young man. This is his first time in the developing world, and he admits he was shocked at the backwardness of the people around the FOB. "It's 'Jesus time' out there," he says with disbelief. The absence of any modern amenities (cars, electricity, running water, health clinics, etc.) is something he had not believed existed.

He also cannot understand the persistence of the Taliban. After a battle in which his platoon killed several of them, he overheard the Taliban leader congratulating his group on their radios because they had been able to inflict a minor wound on a single Canadian. "I don't get it! Why don't they care about their men the same way I care about mine?" he asks.

In other ways, Lieutenant Bolduc-Leblanc displays more maturity and professionalism than someone twice his age. He routinely goes out on patrols in which he engages the local population in conversation. Often he holds *shuras* with the local elders. During his time here, he estimates that he has spoken and shaken hands with at least a few dozen Taliban. "These guys will shoot at me, then hide their weapons and share a cup of tea with me." I asked if he found this intensely frustrating. The same situation has led many soldiers in many armies to abuse and even murder civilians, often with far less suspicion than Lieutenant Bolduc-Leblanc has had. But he describes these events as barely annoying.

"My rules of engagement are clear. We cannot open fire unless directly threatened, and we cannot arrest a civilian without clear evidence of wrongdoing. Until one of those conditions is met, I will extend my hand in friendship to anyone and everyone I meet here."

That is counterinsurgency at its best.

Twenty-five-year-old Lieutenant Josh Makuch could be a poster boy for the benefits of multiculturalism. Although he is nominally an anglophone Ontarian, I lost track of the number of ethnic groups represented in his DNA. These have given him a broad and sophisticated world view as well as almost flawless French.

When unilingual anglophone infantry officers graduate from the Combat Training Centre, they must choose to serve in one of two anglophone regiments. For Lieutenant Makuch, this would have meant being posted to Shilo, Manitoba, or Gagetown, New Brunswick. His French-language skills gave him a third option: by joining the Van Doos, he could be posted to Quebec City and stay close to Montreal, where he had done his undergraduate degree.

Shilo, Gagetown or close to Montreal? It was an easy choice to make. Lieutenant Makuch arrived in Quebec and joined the combat team in August of 2008. There were only nine months left before deployment, and he had to work hard to integrate himself into the platoon's leadership team and to be accepted by the men. By the time they went to war together, he had achieved that.

He describes his time here as being "seven months spent at Maslow's fifth level." For those of you unfamiliar with Maslow's hierarchy of needs, the fifth level is "self-actualization," in which one is achieving one's full potential as a human being. It is a profoundly rewarding experience to be at this level, but it is something few people ever attain.

Lieutenant Makuch's self-actualization has come as a result of the heavy responsibility he has been given at such a young age. "I matured more in the first five months of this tour than in the previous five years," he states. "I have to stand in front of forty men and explain to them what we are going to do and how we are going to do it. And we all know that our lives depend on my plan being sound."

Hearing him express these feelings, I was reminded of the way young doctors will describe their first night on-call by themselves. The sacred trust, the awesome responsibility and the feeling of being extraordinarily privileged to be in this position are similar, but much more intense for infantry officers. And like a young doctor, Lieutenant Makuch has learned that even the best decisions sometimes lead to the worst possible outcome—Master Corporal Charles-Philippe "Chuck" Michaud was one of his men.

Lieutenant Josh Makuch, commander, Third Platoon

Of the three, Lieutenant Makuch is the one who was interested in going to war for "the experience," and he sees the mission in more abstract philosophical terms than I do. "I agree with our goals here and they may well be worth my life. But I am not ready to die for the cause. This is not because I am scared of dying. I am just so curious about what the rest of this life has in store for me."

Lieutenant Makuch is unsure about his future. Being chosen for this job marks him as an up-and-comer in the CF, but he has yet to decide whether or not he will stick it out for twenty years. "I have already had the best job the army could ever give me: commanding a platoon in combat. No matter what happens next, I will never be called to do this task again."

A few years from now, you might bump into the young man pictured here. He might have somewhat longer hair and be living a bohemian lifestyle as he decides what he is going to do next. If you recognize him, take the time to talk to him and listen closely to what he has to say.

He was a warrior prince once; he led Canadians in battle. You could learn a lot from him.

Addendum, August 25—A close call: I have not spoken much about the other medical types at this FOB because my contact with them has been limited. There has been no medic assigned to the UMS for weeks. A Bison ambulance crew was here when I arrived, but they left after four days. Another Bison dropped by for a few days, then they were reassigned as well. One of the four combat team medics left on leave right after I got here, and another one left a week ago on a two-week-long mission. The gang here is just as impressive as their colleagues, as this brief entry will demonstrate.

At 2100, one of our patrols left to set up an ambush in an area where we suspected the Taliban might be transiting. Things were going well till around midnight when a trooper came to tell me that a member of the patrol had fallen into a well. My heart stopped. On June 7, 2008, Captain Jonathan Snyder had been participating in a nighttime combat patrol. Somewhere in Zhari district he fell into a *kariz*, a kind of open-pit well used by Afghan farmers. Weighed down by nearly a hundred pounds of gear, Captain Snyder drowned. I had the sick feeling that in this case the result would be the same.

Things ended differently this time. One of the reasons for this was the rapid reaction of Master Seaman Charles Cloutier, the senior medic of the combat team. Although he was some distance away from the well when our soldier fell into it, MS Cloutier immediately recognized what had occurred and started shoving people out of the way to get closer to the victim. When he got to the side of the well, he quickly

Master Seaman Charles Cloutier,
senior combat medic (after lifeguard duty)

Corporal Alex Cloutier-Dupont, combat medic

organized the other members of the patrol. They fished out a somewhat banged-up, but very much alive, Lieutenant Josh Makuch. MS Cloutier checked the lieutenant and, detecting no major injuries or bleeding, organized the evacuation back to the FOB.

Once they arrived at the UMS, MS Cloutier and I carried out a thorough assessment of his patient. After an hour of observation, we discharged the lieutenant in good condition. Later, when MS Cloutier described his terrible anxiety as he ran towards the well, I could see that he felt as strongly about any wounded Canadian as platoon commanders feel about their men.

Anytime Canadian soldiers go down, for any reason, they can be sure that Master Seaman Cloutier will come for them. Or die trying. That is his commitment to them. He is their "doc."

The only other member of the Sperwan Ghar medical crew here now is Corporal Alex Cloutier-Dupont. I could go on about him at length, but it would sound boringly similar to what I have written about the other combat medics: he is very good at his job, in excellent physical condition, always good humoured and keen to help out wherever and whenever he can. I will therefore limit myself to a single observation. Take a close look at the following photograph of him. Does anything seem unusual?

Military readers may notice that Corporal Cloutier-Dupont is not wearing the standard Canadian Army tactical vest. Instead, he is wearing a modular vest that is far more functional for a combat medic than the one the army issues.

As with the special medic pack, which he has also bought, this piece of equipment cost him six hundred dollars. A week's pay, so that he can do his job better. Do his *government* job better.

AUGUST 24 | The Internal Contradiction of the Taliban

A quiet day. This gives me a chance to write about something which happened a few weeks ago.

It was my last day at FOB Ma'Sum Ghar. The combat team based there had been out on a mission for a few days. They had been in a heavy firefight on the second-last day of the operation, not far from the FOB.

On their way back to Ma'Sum Ghar, they were flagged down by a wounded Afghan. He was lying beside the road, propped up against a rock. He stated he had been a bystander during the fighting the day before and had been hit during the exchange of fire. He had a number of bullet wounds, some of them large and gaping. None of them were bleeding, and all appeared to be several hours old.

Master Corporal Turcotte's ambulance crew picked him up and treated him. As they packed and dressed his wounds, they noticed something bizarre: the wounds appeared to have been cleaned and... he had an IV catheter in place on one of his arms. *What the hell?* He had received medical care of some kind after being wounded. So what was he doing on the side of the road?

When the Canadian medics began to question him about this, he fell silent. That made everybody suspicious. These suspicions were confirmed when we checked his skin for gunpowder residue: the test was strongly positive. He was evacuated to the KAF hospital in good condition... but with a military police escort.

As mentioned earlier, we treat Taliban prisoners the same as anyone else, and I make sure these prisoners know that it was the Canadians who took good care of them. It seems that our enemies have finally understood this. Although I have heard of similar incidents before, this is the first time I have had direct knowledge of a wounded Taliban being deliberately placed in the path of our troops so that we will pick him up and treat him. I've discussed this with other senior officers, and apparently this is not a rare occurrence.

You cannot help but wonder what effect this will have on the ordinary Taliban trooper. He is told that we are infidels who should be tortured to death if we are captured. Then he is told to leave his wounded comrade-in-arms in the path of one of our convoys because he will be well treated. At some point, the contradiction of those two statements has to make all but the most fanatical ideologue question the legitimacy of the first declaration.

AUGUST 25 | The Observer Observed

After three months of observing everything around me, I have spent the last forty-eight hours being observed myself. A Canadian journalist has joined us on the FOB and has spent a fair bit of time with me. He has interviewed me about the upcoming release of FOB *Doc*, and we have had a number of informal conversations.

This being his fourth visit to Afghanistan, he has learned a lot about the country. He is familiar with the geography, understands the politics and knows something about half of the presidential candidates (forty-one people—some of them women—ran for the position in last week's elections). As he is the first "journo" I have spent any time with, I thought I would read his articles and write an entry explaining whether I agreed with him or not. But something happened this evening that is more newsworthy.

I have been spending a fair bit of time with the Afghan soldiers. I regretted not having done this previously and was determined to make up for it before I left. While I feel that my readings have given me a clear sense of Afghanistan as a country, I was hungry for more personal contact with its people.

This is not a common thing for Canadian soldiers to want to do. By and large, they prefer to keep to their own when not on operations with the ANA. The Afghan soldiers are not shy about making remarks about this. The frequency of my visits is something they seem to appreciate.

The journalist became aware of the relationship I had with the Afghan officers and asked if he could come along the next time I had dinner with them. I was happy to arrange that, and got the best interpreter on the camp to facilitate our discussions.

A few minutes before the evening prayer call (which defines the end of the day's fast during the month of Ramadan) I went to collect the journalist. As we walked over to the ANA barracks, I commented on the tastiness of the meal we were about to receive. What he said next stunned me: he had no intention of eating anything because he was afraid the Afghan food would make him sick.

I should have stopped right there and flatly refused to bring him to dinner with people I consider my friends. I did not, and the result was predictable. The Afghans sat us down on the thickest cushions, served us first and provided us with a series of courses. My countryman rejected everything that was offered to him, with the exception of a few bites of bread. He gave the excuse of having a "bad belly," which fooled no one. The Afghans commented that "only the Doc likes our food." The protestations of the journalist to the contrary were unconvincing.

This refusal to participate in a social event he was there to document did not stop him from taking numerous pictures and writing an article about his meeting. I was left with the feeling that I had facilitated something that was at least mildly exploitive.

AUGUST 26 | The Bomb

At least forty-one dead. A number that is sure to rise because many of the wounded, who currently number sixty-six, are critical.

The Taliban set off a massive bomb last night in Kandahar City. They packed five cars full of explosives and detonated them. A city block was wrecked, and more than forty shops were destroyed, many of them the only source of a family's livelihood.

The story on the CBC website about this event gives us the total of Coalition deaths for the year to date. The story emphasizes that this is the most in a single year since the beginning of the war. It does not explain that this is due to the massive influx of American soldiers into Afghanistan and that, with these additional troops, we are challenging the Taliban far more than we used to. As in all these stories, the total number of civilians killed by the Taliban this year is not mentioned. The fact that most of the people the Taliban kill are civilians is also omitted.*

Data without context, again.

Addendum, August 27—Inside the Blast Radius: The second Bison ambulance crew to spend time with me at this FOB had been quickly reassigned to Kandahar City for the election. They were to be the medical element of an additional QRF (quick reaction force) located at Camp Nathan Smith (CNS). This is a base on the outskirts of Kandahar, separate from KAF. CNS is the home of the Provincial Reconstruction Team. Units located here have rapid access to the eastern half of Kandahar City.

The medic of that Bison is Corporal Marie Gionet, a remarkable thirty-one-year-old woman who earned an anthropology degree before joining the CF Health Services five years ago. She was attracted by Egyptology but realized that not many people can earn their livelihood doing this. She describes joining the CF as a wise career move. In Afghanistan, you could argue that she has the best of both worlds: a secure career in the military and a job where an attractive lady still gets to wear shapeless clothing, live cheek-by-jowl with a bunch of smelly guys and work in a hot, sandy environment.

On the evening of August 25, Corporal Gionet heard a blast so loud that she thought it had taken place right outside the camp walls. She rushed to get her gear on and she reported to the sergeant in command of the QRF. He told her to stand by until they had a clearer idea of what was going on. She went back to her Bison and got ready to head out.

The order to deploy into Kandahar City came thirty minutes later. Corporal Gionet was shocked to learn that they would be going to a

---

* "Kandahar Blast Kills Dozens," CBC.ca, August 25, 2009, www.cbc.ca/world/ story/2009/08/25/afghanistan-violence025.html.

Corporal Marie Gionet, Bison medic

blast site over four kilometres away. This was her first inkling of how massive the bomb had been. Basing the ambulance at CNS proved to be a prescient move: this supplementary QRF was the first Coalition force to arrive at the scene of the blast.

When the QRF arrived, Corporal Gionet was faced with a scene of unbelievable destruction. An area the size of three football fields had been blasted and blackened. Many fires were burning, the air was thick with smoke and it was getting dark.

Contrary to what the media had first reported, a single vehicle was involved in the attack—a tanker truck filled with explosives. It had more destructive power than anything we drop from our planes. The priority was to secure the scene and light it. The QRF vehicles formed a circle around the blast area, guns pointing out and headlights pointing in.

Corporal Gionet relates that two events marked her strongly during this incident. The first occurred once the perimeter had been secured and she rushed out of her ambulance to render aid to the wounded.

There weren't any.

Further information confirms that there were forty-one dead after the blast, but that the total number of wounded was seventy-six, not sixty-six as written above. Six of wounded died, bringing the total deaths to forty-seven. But not one of these seventy-six people was still on the scene when Corporal Gionet arrived. The Afghan civilian medical personnel had, in her words, done a spectacular job. They had secured the scene—ensuring that no secondary explosions (whether intentional or accidental) or any other hazard threatened the rescuers—triaged the patients effectively and organized an efficient entry-exit system for the many ambulances to come in, pick up a patient and depart. The job of saving lives had been done as well as it could have been done. By the Afghans themselves. Without anybody's help.

This had quite an impact on Corporal Gionet. As a medical professional, she grasped the sophistication required to accomplish what the Afghans had done. "This was the first time I have seen a non-military branch of the Afghan government functioning at a high level without any outside assistance," she told me. "I had been unsure about the mission's chances of success until I saw that, but I'm more optimistic now."

This reminded me of how distorted our perception of Afghanistan can become because we spend all our time fighting the Taliban in Zhari-Panjwayi. Not too far from here is a city of a half-million people that works reasonably well, by developing world standards.

These people dealt quickly and efficiently with the biggest mass casualty event Afghanistan has seen in two years. All that was left was to pick up the pieces of those who could not be saved. Corporal Gionet went through her entire supply of body bags. She then started to use baggies, and ran out of those as well. One of the baggies was being requested by a soldier who called on the radio to say that he had found a hand, but that it was not an adult hand. He kept repeating he needed a small bag for the small hand. I wonder if he was not saying that it was a child's hand in order to avoid confronting what had happened to the child.

There were no Afghan or Coalition military personnel or installations in the vicinity of the blast—only civilians. And how did our enemies, the authors of this atrocity, choose to follow up on their actions? Did they express any regret? Did they say it had been a mistake? No. A few of them opened fire on the QRF. The ANA soldiers present quickly drove them off.

For the next four and a half hours, the Canadian QRF kept the site secure while Canadian infantry searched through the rubble with digging equipment, search dogs and their bare hands. They found only more body parts.

Sometime after midnight, an American unit arrived to take over from the Canadians. As Corporal Gionet was getting ready to leave, she had her second head-spinning experience of the evening.

Although the Afghans had conducted the evacuation of the wounded from the blast site efficiently, they had brought all these patients to hospitals with limited resources. Some of the walking wounded were therefore given first aid and told to return in the morning for definitive treatment, such as suturing or casting. One of these partially treated patients was brought to Corporal Gionet.

The patient in question was an eleven-year-old girl who had been brought to the Bison on her father's back. The parents asked if it were possible for their child to be seen by a female medic, but Corporal Gionet got the impression that this consideration took a back seat to getting their child well treated. She invited the patient and her parents into the ambulance. Then, her world shifted.

The mother sat down across from Corporal Gionet, promptly removed her burka and fairly threw it at her husband. She then began speaking in fluent English, describing her child's injury and thanking Corporal Gionet for agreeing to see her.

As a Bison medic assigned to a combat team, Corporal Gionet's contact with Afghan civilians has almost exclusively been in the context of a combat operation. The connection she was able to achieve by caring for the child would have been remarkable in and of itself. But she was also able to connect directly, without interpreters, to another woman. "This was the first woman I have met here that I didn't have to search," she said. She found the experience extremely rewarding.

I wish every Canadian could have heard the conversation between Corporal Gionet and the mother. This Afghan woman could not comprehend why Corporal Gionet would have come all the way from Canada to help the Afghans. She emphasized to Corporal Gionet that this was very dangerous, as if she was unsure whether the corporal fully understood the risks Coalition soldiers face here. But as difficult as it was for this Afghan to grasp that Canadians would come here and risk their lives to help her, she and her husband were nonetheless deeply appreciative.

She then said something that should be juxtaposed with the media reports about the election. She said that there had been far *less* violence on election day than she had feared there would be. The Taliban attacks, other than in Zhari-Panjwayi, had been pinpricks, in her opinion. The media had made it sound like the roof was caving in.

Corporal Gionet finished taking care of the child. The girl had a nasty laceration on her knee, which was closed and bandaged. Throughout the treatment, the child remained calm and stoic. Once Corporal Gionet was done, the daughter reattached herself to her father's back and the family headed off.

In talking to the mother, Corporal Gionet had discovered that the young girl was going to school. The mother felt very strongly about this—in a city where the Taliban will throw acid in the faces of girls who try to get an education. If they do not kill them. This family is fighting the Taliban as much as we are.

AUGUST 27 | Quick Draw

Earlier I introduced the "Battle Captain" of the armoured squadron. The equivalent in the infantry is the "LAV Captain" (*"Capitaine d'assaut"* in francophone units), an individual who plans operations and missions. The LAV captain of Combat Team Cobra is Captain Sacha Boisvert-Novak. From my trips to the command post and the card table, I have gotten to know him and have enjoyed his company.

Captain Boisvert-Novak knew he wanted to be a soldier from childhood and joined up when he was only seventeen. He had his university education paid for by the CF, earning a degree in political science. Given the complex nature of international conflict in the twenty-first century, this will no doubt serve him well.

Captain Sacha Boisvert-Novak, battle captain*

After graduation, Captain Boisvert-Novak completed his infantry officer training as well as paratrooper training. He then reported to his infantry battalion and began work-up training to come to Afghanistan on Roto 4. He spent most of his time on his first tour as a liaison officer with the British Gurkhas. Returning to Canada after Roto 4, he immediately volunteered to return to Afghanistan. His wish was granted, and he was given that most coveted of positions for a young officer: infantry platoon commander in a combat team. But halfway through the year-long work-up training for Roto 7, his assignment was changed.

Captain Boisvert-Novak's other assignment on Roto 4 had been to oversee the digitization of many of our command and control systems. As a combat officer he was not thrilled to be surrounded by techies and computers instead of infantrymen, but he did a fantastic job. Maybe a little too good—when Major Jourdain, the combat team commander, was rounding out his leadership team, he came looking for Captain Boisvert-Novak. As battle captain, he has made the command post "100 per cent more efficient" (in the words of Major Jourdain) because of his intimate knowledge of all the new technology.

Captain Boisvert-Novak, however, was bitterly disappointed. The accelerated promotion (coming two years sooner than it normally would) and the esteem of his superiors could not fully erase the frustration of no longer commanding men "at the sharp end of the stick." But he is a soldier first and foremost; he took up his new post without complaint and with considerable energy. He is the only veteran among

---

* Who wishes it known that he quit smoking shortly after this picture was taken.

the officers of the combat team. As battle captain, he draws on his experience to advise the commander and to counsel the junior officers.

Joined the army at seventeen. Paratrooper. Volunteered for a combat tour, then a second one. Has already volunteered for a third. Civilians reading that curriculum vitae may decide that Captain Boisvert-Novak enjoys war, for some deranged reason. The motivation for such a career path is best explained by David Grossman in *On Combat*:

> Everyone has been given a gift in life. Warriors have been given the gift of aggression. They would no more misuse this gift than a doctor would misuse his healing arts, but they yearn for the opportunity to use their gift to help others. These people, the ones who have been blessed with the gift of aggression and a love for others, are our warriors.*

Here's how a warrior like Captain Boisvert-Novak puts these words into action. If you look in the dictionary under "phlegmatic," you will see a picture of Captain Boisvert-Novak. Whether he is helping to coordinate the defence of the FOB while we are under attack or winning (or losing) a gigantic pile of poker chips, his face remains inscrutable. I had formed an impression of him as being unshakably calm in any situation. That impression was dramatically confirmed at supper yesterday.

Captain Boisvert-Novak and I, along with a couple of the combat team's senior NCOs, were dining together at the same table. The discussion was lighthearted and jovial, mostly centring on how best to ingest massive quantities of alcohol while on leave. Everyone was enjoying themselves, things were quiet and the day's work was done. So we lingered, remaining seated at the table long after our meals were eaten and the rest of the soldiers had left the mess tent. We were comparing stories of earlier excessive alcohol intake when the

---

* David Grossman and Loren W. Christensen, *On Combat: The Psychology and Physiology of Deadly Conflict in War and in Peace*, 3rd ed. (Warrior Science Publications, 2008) at 181.

unmistakable sound of an automatic rifle on "full auto" was heard coming from *much too close.*

In unison, everyone seated at the table dove onto the concrete tent pad. The firing continued, but no holes were appearing in the canvas wall of the mess tent. Either the shooter's aim was off or he was hitting some of the concrete barriers surrounding our tent. He could also have been shooting at something other than the mess tent.

I must explain that whenever we leave the FOB, we wear all our protective clothing. We are heavily armed and ready for anything. But when we go to dinner, we are only wearing our combat uniforms or gym clothing. The only weapon we carry is a 9 mm pistol.

With that background in mind, we return to the three senior soldiers and me as we land on the mess tent's concrete floor. There was gunfire outside. Without leaving the tent, we had no way of knowing what was going on. Everybody was thinking about the worst-case scenario: Afghan soldiers who had never shown signs of disloyalty suddenly turn on their Coalition allies. Had a Taliban infiltrator made his way into the FOB?

Civilian readers might think that staying close to the floor inside the tent would be a reasonable option here. We could aim our weapons at the doors and challenge anybody who tried to come inside. This group of Canadian soldiers felt differently. Anyone attacking our FOB would have to fight their way in. In unison, we stood up and started running to the door.

In the few seconds it took us to get to the other side of the mess tent, we all had our pistols out of our holsters. I was so focused on the door that I experienced a classic case of tunnel vision.* But while

---

* This occurs when stress overloads the nervous system and the body starts to exclude certain stimuli. Soldiers in combat will think that their rifles are making barely audible popping sounds. Others will feel no pain from severe wounds. What I experienced is common: the loss of peripheral vision. If you recognize this when it happens, it can be compensated for by scanning right to left. In my case, I got myself together (and my normal vision came back) a few seconds after I left the mess tent.

FOB Sperwan Ghar mess tent (letters A and B indicate positions relevant to the story)

I could not see my comrades, I could clearly hear the metallic *chick-kachick* of all our pistols chambering a round. We did not have rifles, frag vests or helmets, but we were ready to fight if necessary.

Because of where I had been sitting, I reached the door first. I went outside, turned to my right (the direction the firing had come from) and took cover behind a concrete barrier (position A in the photograph). That was far enough for me, but not for Captain Boisvert-Novak. I watched in amazement as he went running *across the open ground in front of me* to the next good position of cover some ten metres away. No frag vest, no protective gear, just a desire to protect his comrades.

From position A, I could not see very far at all. Captain Boisvert-Novak had sized that up in a heartbeat and gone to position B, from where he had an excellent view of the nearest side of the ANA barracks. I heard him call out to someone, asking where the firing had come from. In a few seconds, he had determined that the enemy shooters were still outside the FOB walls. The loud gunfire we had heard was likely someone on our side shooting from inside the FOB. Only then did Captain Boisvert-Novak turn and lead us back to the shelter of the command post.

As we headed inside, the heavy machine guns on the hilltop opened fire. Combined with the fire from the defensive positions on the FOB perimeter, this quickly drove the attackers away. Throughout this episode, Captain Boisvert-Novak looked like he was out for a Sunday stroll. As I said, phlegmatic.

AUGUST 28 | Doctor in an Undoctored Land

I have made a conscious effort to get to know the ANA soldiers at this FOB. Effort is perhaps too strong a word. All I have done is sit down to dinner with them two or three times a week and dropped by occasionally during the daytime for a conversation. But these regular visits have marked me as someone with a sincere desire to connect with the Afghans. This affection has been returned several times over.

I also warmly welcome the Afghan soldiers who come to the UMS and I try to make them feel at ease with my rudimentary Pashto. This has led to an increase in visits by Afghan soldiers to the UMS. This exposure to patients from another culture prompts me to make two observations.

In these parts of the world, modern Western medicine represents something of great value, something the people here could never afford. When they can access such medicine for free, they come to see the Western doctor with a minor ailment: a stuffed-up nose, a sore back or, my favourite, "total body pain" (a complaint I have now heard from at least five distinct cultural groups). They do not really think the problem will go away. They only want to have the experience of being seen by someone who appears to them to be a miracle worker.

A lot of Westerners fail to appreciate this and go down one of two erroneous paths. The first mistake is to assume that the patient has a serious condition. This may lead doctors to provide treatments that are unnecessary and sometimes harmful.

The second mistake lies at the other end of spectrum. This occurs when Westerners assume that the patient is malingering. In these instances, the doctors often get angry and rudely show the patient the door.

The best way to deal with these situations is to respond as you would during any other patient encounter. Sit down, give the patient your full attention, take a thorough history and perform a careful physical exam. These patients want the same thing that patients in our emergency departments want: to be listened to, and to have the feeling that someone cares about them.

Beyond that, they often want a taste of high-tech medicine, and frequently ask for IV medication. But these people are not all that different from us. By giving them a sympathetic ear, I can achieve as much or more healing as I could by shooting them full of antibiotics. I have been here nearly four weeks now, and I have not given a single injection or intravenous drug to an Afghan soldier. And yet they seem very pleased with the service they receive.

The second observation has to do with a subset of patients who are unlike any I have ever had to deal with in emergency medicine in Canada or anywhere else in the world. At least once every three or four days, one of the Afghans on the base will come to me with a complaint having to do with sexual function. Not sexual *dys*function, but sexual function: things are going *too* well.

Usually, this takes the form of wet dreams. As observant Muslims, the patients are disturbed by nocturnal emissions because they are "unclean." The first time I heard that one, I recommended the patient masturbate before going to sleep. I was informed that, because of the Islamic religion, this was not going to happen.

Talk about irony! Theologically enforced sexual abstinence causing a desire that theologically enforced rejection of masturbation renders one unable to relieve. I was left to recommend that fallback of the British boarding school, the cold shower.

At the other end of the masturbation spectrum, a member of the interpreter staff arrived with a complaint that he was initially reluctant to describe. After some beating around the bush, he came out with it: he was masturbating so often and so vigorously that he had developed arm and back pain.

The physical exam was . . . unremarkable, as we say. The patient was discharged with anti-inflammatory medication and reassurance that this was normal behaviour for a nineteen-year-old male.

The things that bind us together as human beings: parents love their offspring, children need lots of fresh air, the elderly are smarter than anyone thinks and adolescent males will jerk off until their dick and/or hand drops off.

Addendum, September 6, 2009: As if to prove the above observation, a Canadian soldier came in today with the following complaint: "Every time I masturbate, I see little brown specks in my sperm." And how long has this been happening? "Twice a day for two months." And this concerns you now because . . . ? "I dunno. I thought it would go away."

AUGUST 29 | Company Sergeant-Major

Since I have re-enlisted in the CF, I have been gratified to see the esteem that ordinary Canadians have for those who wear the uniform. Even individuals who oppose our mission in Afghanistan make a clear distinction between the mission and those who carry it out. There is none of the vile rejection of soldiers that was seen in the United States when American soldiers returned home from Vietnam. Instead, a common slogan of the anti-mission side is that they support the troops and do not want to see us hurt or killed in a mission they feel is flawed. I disagree with that view, but I respect it.

This affection for the troops, however, does not translate into an understanding of our world. To appreciate this next section requires a basic knowledge of the ranks of the combat team's leadership. I will provide an abbreviated version of it here.

The army is divided into two distinct groups: officers and enlisted men. An adequate civilian analogy would be that the officers are management whereas the enlisted men are labour. The military reality is much more nuanced. While it is true that the officers lead and make the decisions, they do so in close collaboration with the senior enlisted men. Although the most junior officer has the authority to give an order to the most senior enlisted man, in practice that would never happen. Instead, officers work as partners with enlisted men who have been in the army roughly ten years longer than they have. Like parents, they may have vigorous disagreements behind closed doors, but they will never oppose one another in front of their subordinates.

The most senior enlisted man in the combat team is the company sergeant-major. This position is held by a master warrant officer, the second-highest rank among the enlisted men. When I joined my battalion as a junior infantry platoon commander, there was a sign on the orderly room wall that summarized the various ranks in the company:

MAJOR: Commands the company. Faster than a speeding bullet. More powerful than a locomotive. Able to leap tall buildings in a single bound. Walks on water. Raises the dead.
Relationship to higher authority: Has lunch with God every few days.

CAPTAIN: Company second-in-command. As fast as a speeding bullet. Wins tug-of-war against a locomotive two out of three times. Able to leap tall buildings with a running start. Can swim across the ocean. Performs open heart surgery with a bayonet.
Relationship to higher authority: Has weekly meetings with God.

LIEUTENANT: Platoon commander. Pedals a bicycle faster than a speeding bullet. Carries a heavier load than a Mack truck. Can clear a multi-storey building if there is a trampoline to assist him. Able to swim across Lake Ontario. Can perform life-saving CPR for hours.
Relationship to higher authority: Talks to God on the phone.

COMPANY SERGEANT-MAJOR: Catches bullets and eats them. Throws locomotives off the tracks. Lifts tall buildings and walks under them. Freezes water with a single glance. Tells you when you can die. If he does, drop dead immediately. Stay dead.
Relationship to higher authority: IS GOD!

Any questions?

Now that we have clarified the rank structure, we can go on. Because no description of the leadership of a combat team would be complete without describing the man who holds the thing together, the company sergeant-major.

Major Jourdain, like all combat team commanders, has a second-in-command. This post is ably filled by Captain Hugo Dallaire, a senior captain of long experience. He is capable of taking over and running the combat team if anything were to happen to the major, and he did so during the commander's leave. But if Major Jourdain has a right-hand man, it is his company sergeant-major.

This person is the essential link between the major and the men. It is the sergeant-major that the commander turns to for assistance in dealing with morale and discipline problems, providing invaluable advice when the commander has to make the most difficult decisions.

Earlier I quoted David Grossman's explanation of the motivation of the warrior. Grossman goes on to explain that a person is not born to be a warrior but can make the choice to become one. If ever there was an exception to that rule, it is Master Warrant Officer Guy Lapierre.

MWO Lapierre can remember wanting to be a member of the CF since he was five years old. He spent his childhood and adolescence dreaming of joining the Canadian Navy. When he turned seventeen, he headed straight for the recruitment centre. The power of the open ocean and the excitement of foreign ports were only days ahead. Then a rather large fly landed in his career ointment. The economy was in recession and the army was having no trouble recruiting. When MWO

Lapierre came looking for his long-awaited job as a sailor, he found that they had all been taken. He was told that the waiting time to get a position in the navy would be a year or more.

Seventeen-year-olds are not known for their patience. The recruiting officer must have sensed this. There is no other way to explain what he proposed next: "You can't get into the navy for at least a year but... you can be in the infantry in three weeks!"

Translated into civilianese, that would be: "If you want a career on a clean boat, wearing clean clothes, eating three square, hot meals a day, you have to wait for twelve months. If you want to carry a heavy pack through swamps while eating scraps of freeze-dried crud, you can start working right away."

As often happens when males are in their teens, testosterone won out over patience and good judgment. MWO Lapierre signed up on the spot and found himself in an army uniform within the month.

MWO Lapierre's high testosterone levels now put him at a distinct advantage. After his basic infantryman's course, he was sent to the paratrooper school. He was then assigned to the Airborne Regiment, the most elite formation in the CF. He must have been one hell of an impressive kid; he got into the infantry a year after I got out, and I knew soldiers who had been trying for three years to get into the Airborne. Being accepted into that regiment after basic training would be like being invited to play high school football... in Grade 7.

MWO Lapierre, who had so wanted to be a sailor, proceeded to have a career dominated by the most intense infantry experiences imaginable. During a decade as a paratrooper, he made the rounds of the more arduous peacekeeping missions Canada was involved in, including tours in Cyprus in 1986, Bosnia in 1993 and Haiti in 1997.*

---

* He missed the disastrous mission to Somalia because it occurred during one of the few times he was posted to a "straight leg" infantry battalion. ("Straight leg" is a slightly derogatory term used by paratroopers to denote non-parachute infantry. The term evokes the need to bend one's legs when doing a parachute landing.)

The most impressive part of his résumé, however, would have to be the two years he spent testing paratrooper equipment.

The conversations during these two years would have gone something like this:

(Note: Before any other old paratroopers out there think I am exaggerating, let me tell you that I have seen the video—not of the conversations—the video of the jumps. If I hadn't seen it, I wouldn't have believed it. But it happened exactly as I am about to describe.)

"Lapierre! We have this new rucksack/piece of gear/whatever. But there's a chance it will completely screw up the flight characteristics of the free-falling paratrooper, get tangled in his chute and he will crater. Strap it on, go jump out of a plane and tell us how well it works. Or not."

"Yes, Sir!"

"Lapierre! That seemed to work when you jumped by yourself, so we want you to do the same jump, but 'tandem.' Attached to another paratrooper. That way, we can drop paratroopers more closely together. But there's a chance it will completely screw up the flight characteristics of the free-falling soldiers. They could get tangled in their chute and crater. Go jump out of a plane and tell us how well it works. Or not."

"Yes, Sir!"

Even the most determined soldier would be having second thoughts about his career choice at this point. But the main event was still to come.

"Lapierre! We want to see if we could drop a paratrooper with a big bunch of gear at the same time. They could drop food into famine areas or large amounts of ammunition to our forces, with pinpoint accuracy. So we want you to strap this gigantic barrel to your chest harness. It is five feet high and two and a half feet across. It weighs 630 pounds. You will fall much faster than normal paratroopers do, and there's no telling what might happen. It could get tangled in your chute, and you will crater. With the barrel on top of you. Strap it on, and go jump out of a plane and tell us how well it works. Or not."

"Yes, Sir!"

There is an old joke about undesirable jobs whose punch line was "parachute tester." MWO Lapierre did it for real.

He describes his time at the Airborne School as having been the most enjoyable of his career. But he has the warrior's skills, and he lives by the warrior's code. There were evil men doing evil things, and his country was at war against them. There was only one place he wanted to be.

He started to angle for a combat posting on Roto 4. Having seen war in Bosnia and misery in Haiti, he had no illusions about what he would be facing. He was nonetheless frustrated when he was not chosen. For the men of Combat Team Cobra, that was a good thing: it meant that he was available to come with them on Roto 7. Major Jourdain knew a good thing when he saw it and snapped him up. This made it easier to staff the rest of the combat team. MWO Lapierre's reputation was such that soldiers from other companies were asking to transfer into Combat Team Cobra to serve under him.

If I tell you that MWO Lapierre is the very picture of what the ideal sergeant-major should be, most civilians will think back to the tongue-in-cheek description at the beginning of this entry and imagine that he is a fire-breathing terror. But while he can be harsh when the occasion calls for it, that is not his leadership style. On the contrary, this soft-spoken man motivates his troops by being tougher on himself than on anyone else.

He starts off by being in amazing physical shape. He has been in Ironman competitions, and he has come at or near the top of any group physical fitness test that he has ever participated in. In a group as fit as the paratroopers, that would be impressive enough. Call that Airborne tough.

But what does it become when you learn that MWO Lapierre broke his back in 1996? And was told he would never be in the infantry again, much less jump out of airplanes? And then attacked his rehab program with such determination that he was doing parachute jumps again eighteen months later? That is sergeant-major tough.

Master Warrant Officer Guy Lapierre in his element: the field

MWO Lapierre brings the same energy to everything he does. He pushes himself to always be more upbeat, more confident, more "together" in every way a soldier can be than any of the men who serve under him. In private conversation, he is candid about his weaknesses. For instance, he admits that he is not as good a public speaker as other men in his position. He compensates for this by working much harder than they do to get to know his men. When he speaks to them one-on-one, the impact is magnified.

The thing he enjoys least about his job is dealing with the interpersonal conflicts that are inevitable in any large group. This falls to him when it cannot be resolved at a lower level, so he gets to deal with the worst cases. But he knows his men so well that he can see the value in each one. This makes it challenging to resolve their quarrels—he can always see both sides.

When I asked MWO Lapierre to summarize what it meant to be a sergeant-major, he replied without hesitation. He sees himself as a teacher, one who demonstrates for the undisciplined the advantages of superb self-discipline.

Like all Canadians, MWO Lapierre is proud of our role as peace-keepers. But he also describes, with passion, the outstanding performance of Canadian combat soldiers in every war we have ever been involved in. He sees no contradiction in being good peacekeepers and good warriors. The job we have here in Afghanistan calls on the attributes of both.

MWO Lapierre is living the crowning achievement of an outstanding career. He does not enjoy being at war but, like most of the soldiers here, he has been given "the gift of aggression." He is where he needs to be, not where he wants to be. He is serving his nation to the best of his abilities.

What is he getting out of it? He speaks with remarkable sensitivity and insight about achieving as much personal growth as possible from the experience. He feels that most of this growth will come from having been a member of a team, a team involved in the most valuable work a group can possibly do: bringing hope where there was none before.

AUGUST 31 | RCIED: Radio-Controlled Improvised Explosive Device

Every day, small groups of Canadian soldiers go into some of the most hostile territory on Earth. Reconnaissance patrols seek to obtain information. Ambush patrols lay traps for Taliban infiltrators. Some patrols escort our officers to a *shura* with a local elder. Others are "presence patrols" that make the point that we can go wherever we like. The territory the media likes to describe as being under Taliban "control" is territory they cannot stop even a few of our soldiers from traversing.

It is during these patrols that the skill of the Canadian soldier becomes overwhelmingly apparent. By day and by night, these men and women will engage in an activity that requires the peak level of the warrior's craft. Camouflage, tactical movement, silent communication and combat skills must all be of the highest order.

The patrol that left at first light this morning was tasked with an engineering function. Led by Lieutenant Jonathan Martineau of the 5th Combat Engineer Regiment, their goal was to weld grates onto a culvert that passes under the main access route to the FOB. It is easy for the Taliban to sneak an IED into such culverts. They use the cover of darkness, civilian passers-by or even a wandering herd of sheep to gain access to the culvert undetected. Because they do not have to dig, it takes only seconds for them to place their lethal device. This obliges us to clear the road at least once a day, a time-consuming and occasionally dangerous task. The heavy metal grates would make it more difficult to access these culverts.

Accompanying the patrol this morning was Corporal Pascal Girard, the thirty-two-year-old combat medic assigned to Captain Lussier's First Platoon. This platoon had just come back from two weeks of QRF duty. This was an exhausting time for Corporal Girard. When the QRF was called out, as it could be several times in a single day, it was common for Captain Lussier to assign only a portion of his men to the task. But it was necessary for the platoon medic to go out every time.

With his platoon back at the FOB, the soldiers of First Platoon now had to assume their share of the patrols. Most of these would not involve all the men of the platoon, but a medic has to go every time. Master Seaman Cloutier, the senior combat medic, tries to even this out between the medics on the FOB. The fact remains that these young people work hard and are exposed to tremendous risk. I have never heard any of them complain about that.

The diagram accompanying this story offers a visual representation of the ground. When the patrol arrived at the culvert, Corporal Girard, the medic (M), took his place in the security cordon. From here he could cover the footpath which headed northeast. With his back against the wall of the abandoned family compound, he was invisible to anyone coming from the south. Because of the position of the sun, anyone coming from that direction would cast a shadow that would alert Corporal Girard to their presence before they came around the corner. Lieutenant Martineau (L) stood close to the culvert, supervising his engineers (E). Sergeant Luc Voyer (S), commanding the infantry, stood between the lieutenant and the medic, with an interpreter, or "terp" (T). Other infantrymen (I) completed the security cordon.

While the engineers were performing their tasks, two children (C) walking down the footpath from the east approached Corporal Girard's position. Sergeant Voyer went to meet them and began

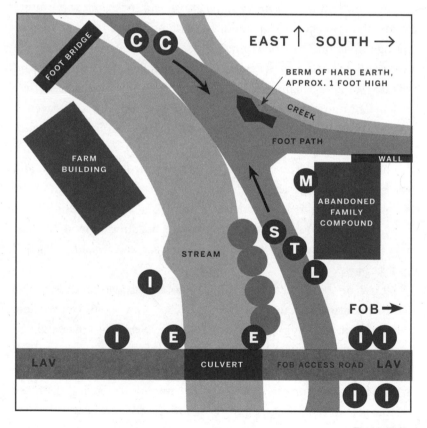

The blast site

talking to them through the terp, immediately to the west of the berm of hard earth shown in the diagram. The children, a boy and a girl both about ten years old, offered the soldiers pomegranates. Sergeant Voyer asked them where all the adults were. The children explained that, it being Ramadan, most people were staying inside and not exerting themselves. Corporal Girard saw that the sergeant and the terp were now exposed to anyone coming from the south. The compound to the south of the footpath blocked the view of the infantrymen near the road. He therefore moved further east to better protect his sergeant. Then a massive explosion occurred. The sergeant, the terp and Corporal Girard disappeared in a cloud of smoke.

Corporal Girard was hit by some gravel and rocks, but was unhurt. Remembering where the abandoned compound had been, he headed in that direction. When he found it, he turned west and followed the wall until he got out of the smoke. Then he called to his sergeant and the terp, guiding them out of the smoke by his voice. Sergeant Voyer reached him first. Having gotten his bearings, Sergeant Voyer went a short way back into the smoke, found the terp and brought him out.

Lieutenant Martineau could not believe they were all still alive. He had thought they were dead, given the size of the explosion and their proximity to it. His relief would be short-lived. Once out of the smoke and with the terp headed to safety, Sergeant Voyer and Corporal Girard both looked at each other and said, simultaneously: "The fucking kids!" Then they *ran back to the blast site, still completely obscured by thick smoke.*

It was an extremely brave thing to do. It was also foolhardy. The Taliban routinely plant secondary devices to kill Coalition soldiers who have the life-saving reflexes displayed by Sergeant Voyer and Corporal Girard. Lieutenant Martineau ran after them, screaming at them to stop. Although none were under his command, he has lost three engineer brothers on this tour. He had no intention of losing any more friends. He ordered the men to return to the road. Reluctantly, they obeyed.

As the smoke began to clear, the engineers moved around the south side of the blast site, checking for secondary devices and casualties. Corporal Girard and Sergeant Voyer stood on the edge of the smoke cloud, peering into the haze with their rifle scopes and listening for screams or moans.

Back at the FOB, we had no idea how bad this could get. I ordered all preparations to be made for a MasCal and my team responded superbly: within fifteen minutes we had three medics, ten TCCCs, two terps and a dozen stretcher-bearers standing by in and around the UMS. Our triage and holding areas were ready, and all our resuscitation gear, including our pediatric bag, was ready to go.

The engineers continued to inspect the blast site from the east and then from the north, crossing the stream at a small footbridge. Corporal Girard and the other infantrymen rearranged themselves to cover the perimeter.

As the engineers walked past the east side of the farm building, they noticed that two Afghan men were inside. There was no good reason for these men to be in that spot. They claimed to be working on the grapes, but these were already all hung to dry. The engineers brought the men back to the main body of troops to question them further. Along the way, they found three more Afghan men in another farm building farther south (not shown in the diagram), and they brought these men along as well.

The engineers had not seen any casualties, but Corporal Girard was still not satisfied. He headed down the footpath to stand right on the spot where the children had been when the explosion occurred. This was clearly against the lieutenant's wishes. Corporal Girard figured he would ask for forgiveness rather than permission.

The explosion had taken place less than ten feet from where they had all been standing. Once there, Corporal Girard realized that their lives had been saved by the berm of hardened earth. It had deflected the force of the blast and most of the shrapnel over their heads. There was nothing on the ground, such as bits of clothing or blood or tissue, to suggest that the children had been wounded. It was evident that they had run away to the east. Only then did Corporal Girard relax.

With the site now secured, the engineers proceeded with what they call "exploitation." This involves examining the blast site to learn as much as possible about how the enemy makes their weapons, so as to better defeat them.

No one had been standing on the mine when it went off. This ruled out any pressure plate or tripwire mechanism. No wires were leading away from the blast site. This left only one option: it had been an RCIED, a radio-controlled IED. The mine had been deliberately set off by someone who had been watching the place where it had been hidden. There was nothing accidental about this detonation. Someone had watched the Canadian soldiers and the Afghan children together and decided to trigger the blast.

That "someone" had to be close. The two Afghan men hiding in the farm building to the north of the stream were very suspicious. They told contradictory stories to explain what they had been doing in the area and how they had gotten there. They were tested for explosives residue. One of them tested strongly positive for military-grade explosives. Both were taken into custody. Tests on the other three men were negative. They were released.

The men were brought to the FOB, where we followed our standard procedure for detainees. The first step is to examine them medically, to document their state of health and any injuries they may have had prior to entering a Canadian or Afghan detention facility. If anyone mistreats these detainees, the military police and any investigative body will be able to refer to these documents. If injuries are later found that were not noted on the initial exam, then whoever is responsible for the detainee has some serious explaining to do. I had done a few of these "detainee medicals" during my first tour, and this one was no different.

After the two Afghan men had been interviewed, it was the opinion of the officer in charge of the process that the older man had been coerced by the younger one, either to participate in the mine attack or at least to vouch that they were both farmers.

Even if the Taliban had killed both of the children, it is unlikely you would have heard about the incident in Canada. This is incomprehensible to me. The only way we can justify our actions here is that they are occurring in the context of a moral war, and a moral war is defined by the degree to which our enemies are evil. The people we are fighting will not hesitate to kill children if there is a chance that they might wound one of us. So why does the media so rarely report these stories?

I felt no rancour towards this man as I examined him. He was a detainee now, and I would no more have mistreated him than I would have harmed my own daughter. I regretted that his world view was so opposed to mine that we had to struggle against one another with lethal force. And I wondered whether he and I could ever come to an

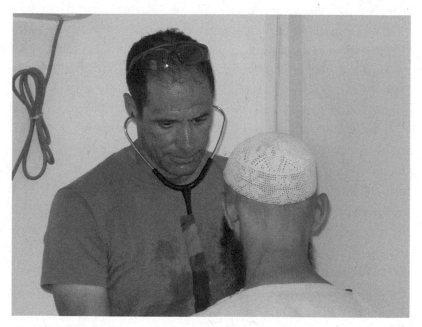

Face to face with evil

accommodation that satisfied his obedience to his god while respecting my passion for human rights.

Addendum—March 27, 2010 About Detainees and Torture: "It's worse than a crime. It's a mistake"—attributed to various French diplomats of the Napoleonic era, referring to the execution of the Duke of Enghien.

A number of post-hoc justifications have been advanced through the ages to rationalize the use of torture. These range from the utilitarian—"We needed to obtain information"—to the theological—"It is God's will."

The reason people torture in the first place is much simpler: for those who are capable of it, the act of torturing is enjoyable. If you do not think this is possible, watch a seven-year-old child burning ants. An individual whose ego is not well developed can feel greatly empowered by inflicting pain on another creature. For those who have been brutalized themselves, this can be tremendously gratifying. The gratification comes at the cost of even more long-term psychic damage, but the torturer is unable to appreciate that.

It is this underlying emotional trauma, or childlike immaturity, that renders the torturer incapable of accepting that torture has a dismal track record. But the evidence is overwhelming: quite apart from the fact that it is it utterly immoral, torture is also spectacularly counterproductive.

Prisoners who have valuable information represent a tiny minority of torture victims. There has never been any proof that these individuals are more likely to reveal this information under torture. Meanwhile, the great mass of those who are tortured have no useful information to divulge and will blurt out anything they think the torturer wants to hear. This leaves the side doing the torturing with a mass of misleading and contradictory data. The intelligence services must then expend an inordinate amount of time sorting through this junk, which distracts them and diverts resources that could and should be used more effectively. Even worse, torture guarantees that if the victim was not an enemy before, he or she almost certainly will become one.

I am bringing all this up because, shortly after I returned to Canada, the controversy over our handling of Taliban prisoners of war, a.k.a. detainees, exploded. This debate, like many others about the war in Afghanistan, has been marked by misinformation, a lack of context, political manoeuvring and hyperbole that is way over the top.

Let's begin with some cultural context: harshness and physical violence are commonplace in Afghan society. Many Afghan men beat their wives, virtually all parents beat their children and superiors in any field occasionally beat their subordinates. I alluded to this earlier when I related that the Afghan officers I met during my first rotation would occasionally throw rocks at underperforming soldiers. Individuals who may have been involved in atrocities against Afghan soldiers, as would be the case with suspected Taliban prisoners, can be in for a rough ride from their Afghan captors.

It does not follow that the Canadian Forces had direct knowledge of systematic abuse. Our CDS, General Walter Natynczyk, has been pilloried for not being aware of a single memo in which a military policeman reported seeing an Afghan policeman hit a Taliban detainee with a shoe. It is a grotesque exaggeration to extrapolate from this that CF commanders had *definite* knowledge that "100 per cent of detainees" were being viciously tortured and that they ignored this information. We certainly had our suspicions, and those suspicions led to occasions on which we would stop transferring detainees to the Afghans. We even sent officials to monitor conditions in the Afghan jails. Our actions have led to vastly improved conditions for detainees when compared with the situation in 2006, when most of the incidents are said to have occurred.

What was happening to the Canadian Forces in Afghanistan at that time? In the four years leading up to that point, we had been stationed in Kabul. During that period, we had lost eight soldiers, only three—three—to enemy action, less than one per year. Then we moved into Kandahar province and took on the reorganized and reinvigorated Taliban on their home turf. The intensity of the combat we faced was several orders of magnitude greater than anything we had experienced before then, and we started dying at the rate of two a *month*. On top of that, our infrastructure was still getting organized; things were chaotic. It would have been impossible to track each detainee we turned over to the Afghan security services. It is easy now, in the calm of an Ottawa parliamentary committee room, to criticize the CF for having failed to protect these individuals. None of the persons doing the criticizing, however, have offered much insight into how this oversight should have been implemented.

Finally, nowhere in the detainee debate is there any kind of comparison to what our enemies are doing. Hundreds of Afghan soldiers and policemen have been captured by the Taliban since the beginning of the war. Nearly all of these men were tortured to death within days, if not hours. I described finding the bodies of some of these unlucky men on two occasions in my first book. There is no "detainee issue" on the Taliban side because there are no detainees. This is an important distinction to make. Our Afghan allies are imperfect. Some of them can be brutal, even sadistic at times. But they are nowhere near as bad as those we are fighting.

This is a civil war. We cannot fight it without the Afghans, nor would we want to. What we must do is continue to fight it in as moral manner as possible and, in doing so, show the Afghans a different way of thinking.

Again, education (writ large) is the solution.

"The highest result of education is tolerance"—Helen Keller.

SEPTEMBER 1 | Chuck

Corporal Pierre-Luc Vallières turned twenty-three today.

His best friend in the combat team, Master Corporal Charles-Philippe "Chuck" Michaud, would have turned twenty-nine next March. I would have liked nothing better than to have talked to Chuck myself and to have told you his story, but that is not possible. He was wounded on June 23 and died of his wounds on July 4. So I will tell you

Corporal Pierre-Luc Vallières

the story of his friend instead. Through that, you will get a glimpse of our absent brother. We are known by the company we keep, and Chuck kept very good company.

Corporal Vallières and I got together in a bit of a roundabout way. It is inevitable that a writer who is chronicling the lives of a group of soldiers at war will focus on the leaders. I have tried not to fall into this trap, writing about our front-line troopers in the tanks, artillery, engineers and health services.

I realized, however, that I had not yet included a member of the branch closest to my heart. I asked Sergeant-Major Lapierre to choose a soldier he felt best represented the combat infantryman. He suggested someone to Lieutenant Makuch, and the lieutenant agreed. They both felt Corporal Vallières was one of the best soldiers in the combat team.

Corporal Vallières's relationship to the army was ambiguous at first. He joined the cadets and knew early on that he wanted to follow in the footsteps of his uncle, a career military man. But when he became eligible to sign up at age seventeen, he chose the intermediate step of joining the reserves so that he could remain in his family's construction business. His loyalty to his family also led him to turn down a chance to go Afghanistan with Roto 4.

It is axiomatic that the younger generation will be criticized by those who came before them. People in their forties and older always feel that people in their twenties are irresponsible, unwilling to work diligently and less good citizens than they were. Nonsense. The youth of today must be as honourable, hard-working and motivated as any generation that has gone before. That is the only way to explain the existence of people like Corporal Vallières.

When I asked this young man why his superiors held him in such high regard, he was not sure what to say. But when I prodded him a bit more, he answered, "Because I always say yes." You have no doubt heard the cliché about soldiers never volunteering for anything. Here you have one who always will.

Corporal Vallières's time in Afghanistan has given him the best times of his life. These have been due to the relationships he has had with the men in his section. Like all the best team players, he spontaneously expresses that he is exceedingly proud of these men: "Our sergeant (the section commander) is the best sergeant in the company, and our section is the best section in the combat team." He says this not with the arrogance of someone wanting to put others down, but with the sheer joy of someone who is very happy to belong to this group.

Chuck was not just a member of that group; he was at its centre. Corporal Vallières describes Chuck as being his best friend. But then he offers that "a lot of people felt the same way about Chuck. When you were with the big guy, he always made you feel great, like best friends do."

Chuck was the section second-in-command while Corporal Vallières was third-in-command. This was the first time Corporal Vallières had been in a leadership position, and he was a reservist, often seen by regular soldiers as being less competent or capable. It is not

Corporal Vallières on patrol in a Panjwayi village

uncommon in these situations for the senior regular soldier to keep a tight rein on the junior reservist.

The way Chuck treated Corporal Vallières reveals the kind of man he was. Rather than constantly looking over his shoulder, Chuck gave his young subordinate a lot of trust and independence. Corporal Vallières was given many tasks to complete independently, particularly with regard to navigation. He found this very rewarding.

But was he really all that independent? Corporal Vallières also had the impression that, whenever the situation became more than he could handle, Chuck would somehow magically appear at his side. He would then smoothly intervene in a way that recognized all the good decisions Corporal Vallières had made up to that point.

This was most apparent when the men were under fire. At those times, Chuck was as calm as he would have been in his own backyard. He would give orders or advice, depending on the circumstances, in a manner that demonstrated he was in complete control of himself and the situation. This was what defined Chuck: he took care of his people, in combat and back at the base. Corporal Vallières insisted that was what Chuck did better than anyone else.

But if Afghanistan has given Corporal Vallières the tremendous highs of leadership in combat, it has also given him devastating lows. Trained as a TCCC, Corporal Vallières was one of two soldiers who gave first aid when Chuck was hit last June. His friend had devastating injuries that were life-threatening, and Corporal Vallières, assisted by Private Pierre-Luc Rossignol (the other TCCC in their section), had to work quickly to stop him from bleeding to death. They soon received assistance from Corporal Sébastien Aziz-Beaulieu, a TCCC who is also the company's sharpshooter, and Master Seaman Charles Cloutier, the senior medic of the combat team (see addendum, August 23 entry).

And how did Chuck behave through all that? He was terribly wounded, but his frag vest had prevented the mine from tearing out his heart and killing him on the spot. His helmet had protected him from serious brain injury. He was fully conscious. And so Chuck acted as he had always acted: he looked after his men. He encouraged Corporal Vallières and Private Rossignol, telling them they were doing a great job. When he saw tears welling up in Corporal Vallières's eyes, he comforted him. Every moment that he was with them, right up until the helicopter came, he never stopped being Chuck.

It was a sad, sad day for Corporal Vallières. His friend and mentor would be permanently handicapped. Despite the fact that Major Jourdain and others praised him for helping to save Chuck's life, Corporal Vallières brooded about the future. How would Chuck adjust? How would his wife react? How would he earn his living? How would he pass the time?

But if Corporal Vallières felt sad on June 23, what he felt on July 4 was pure rage. When he learned that Chuck had died, nothing made sense anymore. For a month, he could not think of a single good reason for Canadians to be in Afghanistan.

Then one day, while the patrol was passing through a small Afghan village, he came upon a young child with a badly infected wound on his forehead. Opening up his TCCC kit, Corporal Vallières debrided and cleansed the wound and gave the child a proper bandage. Shortly afterwards, his unit secured another village, one that had not been visited by Coalition forces for some time. There they found a child whose broken leg had not been set properly because the Taliban had prevented the parents from seeking medical attention at the government hospital. As a result, what should have been a minor orthopedic problem, solved by a few weeks of casting, had become a lifelong handicap. The Taliban do this because, in their bizarre way of thinking, visiting the hospital expresses support for the government.

Corporal Vallières struggled for a few moments as he tried to express how the encounters with these children had made him feel. He finally summed them up by saying: "These kids did not ask to be born here." But, in their way, these kids asked for *him* to be here. And that was a call he was happy to answer, a call he felt he had to answer.

There it is again. The gift of aggression, combined with empathy. The way of the warrior. The way of Chuck.

Addendum—The Picture: One of the enduring regrets Corporal Vallières has of this tour is that he did not manage to take a single photograph of all the men in his section before Chuck was wounded. Looking through all the pictures the section has, there are only three that show their lost brother. In one of these his face is turned; in the other he sits in darkness. The only one that shows him well is the top photograph on the next page. Chuck is in the middle. Someone who kept everybody under his wing would not stand anywhere else.

Addendum—The Ghost: Within days of returning to Canada, Corporal Vallières will travel to Edmundston, New Brunswick, to visit Chuck's family. The tears will flow then, and the pain will take his breath away. Corporal Vallières will look around, still wishing that someone got it all wrong, a small part of him still convinced that Chuck will walk through the door, if only he waits for him just a second longer.

But Chuck won't be coming. Only Chuck's ghost will be there with him. Eventually, Corporal Vallières will make friends with the ghost, as he made friends with the man. The pain will come less often then.

The only good picture we have of Chuck in Afghanistan
Left to right: Warrant Officer Jean-François Bastien, Private François Larose, Private Steve Bernier, Private Pierre-Luc Rossignol, Chuck, an unidentified American visitor, Private Michael Brisson-Hovington, Corporal Pierre-Luc Vallières

Section 3-3 Charlie and their ghost
Standing, left to right: Private Guillaume Dubuc, Private Michael Brisson-Hovington, Private Mathieu Grégoire, Private Pierre-Luc Rossignol, Private Mathieu Rivard-Lemieux; Kneeling, left to right: Sergeant Jim Auger, Corporal Pierre-Luc Vallières

But it will never go away.

Addendum—Remembrance Day: Nearly every member of Third Platoon went to Edmundston on November 11 to pay tribute to Chuck, a gesture that was greatly appreciated by Chuck's family.

SEPTEMBER 2 | The Mobile Unit Light Logistics Element

In the August 29 entry, I briefly introduced the final member of the Combat Team Cobra leadership group, Captain Hugo Dallaire. As second-in-command, Captain Dallaire must be ready at any time to replace Major Jourdain. This happens for a predictable amount of time during the major's leave. But this is war; the unpleasant reality is that Captain Dallaire must be physically, intellectually and emotionally ready to step in as combat team commander for the remainder of the tour at a moment's notice.

After his seventeen years in the army, there is little doubt that he can do this. He entered military college at sixteen and went into the infantry after that. He served as a platoon commander for several years, and then was posted as an instructor to the Infantry School of the Combat Training Centre, CFB Gagetown.

After spending a couple of years teaching the next generation of infantry officers, Captain Dallaire was ready for a break. He had always wanted to live out west, so he took up a post in a recruitment centre in Vancouver. His existence there must have been as distinct from what he had lived at the Infantry School as it was possible to be while remaining in uniform. It was a good time . . . but it did not take long before he started looking for a way to get back into a front-line infantry battalion.

As Company Sergeant-Major Lapierre had done, Captain Dallaire tried unsuccessfully to come to Afghanistan with Roto 4. And as with the sergeant-major, the men of Roto 7 are fortunate he had to wait.

It has worked out for Captain Dallaire as well. He led the combat team for a full month during Major Jourdain's absence, conducting two major operations. Both of these operations were helicopter-borne

Captain Hugo Dallaire, combat team second-in-command

attacks. Helicopters are a pleasure to ride in, but they disgorge a combat team over a large battlefield in a matter of seconds. The problems of command and control are far more arduous than those encountered in a land operation.

As a warrior, Captain Dallaire has also benefited from the major's "everybody fights" policy. Captain Dallaire routinely goes on combat operations and has been in more than his fair share of firefights. Tragicomically, the bullets that have come closest to him (missing by a few centimetres) have been fired at him by confused ANA soldiers. This has left Captain Dallaire with a little less tolerance for the failings and foibles of our allies.

When he is not fighting, Captain Dallaire's job is an administrative one. Hearing him talk about the joys of these tasks is reminiscent of John Nance Garner, who, as vice-president under U.S. President Franklin D. Roosevelt, famously described the office he held as "not worth a bucket of warm piss."

For men of action like Captain Dallaire, administrative tasks are barely tolerable. One of these tasks, however, at least had the benefit of comic relief. This occurred when Captain Dallaire was put in charge of the Mobile Unit Light Logistics Element, or MULLE program. In an army filled with arcane acronyms, this one at least had the benefit of being wonderfully and accurately evocative.

There are few things more terrifying to a front-line soldier than to hear that somebody higher up has an "idea" that will improve things in their combat unit. The probability that the idea will involve extra work or increased danger for little or no benefit is over 99 per cent. The MULLE program would *not* prove to be an exception to the rule.

"Logistics" is another term for "supply": the provision of all the items needed by a unit in the field. The "mobile unit" in question was an infantry platoon of the combat team. Once dismounted from their LAVs, these men would revert to being "light infantry." Much of the fighting in Zhari-Panjwayi needs to be done in this mode: the under-developed and agricultural nature of the terrain makes it impossible to reach most areas by road.

Obliged to carry all their weapons, supplies and ammunition on their backs, foot-borne infantry can only cover a limited distance. This is particularly true in summer, when the men have to carry a phenomenal amount of water as well. If there was a way to lighten their loads, they could patrol further and pursue the insurgents more effectively.

What to do? Well, someone with a historical bent remembered that during the Afghan resistance against the Russian invasion, the CIA had provided the mujahedeen with several thousand Tennessee mules. These were used to ferry supplies over mountain passes from Pakistan into Afghanistan. Could the same thing not be done again?

Well, no. The CIA mules had been used along well-worn mountain trails that had existed since the time of Alexander the Great. The terrain in Zhari-Panjwayi could not be more different. Our patrols must negotiate horribly broken terrain, vine-choked grape fields and deep, narrow irrigation ditches. Whoever came up with this idea had never tried to patrol Zhari-Panjwayi on foot. At times the terrain can be impassable for even two-legged animals, much less four-legged ones.

But the *idea* had come down from on high, and it was up to Captain Dallaire to implement it.

In all his infantry training, nothing had prepared Captain Dallaire for the job at hand. In short order, he was required to learn about horseshoes, saddles and mule medicine, among other things. One of the company's NCOs, Sergeant Martin Germain, had experience with horses and took over much of the preparation and training of the animals. There was much to do, because six of the ten mules deployed to the FOB were so malnourished that they were not healthy enough to carry a load.

The only redeeming feature of having so many tasks added to his workload was that Captain Dallaire was able to send a message to KAF asking for an emergency resupply of mule food. The consternation this caused in the chain of command was almost worth the aggravation. Almost.

Being soldiers, the members of Combat Team Cobra gave it their best shot and took the mules out on two patrols. The mules had no trouble . . . until they got into broken terrain.

To describe what happened next, I quote from Major Jourdain's formal assessment: "Mules are well known for their stubbornness, and our experience with them proved that a mule that decided it would not move could not be moved."

It wasn't that they didn't try; Major Jourdain's report goes on to say: "The six infantrymen that were in charge of them tried all feasible means to move the animals."

I doubt that any other phrase composed in any other report written during this war conjures up a funnier image than that one.

On both patrols, the mules ended up as gifts to the nearest local farmer. You can imagine the scene: "Excuse me, sir, can I interest you in a used mule? We only need to unload the machine gun ammunition on his back and he is yours. Please note that this item is non-returnable."

Major Jourdain concluded his assessment by writing: "Mules are not a viable logistical option for Canadian soldiers operating in our present settings."

"You're fired!"

The MULLE Program. March 2009–June 2009. R.I.P.

Addendum, September 3: Scooped! Although I wrote this yesterday, I've been beaten to the publication punch. The story of the Panjwayi mules appeared in a Canadian Press story today, albeit with fewer colourful details.

SEPTEMBER 3 | First Day of School

This was Michelle's first day of school. Yet another milestone in her life that I will have missed. At times like this, I cannot help but ruminate on the cost my family is paying to prosecute this war.

I have done my best to minimize the impact of my absence on my daughter. With three exceptions, I have kept my promise to call Michelle every day. This was true even on those days she refused to speak to me. I would ask Claude or whoever was looking after Michelle to put the phone to her ear so that she could hear me say that I loved her. That seems to have helped. Since I always call at the same time of day, Michelle will either answer the call herself (when did she learn to do that?) or yell "Daddy!" when her mother picks up the phone.

The videos I had mentioned in the first entry have also been a big hit. These have been augmented by videos I have made here. She seems to like these best of all. Claude thinks that is because these videos give Michelle a sense of where I am and what I am doing. Michelle now knows the difference between Ma'Sum Ghar and Sperwan Ghar. And she knows Sperwan Ghar is my last stop before coming home.

Her language skills have skyrocketed during my absence, and she now describes her actions and emotions quite eloquently. Her development in this area has filled me with pride and happiness. This has only made the pain of not being able to be there to witness it even more heart-wrenching.

Her mathematical ability has also improved. When I left, counting from twelve to twenty was a bit of a haphazard affair. Now she rattles the numbers off with confidence. So much so that, when I told her yesterday that I would be home in "twenty days," she corrected me. "No, Daddy. It will be twenty-three days."

More pride, more pain.

SEPTEMBER 4 | Pit Bull

To get the full impact of this entry, it is essential that the reader not look ahead at the next photograph.

One of the real characters on my various medical teams has been Master Corporal Sylvain "Pops" Vilandré, the crew commander of one of the Bison ambulances at FOB Ma'Sum Ghar.

"Pops" would put himself through a punishing workout every day. Many of us cannot find the discipline to do that in the kind of heat we have been subjected to. I go running every morning, but I am barely on speaking terms with the weight room.

While we were together, Pops had come to me to put his affairs in order. If a soldier wishes, he or she can pre-select their pallbearers and also one special individual who will accompany the remains back to Canada. This is a job one gives to the closest friend one has in the theatre of operations. Given the importance of physical exercise in his life, "Pops" chose the person who had been his workout partner during pre-deployment training, a woman serving in the artillery.

Pops told me that this woman was one of the few people he had ever seen who pushed themselves as hard as he did. He had enormous respect for her, and she was one of his best friends. A few days ago, I bumped into her.

Twenty-one-year-old Bombardier Kina Lord is someone you can't help but like as soon as you meet her. Her thousand-megawatt smile is permanently turned on, making everyone around her happier. She has only been in the reserves for three years, although she was in the cadets for six years before that. She thinks she has found her niche in the artillery, to the point that she will likely join the regular force at the end of this tour. She enjoys pushing herself physically, and the army has given her the kind of challenging work she wanted.

While this tour is Bombardier Lord's first trip out of Canada, her return will not be her first trip *into* Canada. Like Michelle, she was adopted, in her case at age five, from Bulgaria. It is heartening to hear her speak perfect Québécois French. She has been a Canadian, in every sense of the word, for some time now.

I spoke to her sergeant, who confirmed what was blatantly obvious: Bombardier Lord is the hardest-working member of her unit. She has a job that requires her to get up earlier than anyone else, and she does this without objection. The only problem her sergeant has ever had with her has been to convince her to take it easy when she is hurt.

I have no trouble believing that. I was watching her gun crew fire some practice rounds into the desert two days ago. She had sprained her back and was banned from lifting the shells. When a call came from the command post for someone to help with a routine task, the sergeant assigned Bombardier Lord to the duty. She *sprinted* off to the post. The sergeant told her to take it easy, but it was pointless. She was gone.

Bombardier Kina Lord, 4' 11" ("and a half!")

Although she regularly helps carry the heavy artillery shells, her official job is to drive an armoured vehicle. The vehicle in question is a variant of the M113 armoured personnel carrier. I think we can all agree there is something sexy about a woman who can control twelve tonnes of weaponized heavy machinery.

Then Bombardier Lord steps out of her vehicle, and you can see how hard she has had to work to earn the respect she has gained in this masculine world of war. This kid has so much heart, it must take up all the space in her chest.

SEPTEMBER 5 | RIP Out (Relief in Place—Out)

I learned today that in another twelve days, I will be out of the FOB. A few days after that, I will be on my way to Third Location Decompression, the mandatory "cooling off" period for Canadian soldiers coming back from the war zone. And then I will be on a plane home. It is getting close enough to taste.

The same is true of everybody here. The first troopers to go home from this tour will leave ten days after me. A couple of factors are at play here. The first has to do with what the troops see when they look back at what they have already been through. The lion's share of their tour is over. Having survived so much danger already, the troops have "downregulated" (see the June 17 entry) their perception of risk. Getting shot at no longer gets much of a rise out of them, unless the fire is very close or accompanied by high-explosive projectiles. Machine gun fire within a kilometre of the FOB but aimed in another direction will barely elicit a comment; in the middle of a poker game, a couple of heads will turn towards the sound, and an eyebrow may be lifted. Life, as they have come to know it, goes on.

The demeanour of the troops is very different from what it was a few months ago. Much of the fear and uncertainty they felt at the beginning of the tour has been replaced by confidence. This is partly the self-assurance of the seasoned combat veteran, which is well earned. The rest is the feeling of immortality that is the birthright of the young. This feeling asserts itself even when confronted with undeniable evidence to the contrary, as has been the case here.

The members of the combat team have already come through more than four-fifths of the dangerous missions they will be asked to execute. To them, it seems reasonable to deduce that they will come through the remaining operations unscathed. Reasonable, but erroneous. The danger of dying on any particular day in Zhari-Panjwayi is always the same. Statistically speaking, the last day is as dangerous as the first.

Those of us who have been here before must convince the younger soldiers of this. This brings the second factor to the fore: what comes "after." For all the camaraderie and excitement of life here, very few soldiers are not eager to go home. For most, home means family, friends and familiar surroundings—all the things that give us pleasure, all the things that give our lives meaning. To paraphrase Yoda, we are all thinking much more about where we are going and much less about where we are.

This is a dangerous time. Sergeant-Major Lapierre is more aware of this than most. We had a meeting for the various section commanders last night at which he emphasized the need to remain vigilant. The threat level is unchanged; the enemy is still out there; this is not the time to let our guard down.

One way to keep soldiers focused on the present is to require the routines of military life to be performed in an exemplary fashion. The sergeant-major directed that all section commanders not allow "dress and deportment" to slip. This starts with the small things: shaving, haircuts and the cleanliness of quarters. It goes on with the not-so-small things: making sure our weapons are clean and our equipment is fully operational.

The sergeant-major had just the thing to kick-start the process. Time for some armoured-vehicle spring cleaning! LAVs are the "home away from home" of the troops when they leave the FOB. It takes a full day to thoroughly clean one out because there seems to be no limit to what can be stuffed into the various nooks and crannies of these conveyances.

This also prepares the vehicles for the transfer to the incoming roto. On a couple of occasions, Major Jourdain has emphasized to his troops that the FOB and its equipment was in tip-top shape when they took over. He has made it a point of pride for his soldiers to match or exceed this for their replacements.

Keep the troops happy. Keep the troops busy. Keep the troops focused.

Keep the troops alive.

SEPTEMBER 6, MORNING | The Way We Will Win This War . . .

A day of bitter disappointments.

It began with Captain Dallaire dropping by the UMS to ask me to inspect another detainee. While passing through a village early this morning, some of our patrollers thought they recognized one of the area's main Taliban commanders. He was in the company of three other men, so all four were brought to the FOB for questioning. Before the inquiry could start, I would have to examine them, as per our standard operating procedures. I began with the presumed "high value" detainee. To my dismay, none of the distinctive marks we had been told to look for to identify the Taliban commander were present.

I continued with my examinations, including that of one man who had lost his right leg. He walked using a crude prosthesis. When I asked him how he had been wounded he answered, as so many Afghans will: "It happened during the Russian time."*

I will always remember this man. He interacted with me in a friendly manner... until the time came to examine his skin for identifying scars. To fully appreciate what happened next, I need to give you a bit of back story.

The first time I had examined a detainee was during Roto 4, on my second day in the country. I was still getting the feel of the place, so I followed the lead of the military police. When it came time to inspect the skin, they had the patient undress completely. I had worked in jails when I was younger and had participated in a number of strip searches. This seemed no different. The man was a confirmed Taliban soldier, and the military police were being very cautious. As I performed my examination, the two officers watching the man had their hands on their holsters.

During that first tour, I learned how private Afghan men consider the genital area to be. Since returning, I have tried to accommodate this as much as possible. I explain to the detainees that my exam is for their protection, to document that they have no injuries at present.

---

* Although it does not lessen the tragic nature of what is going on today, it is worth remembering that the sum total of all the casualties caused by the war since the Coalition invaded in 2001 is only a small percentage of the number of Afghans who died in the same length of time during the Russian occupation: possibly as many as a *million people.*

When the time comes to examine the skin of the buttocks and genital area, I have the soldiers escorting me turn their backs. Then I tell the detainees to loosen the sash holding their baggy trousers on their waists. Rural Afghans never wear underwear, so I can then do a visual inspection of the buttocks and genitals without touching the detainee and without having them lower their trousers. They only have to hold the garment away from their body.

Until today, that had seemed to satisfy the detainees I had examined. But not this man. Standing on his good leg, he stated clearly although still respectfully that he would not let me look at his groin. He was in a room with three armed Canadian soldiers, and yet he insisted that his limits be respected. He said that he was not a Taliban and that although he could accept that we needed to arrest individuals who appeared suspicious, he felt there was "no reason you need to look at my ass."

I had not run into this situation before and wondered what the best course of action would be. My instinct as a physician was to respect the man's wishes, but there was the small matter of the war to consider. So I conferred with Captain Dallaire, who told me that I could dispense with that part of the exam. Perhaps if the first man I had examined had been our high-priority target, he would have felt differently. Since that had not been the case, I think Captain Dallaire made the right move. I therefore completed the exam with a pat-down.

In the end, we found no hard evidence of wrongdoing on the part of these men. Having disrupted their day, albeit for sound reasons, we would now do our best to make it up to them. They were given food and something to drink, then they were loaded into our LAVs and taken back to their village. One of our senior NCOs even gave them a case of fruit for the road.

One of our interpreters overheard the (now former) detainees as they spoke among themselves while they ate the meal we had provided. He said that they had much praise for our treatment of them. They understood why we had arrested them, and they recognized we had treated them fairly. This compares quite favourably with what these men have grown to expect from foreign invaders, including al Qaeda. This is why the Taliban leave behind their wounded soldiers for us to treat. I can only hope that, eventually, our way of thinking will win out. A world where the opposite is true is too awful to contemplate.

SEPTEMBER 6, AFTERNOON | ... and the Price We Have to Pay to Do So

I did not sleep well last night and so, after finishing my medical exam of the detainees, I had a nap. When I woke up, I went to the command post to find out what had happened to the detainees. It was then that I learned how these men had been treated after I had left. Although I was proud of the way we had behaved towards them, I was still very disappointed that we had failed to capture any Taliban leaders.

Far worse news was waiting for me back at the UMS. When I walked in, I saw my medic team huddled around our various communication devices. I did not have to ask what they were watching and listening to. Their grim faces made it clear: we had been hit again. One of our vehicles had struck an IED, and two Canadians were dead. But who were they?

In the June 5 entry, I described the communication network we now have at our disposal. Even out here on the FOB, we are able to maintain excellent "situational awareness" of the combat activity in our area of operations. Although there is a great deal of secrecy surrounding the identity of our dead, we can now seek other clues. It was the search for these clues that was going on when I walked in. As sad as my medics were that Canadians had been killed, they were desperately hoping that their close friends were still alive.

The radio call sign of the unit that had been hit narrowed down the list of medics who could have accompanied them to only two, both good buddies of the crew here. The possibility that one of them might be dead was very upsetting to my people.

We scrutinized the quality and detail of the medical reports coming from the stricken convoy. Most of it was a routine recitation of vital signs and injury descriptions. And then we saw it: the description of a particular therapeutic manoeuvre that only a medic would have done. We focused on that line of disembodied text, telling ourselves it was inconceivable that someone who was not medically trained would have attempted such a manoeuvre. This had to mean our friend was alive.

A few hours later, our suspicions were confirmed. Both of the dead were engineers. How that group has suffered on this tour! I wrote an e-mail to Warrant Officer Comeau to express my condolences . . . again.

In the pantheon of pain, these deaths seem somehow worse because of their timing. For the past week, we have been busy on the administrative side with the preparations for the RIP Out. People have been closely studying the flight manifests to see when they are going from the FOB to KAF, from KAF to decompression and, best of all, from decompression to home. The end of the tour is in sight.

Every Canadian roto to have fought in Kandahar province has lost between ten and twenty soldiers. Until today, we were at the lowest end of that spectrum. I do not know what the other troops may have been thinking, but for the past several days I have been acutely aware that we have gone a month without a death. And this has been during the "fighting season," the time of year when good weather and drug money from the recent opium harvest give the Taliban mobility and weapons. I had allowed myself to hope that this roto might set a new record for least number of deaths.

Addendum, suppertime: It is in the nature of combat soldiers to hope. Hope for victory. Hope for home. Hope for tomorrow. Maybe only hope for tonight. And so we mourn our dead and go on with our lives.

Captain Vince Lussier turned twenty-seven today. We had a party for him at suppertime, which began with his platoon ambushing him with water-filled condoms.*

---

* Which we keep on the FOB to issue to young soldiers of both genders before they go on HLTA. What did you think?

Happy Birthday, Vince!

Then the war went on. As we were cutting the captain's cake, small-arms fire broke out east of the FOB. The machine guns on the hilltop returned fire, and we all rushed to our defensive positions. And our lives went on.

SEPTEMBER 7 | Ramp Ceremony

We held the ramp ceremony for Major Yannick Pépin and Corporal Jean-François Drouin today. This is something the CF does particularly well.

First, these are well-attended affairs. Two-thirds of the 2,800 Canadians serving in Afghanistan at any one time are based at KAF. Almost all of them, nearly two thousand men and women, will be at the ceremony. They will be joined by a similar number of soldiers from other Coalition nations.

But what about the warriors? The ones who go "outside the wire" to do the fighting and the dying? We cannot all leave the combat area on these occasions, but for those closest to the fallen, the CF spares no expense to have them participate. These emotional rituals are an important part of the grieving process, so our helicopter squadron was assigned the task of bringing all the engineers from the various FOBs back to KAF. Despite only having one Chinook available, it took the time to fly to all three FOBs and picked up everybody who wanted to go. Major Arsenault at FOB Wilson was the last one to board. There were over fifty people crammed into the chopper, the most he had ever seen in one bird. He ended up sitting on the ramp next to the gunner! This effort on the part of the Canadian aviators—born of a camaraderie forged in combat—was greatly appreciated by the troops.

Although majors are the highest-ranking officers to lead their troops into combat, there are only seven majors in the task force to whom this applies: the three combat team commanders, the tank squadron commander, the commander of the artillery, the commander of the armoured reconnaissance squadron and the commander of the engineers.

Major Pépin, the engineer commander, was a combat leader. His troops were spread throughout our area of operations, supporting the infantry with their specialized skills. A lesser man might have stayed at KAF getting "sitreps" (situation reports) and sending orders by radio. It would have been a lot safer, but it would have sent a terrible message.

Instead, Major Pépin travelled extensively throughout the combat area. He personally checked on his soldiers, assessing their morale and making sure they had everything they needed to accomplish their tasks. His constant movements gave him an intimate knowledge of the war zone and made it possible for him to advise the battle group commander on the best way to use our engineering resources. It made him a very effective officer, but it exposed him to awful risks.

If it had been desirable, even necessary, for the engineers in the task force to be present at the ramp ceremony, it was all the more so for Major Pépin's peer group. As many as possible of the six surviving

The majors bid farewell to one of their own

"combat" majors were brought to KAF to act as pallbearers. In the above photograph you will recognize the first man, Major Jourdain, the commander here at Sperwan Ghar; Major Tim Arsenault, the commander at FOB Wilson, is third.

These men had trained together for nearly two years as they moulded the battle group into an efficient fighting force. It must have been almost unbearably painful to carry their friend's body into the waiting Hercules aircraft.

Addendum, September 8: The remembrance process continued the following day at FOB Sperwan Ghar. The Canadian flag and that of the Van Doos will be flown at half-mast till our fallen are buried. This evening, after Major Jourdain returned, we gathered to observe a moment of silence in the memory of our fallen comrades. These moments are important to us. We have lost brothers. We will honour them as we always have, by respecting John McCrae's admonition, from his poem "In Flanders Fields":

Take up our quarrel with the foe:
To you from failing hands we throw
The torch; be yours to hold it high.
If ye break faith with us who die
We shall not sleep . . .

We will keep faith with those who die.

SEPTEMBER 8 | A Moral War

The men we arrested, questioned and released two days ago knew what they were talking about. Anybody who doubts that needed only to witness what has happened here over the past twenty-four hours.

We picked up another suspicious character yesterday. One of our patrols had "probable cause" and tested his hands for explosives. The test was positive, indicating he had recently handled a bomb of some kind. I again performed the detainee medical exam.

Almost everything about this guy was wrong. He claimed to be the mullah of a nearby village. In this culture, elders are revered merely because they are old. All the mullahs any of us had ever seen were at least middle-aged. Their beards were all white or at least shot through with grey. This man's beard was black.

This was so incongruous that, although it is not required on the detainee medical examination form, I asked him his age. He replied that he was thirty-one. Had he been Canadian, that would have been believable. He looked like a young man in our own society: healthy, vigorous and with the sheen of youth barely faded. But we are not in Canada, we are in the Panjwayi. Life here is almost indescribably hard, so hard it uses people up and ages them long before their time. When estimating the ages of adults who have worked as farmers in this area all their lives, it is wise to subtract a decade or sometimes even two. If this guy was a thirty-one-year-old Panjwayi farmer, he should have looked like a forty- or even fifty-year-old Canadian.

Other aspects of his physical exam were incongruous. His hands were soft and free of calluses. His feet were equally supple, with none of the hard corn at the heels that the inhabitants of this area all have. He also had perfect teeth, something I had never seen in the mouth of any adult resident of the district.

I doubt this individual has spent a single day in the fields around our FOB. It is far more likely that he has spent most of his life, at least since adolescence, in a well-funded *madrassa* (Islamic religious school) in Pakistan.

When Captain Dallaire reported the results of his questioning to Major Jourdain, the commander decided to send the detainee onward to KAF for a more in-depth investigation. This does not guarantee that this man will be held. On the contrary, many of the individuals we have detained after finding explosive residue on their hands have been released from KAF within a few days. This can be frustrating for the troops in the field, but we follow demanding rules of evidence before depriving someone of their liberty.

It took a full day to organize the evacuation of the detainee. This had to be done by helicopter with a military police escort, resources that cannot always be rustled up at the drop of a hat. During those twenty-four hours, we gave him food and accommodations equal to our own. We respected his beliefs, providing him with meals at times that did not conflict with the Ramadan fast. Captain Dallaire even interrupted his questioning to allow the man to pray. In this war, where the best a captured Coalition soldier can hope for is to be beheaded quickly, we did not mistreat our detainee in any way.

What most impressed me occurred right before he was to be picked up from the FOB. He had been brought to the helipad and placed under the supervision of a couple of junior soldiers. When the helicopter was delayed, they thought to move him out of the sun and into the shade. These two young Canadians, who less than twenty-four hours ago had watched two of their comrades go home for the last time, spontaneously acted to make the detainee more comfortable.

The same respect for the law and for human rights permeates everything that we do in Afghanistan. For instance, there is a family compound not far from here that is routinely used as a staging point for the Taliban to plant their IEDs. The compound prevents our observers on the hilltop from seeing this area. The Taliban know this and use it to their advantage. It has long been Major Jourdain's desire to flatten this compound, and he has any number of ways to make it happen. In most armies, that desire is all it would take. The compound would be destroyed within minutes, possibly without even warning the inhabitants.

Here in the Canadian area of operations, we clear this kind of demolition with two different levels of legal advisers. Any inhabitants, even if they are no more than squatters, are compensated and cared for. The roof over their heads may be minimal, but it is all they have. We will not destroy it until we are sure that they have at least an equal dwelling to move into.

Canadians have a tremendous amount of pride in the reputation our armed forces have garnered around the world as peacekeepers. Our citizens can feel the same pride about the way we have waged war.

SEPTEMBER 9 | Myna Man

During my visit to the ANA mullah, I had noticed two myna birds running around the room. I knew that Afghans like to tame these birds, but it was incongruous to see two of them in an army barracks. I have met the owner of the mynas several times over the past month.

Abdul Jalala is a twenty-six-year-old Tajik who has been in the ANA for seven years now. He signed a three-year contract and then extended it for a further five years.

Abdul has liked birds since he was a child. He describes the taming process with a fondness for his creatures that is almost parental. It begins when the bird is a hatchling. Abdul will feed it tiny scraps of food by hand and give it water from a dropper. After several weeks

Abdul Jalala, myna man

of this, the bird bonds to him and recognizes him as its parent. It is something to see the tiny creatures run after him in his barracks and even outside.

It is even more fascinating to watch Abdul interact with his birds. He is gentle, affectionate and playful. It is obvious that he loves them. This does not make him unusual. He has no trouble finding other soldiers to look after his birds when he is out on operations.

Sometime after this photograph was taken, I returned to find that Abdul now had only one myna. I was afraid to ask what had happened. I did not want to bring back unpleasant memories if the answer involved one of the stray cats we occasionally see around the base. Curiosity got the better of me, though, and I am glad it did. Abdul told me he had sent the second myna to his kid brother in northern Afghanistan.

Afghans often seem so foreign to Canadians. Here we have a young man, surrounded by the ugliness of war, who has tried to bring a bit of beauty and gentleness into his life. Yet he gladly surrendered half of that beauty to cheer up a younger sibling. Sounds Canadian to me.

The chief of the defence staff, General Walter Natynczyk, came back to town today. This time he came with more than his usual military entourage. Over the years, a steady stream of entertainers, professional athletes and other personalities have come to Afghanistan to provide a welcome diversion for our soldiers. Each group is labelled "Team Canada" for the time they are with us. When one of them arrives in Kandahar, the Canadian contingent at KAF will gather together and be treated to a show. This is a tangible way for these famous Canadians to support us.

Most of them do not go to a FOB, because of the danger. I also imagine the CF subtly discourages such visits because getting non-military individuals into the combat zone creates a number of logistical headaches. The transportation people at KAF are already working around the clock to keep the various combat units supplied; allocating resources to something that does not directly support the mission must strike them as a bad use of their assets.

Then there are the cold hard mathematics of the situation. KAF is home to nearly two thousand Canadians. At a FOB, there is a tenth of that number. In the military, we are nothing if not utilitarian: the greatest good for the greatest number. Even though our lives here are far more arduous and dangerous than the lives of those at KAF, it makes sense (on one level) to divert the "morale boosters" to the main base and away from the FOBs.

Logical it may be, but that does not make us feel any better when we see the parade of visitors and dignitaries who stay "inside the wire" and pass us by. This has been the object of some complaints by the combat troops in the past. General Natynczyk heard those complaints the last time he was here and told the troops he would correct that.

To his displeasure, when he arrived in the theatre of operations this time, he found that FOBs had again been left off the itinerary. But when the general makes a promise, he keeps it. This involved much running around at KAF, but the schedule was altered to include us. The guy does have some pull, after all . . .

Bruce Cockburn's music takes me back to an earlier war

And so it was that, early this afternoon, one of our Chinook helicopters arrived and disgorged a star-studded lineup of musicians, athletes and media personalities. Among them were Pat Côté, a former member of the Van Doos and now an international-level mixed-martial artist, and Montreal Canadiens hockey legend Guy Lafleur. The troopers were pleased with the overall lineup, but they went wild over these two guys.

There was also a man who seemed to have been chosen specifically to raise my spirits. The music of Bruce Cockburn became important for me when I was in my twenties and remains so to this day. I have always been active in social justice movements, and many of Mr. Cockburn's songs were anthems for the various struggles in which I have been involved. He travelled extensively in Central America around the same time that I participated in the Nicaraguan Contra War, and many of his songs dealt with the conflicts then occurring in that area of the world. He sang of the dispossessed, dying like ants under the heel of the elephant. Hearing him sing ten feet from me, the first time I had heard him live, brought back all those memories. It was a very powerful moment.

I had the chance to talk to him in the few minutes after his performance and before he boarded the chopper back to KAF. In that short time, he gave me an excellent explanation for a conundrum in the Canadian political scene that had long confused me: why the left wing of Canadian politics harbours so much opposition to our mission here. This is the part of the political spectrum with which I have almost invariably allied myself. I have a lot of trouble understanding why its members disagree with me now.

When the Taliban were in power, feminists across the country and around the world were vociferous in denunciating that regime. They were quite right to do so. Life-saving surgery was denied to women on the grounds that it would be better for them to die than to be seen by a male physician. Women who had been going to work in skirts were now being told to stay at home and never leave unless covered in full burka and escorted by a male relative. Transgressors were beaten and occasionally killed. Even women who were the sole breadwinners for their family—a common occurrence in a country with so many war widows—were forbidden to leave their dwellings.

Since the beginning of the mission, however, Canadian feminists have been either notably silent or noisily opposed. Earlier this year Judy Rebick, former president of the National Action Committee on the Status of Women, stated: "How has the war helped women in Afghanistan? It hasn't."* Considering that the number of girls being educated in Afghanistan has gone from 12,000 under the Taliban to 1.2 *million* in 2007 and that two women ran for the presidency last month, this statement is breathtaking in its ignorance.

And what about the rest of the left? The people with whom I have stood "on the barricades" are almost uniformly opposed to our intervention in this country. How is that possible? The same ideological

---

* Quoted by Sandra Martin in "Plight of Afghan Women Prompts Fresh Debate," *The Globe and Mail*, April 17, 2009, http://v1.theglobeandmail.com/servlet/story/ RTGAM.20090417.wafghan-martin17/BNStory/International/home.

Bruce Cockburn finally gets his rocket launcher

motivations that led me to support the Sandinista regime in Nicaragua brought me to the Panjwayi.

Mr. Cockburn chose to sing "If I Had a Rocket Launcher," a song he wrote after his first trip to Guatemala. This took place in 1984, when the dictatorship of General Efrain Rios Montt was waging a genocidal war against the indigenous people of that country.* Mr. Cockburn had visited a refugee camp across the border in Mexico that had been attacked twice in one day by helicopter gunships of the Guatemalan Army.

The song, particularly the last line—"If I had a rocket launcher . . . Some son of a bitch would die"—generated a fair bit of controversy.

---

* Although the civil wars in Nicaragua and El Salvador garnered more international attention, Guatemala's was the bloodiest. The best estimates are that 200,000 people, most of them indigenous Mayans, were killed by the army and government-supported death squads.

Left-wingers, for all that they talk about "revolutionary change," were uncomfortable that one of their favourite bards would sing so openly about killing. Some radio stations even took to playing it with the last line faded out, so as not to offend delicate Canadian sensibilities. It did not offend me. I have never had any problem with the concept of killing for a moral purpose. And I could not have agreed more with Mr. Cockburn. There were many people in Central America around that time who needed killing.

I recognized the song as soon as he began strumming the first few bars, and I immediately felt uncomfortable. This time, the side I am on has the helicopters. Was Bruce Cockburn here to express support for the troops but opposition to the mission?

Mr. Cockburn began by admitting that he had been somewhat anxious the first time he sang the song at KAF. From his stage, he could see numerous helicopters. But the crowd went wild, perhaps sensing what he wanted to get across, and what he said to me today: "The Taliban are identical to those dictatorships we fought against back then."

I was both relieved and perplexed that he felt the same way I did.

Relieved, because I have enormous respect for the man. It would have been disconcerting to be on the other side of the debate from him. I am not shielded by the fanaticism of our enemies. When people I admire oppose the mission, I listen to them. They often make valid points. And I worry that they might be right.

Perplexed, because he is an icon of the left-wing politics that I identify with and that has so thoroughly rejected my opinions about this mission. I asked him why he thought our usual political home was so at odds with our current position.

His answer made a lot of sense. This time, the balance of power is the opposite of what it was in those Central American conflicts that united us a generation ago: "our side" has all the heavy weapons. The Taliban are the underdog. Mr. Cockburn opined that support for the underdog is such an ingrained habit for the left that its supporters cannot look beyond that.

Corporal Pascal Girard, combat medic (centre), receives CDS coin from General Walter Natynczyk (left) and Canadian Forces Chief Warrant Officer Greg Lacroix, the most senior NCO in the CF (right)

Mr. Cockburn has at least part of the answer there. Much of the opposition to the war in Canada seems to be driven by an almost reflexive anti-Americanism. This prevents people from judging whether the enemies we face here have gone so far into immorality that it has become moral to wage war to stop them. If that is the case, and I believe it is, then we should accept help from almost anyone to achieve victory. We can disagree with our allies while we fight this war, and go our separate ways once the war is won. But we have to stick together until the job is finished here.

Before General Natynczyk took Mr. Cockburn and the other stars home, he awarded one of his coins (see the June 18 entry) to yet another combat medic. In the August 31 entry I related one of the things Corporal Pascal Girard did to deserve this. He did many more.

As warfare has evolved, the concept of "declaration of war" has become almost an anachronism. Was 9/11 al Qaeda's declaration of war? Hardly. Their operatives had struck at Western targets numerous times before that.

348

The attacks I found most abhorrent were the 1998 bombing of the U.S. embassies in Nairobi and Dar es Salaam, the capitals of Kenya and Tanzania respectively. These embassies were well protected against suicide bombers, but you can always build a bigger bomb. It is estimated that the trucks used in the attacks each contained something in the neighbourhood of ten *tonnes* of high explosive. Even though the bombs detonated far from the embassies, a dozen Americans were killed.

But these buildings were in the middle of congested cities! Hundreds of innocent Africans were murdered, and thousands were maimed. I was enraged. Even if you accept the sick al Qaeda notion that American civilians are legitimate targets, how were these fanatics able to justify this atrocity, even to their own followers? But they did. Killing and crippling thousands of the poorest, most vulnerable people on earth was an acceptable means to their ends. Even the fact that a third of the population of Tanzania is Muslim did not give them pause.

On 9/11, al Qaeda brought this war to our homes. I am using the word "homes" in a dual sense. Twenty-five Canadians died on that terrible day, in the second-worst terrorist attack ever suffered by Canadian citizens.[*] As bad as that was, it is in the metaphorical sense of the word that the attack had the most impact. Al Qaeda's assault was not only against our people but also against our society's core values. On

---

[*] The worst was the bombing of Air India Flight 182 on June 23, 1985, where 280 of the 329 people killed were Canadian citizens. It is dismaying that many Canadians do not consider this a uniquely Canadian tragedy because these victims were "hyphenated Canadians" of Indian descent. For a moving portrayal of the bombing as a Canadian tragedy, see Anita Rau Badami's novel *Can You Hear the Nightbird Call?* (Toronto: Knopf Canada, 2006).

every issue that Canadians identify as important—human rights, rule of law, gender equality, education, democracy and many others—al Qaeda and the Taliban extremists stand diametrically opposed to us. It is essential that we fight these people, and having gotten into the fight, we have to be in it to win.

The comments made by Robert Fowler two days ago stand in contrast to this. He is the Canadian diplomat kidnapped by al Qaeda in Niger in December 2008. Fowler and his assistant, Louis Guay, were held for 130 days. They were released on April 21, 2009.

In his first interview after his return, Mr. Fowler questioned the wisdom of the Afghan mission.* When I saw the headline announcing that, I was nonplussed. When I read the article, however, I found that I agreed with Mr. Fowler on every one of his observations. He referred to the Afghan mission as a "noble objective" to which he "cannot object." He goes on to describe the mission as "complex, challenging." This echoes, almost verbatim, statements I have made.

Where we differ is in the conclusions he draws from his evaluation of the mission's challenges. Mr. Fowler states, "I just don't think in the West that we are prepared to invest the blood or the treasure to get this done" and that "it strikes me as rather extreme that one goes out and looks for particularly complex misery to fix." He then goes on to argue, "There's lots of things to fix that can be done more efficiently and probably more effectively." This summarizes many of the objections to the Afghan mission eloquently and with an admirable economy of words. But strong counter-arguments can be made.

1. *There are "lots of other things to fix."*
True, but irrelevant. There will always be "things to fix." If we were to have a national debate over which country was "most deserving" of our intervention, it would paralyze our body politic ad infinitum.

---

* Robert Fowler, interviewed by Peter Mansbridge, CBC.ca, September 9, 2009, www. cbc.ca/world/story/2009/09/09/f-robert-fowler-transcript2.html.

2. It is *"extreme that one goes out and looks for particularly complex misery to fix."*
Yes, it is. Afghanistan is among the countries where human suffering is at its worst. One can see that as a reason to avoid the mission or a reason to undertake it.

3. *The West is not "prepared to invest the blood or the treasure to get this done."*
Many people agree with this statement. Since it is a statement of political reality rather than personal belief, I hope it is not true. But let us assume that it is. Taken together with the other two objections, the argument Mr. Fowler makes against our mission in Afghanistan can be summarized as: "It is the right thing to do, but it is too expensive."

Let's put that statement in context. We have been in Afghanistan rather longer than we were involved in World War Two (eight years versus six years). When that conflict began in 1939, the Canadian population was 11,267,000. In 2009, that number had tripled to 33,763,000. To get a sense of how much we sacrificed to defeat the Nazis, therefore, you have to multiply our losses in that war by three.

In World War Two, Canada suffered 46,250 battle deaths. That would be the equivalent of 138,750 deaths in our country today. To date, we have lost 129 soldiers in Afghanistan. That is less than one-tenth of 1 per cent of what we lost fighting the Nazis.

As soon as we defeated the Nazis, it was necessary to confront communism. We got into one hot war (Korea) and one Cold War. The former cost us 516 lives. The latter cost us hundreds of billions of dollars. Our participation in the Korean conflict helped keep one of the most bizarre totalitarian regimes ever seen out of South Korea. Our contribution to NATO helped bankrupt the Soviet Union and dump communism into "the ash heap of history" (Karl Marx's reference to capitalism's "inevitable" demise).

Yes, the Taliban are resilient and tough. Yes, Afghanistan is so backwards and desperately poor that progress here will be agonizingly slow. But we have been in fights this tough, and a whole lot tougher, before. We stayed in those fights till we won. We had to then; we have to now.

Further on in the interview, Robert Fowler seems to struggle to express himself. He is quoted as stating that "to get it done, we will have to do some unpleasant things. I mean some deeply hard, this isn't, this is not a nice war."

Having been interviewed live on television myself, I am well aware that even the smoothest speaker will stumble at times and come out with clunkers like this. But Mr. Fowler has correctly identified and plainly spoken some key truths. There is no such thing as a "nice war." To win, we will have to do hard, unpleasant things. I think it is essential that we not shy from this. On the contrary, our government should use language that is unequivocal. I offer a hypothetical example of this here:

The Prime Minister: I rise to address the House about the situation in Afghanistan. Al Qaeda and the Taliban extremists are killing children who want to go to school. There is no excuse, no matter what their religious beliefs are, for such behaviour. People who do such things lie outside of what can be tolerated on this planet.

Beyond that, our enemies subscribe to a world view that is in complete opposition to our own. They have attacked us, and they will continue to attack us. We are as abhorrent to them as they are to us. Our only choices are to fight them now in Afghanistan or elsewhere later.

We have therefore decided to send the hard men and women of the CF to stop them. We will fight in a moral manner. We will not use lethal force unless we are sure that we are engaging an enemy target. Captured enemy soldiers will be treated humanely. We will give our enemies the opportunity to lay down their weapons and participate peacefully in the political process.

But our enemies must never mistake our humanity and our morality for weakness. Those who continue fighting must know that we will hunt them down using every technological means at our disposal. When we find them, we will kill them as quickly and as efficiently as we can. We will do so reluctantly, because we did not want it to come to this. But we will do so without remorse. We are in this war to win.

This morning, I woke up at a FOB for the one-hundredth day in a row.

When I started writing this book, I set myself a goal: to tell a different story about the lives of Canadian and Afghan soldiers every day. These are extraordinary people, doing extraordinary things. They all deserve to be chronicled. But even with this many entries, many other medical and military events occurred that I wish I had had the time and energy to document. Let me mention two of them.

Petty Officer Martin "Bed" Bedard and the FOB Ma'Sum Ghar team have been particularly busy of late. They have had a number of mass casualty incidents, the worst one two days ago. A suicide bomber struck the police station in Bazaar-e-Panjwayi (the village right beside FOB Ma'Sum Ghar). This is the building beside the Panjwayi Comprehensive Health Centre.

The Taliban soldier really was a "suicide" bomber, as he did not manage to kill anyone other than himself. That his victims all survived, however, is largely due to the efforts of the FOB Ma'Sum Ghar UMS gang. Nine critically wounded patients—four policemen and five civilians—were brought to the FOB all at once. In terms of medical intensity, this is the most serious mass casualty event of the tour. Bed had to intubate three of the victims within minutes. One of them was a child. This is a particularly delicate manoeuvre, and Bed pulled it off like a pro. His performance during these events was so outstanding that he was awarded a CDS coin on the spot by General Natynczyk, who happened to be visiting with Team Canada.

Red Ricard did an exceptional job as well. With so many casualties, they had to call more choppers than they had air evacuation medics to crew. With ten seconds' notice, Red got his travelling medical gear together and jumped on the last chopper to escort the final batch of wounded back to KAF. The FOB medical team performed so well that they had all the patients stabilized and evacuated in forty-four minutes, an awesome performance.

The combat team here has continued to execute its tasks superlatively as well. Yesterday, Captain Vince Lussier took his platoon out before dawn. By the time they came back for a late breakfast, he and his men had once again asserted our military dominance of the area.

One Talib had been foolish enough to engage Captain Lussier's light armoured vehicle with an RPG. The shooter had been so inept that Captain Lussier was not sure who the man had been firing at. Not that it mattered. Although he was dressed in civilian clothing, the Talib had clearly identified himself as a combatant. He was cut in half by the LAV's 25 mm gun.

Another Talib had been merely incompetent. He had been detected by one of our troopers while setting our forces up for an ambush. A single bullet from the soldier's rifle ended his life. One shot, one kill.

Yet another armed insurgent died because of bad luck. He was detected in an open field. Though still out of range of our personal weapons when he was spotted, he was not beyond the range of our artillery. Captain Lussier radioed his position back to the guns and, within a few minutes, the enemy soldier was torn apart by a storm of high explosive and shrapnel. Then Captain Lussier did what he has done every other time he has taken his men out to fight the Taliban. He brought them all home safely.

None of this will ever make the news back home.

Addendum, midnight: I have to jot down a few things before I go to bed.

First, we had a late-night medevac for an ANA soldier who had suffered a minor gunshot wound. The medical care was routine. All I did was give a bit of guidance to Master Seaman Cloutier; then I let him run the show. Corporal Vallières came by to help out, and I was pleased to see that MS Cloutier let him do various procedures.

"Procedures" are the things we do to patients, such as starting IV lines, packing wounds and putting different kinds of tubes into various body parts. It is emotionally satisfying to do these procedures because you can immediately see the benefits of your actions. Being the kind of leader he is, MS Cloutier saw the case as an opportunity to share knowledge and skills rather than as a chance to "put cold steel into warm bodies" himself. Within minutes, my crew had the patient stabilized. A little while later, the chopper arrived to take him away. Night vision equipment has made life-saving helicopter evacuation available to us 24/7.

I was also happy that my crew was able to handle this case with minimal supervision because of something else that was going on tonight. I was on my way, for the first time, to winning the evening's poker game. I came back to the UMS, flashing my cash (all of thirty dollars) and telling my people that the honour of the medical section had been restored.

Only that was not true. Major Jourdain had decided to take the night off. Winning the game without him present is like coming first in the hundred-metre dash at the Olympics with Usain Bolt watching from the sidelines.

SEPTEMBER 13 | Unlucky 13

The war in Afghanistan began for Canada in the late fall of 2001. Members of our special operations forces, Joint Task Force-2, were on the ground before the snow fell. Over the next four years, our casualties were light, Then we came to Kandahar. Over the past three years, we have lost more than 120 soldiers here.

To the best of my knowledge, only one infantry company has come through a Kandahar tour without a fatality: the unit commanded by Major Cayle Oberworth and based at FOB Sperwan Ghar during the previous roto. Until today, it looked like one of the companies on this roto might be able to match that. I had served with Bravo Company at FOB Wilson, and Charlie Company here at FOB Sperwan Ghar, but not with Alpha Company.

Alpha Company has been a bit of a vagrant. Lieutenant Colonel Paul, the battle group commander, has given them a number of different tasks. The only one of these tasks that you may have heard of has been the establishment of the "model village" of Deh-e-Bagh (pronounced "Dee-bah"). It has been so successful that it motivated our commanders to implement the change in our tactics that I described in the August 18 entry.

Their other tasks took them hither and yon throughout our area of operations. They did not have a FOB of their own, but rather wandered around the battlefield looking for a job to do or a fight to pick. This obliged them to travel constantly on the roads of Zhari-Panjwayi, which means that the work they do is extremely dangerous. Alpha Company's luck ran out today. One of their vehicles was caught by our eternal nemesis, the IED. The driver, Private Patrick Lormand, was killed.

This would have been bad enough, but as we were preparing to send our comrade home for the last time, we got word that columnist Margaret Wente had written that "our soldiers don't get out much. They no longer chase the Taliban. Mostly, they're trapped behind the wire at the base in Kandahar, where IEDs won't get them."[*] I cannot begin to imagine how that must have made the family of Private Lormand feel, not to mention the families of Major Pépin and Corporal Drouin, who were killed one week ago in the same manner.

This is lazy journalism at its worst. For Ms. Wente to make a statement like this, it would be necessary for her to have ignored all the news coming out of Afghanistan for the past several months. Telling her readers that we are safe from IEDs and are no longer pursuing the enemy is an astounding error. It boggles the mind that a member of the fifth estate could be so out of touch with reality.

If there is one thing the media does a good job of reporting, it is our deaths.[†] Of the thirteen soldiers we have lost on this rotation, all

---

[*] Margaret Wente, "The Tragedy of Good Intentions," *The Globe and Mail*, September 16, 2009, www.theglobeandmail.com/news/opinions/the-tragedy-of-good-intentions/article1290304/.

[†] From our point of view on the FOBs, they do a poor job of reporting everything else. Major Arsenault and the "Bastards" at FOB Wilson were not visited by a reporter until August, when their tour was two-thirds over.

but two of them have been killed by IEDs. This death rate of approximately two per month is what we have suffered on every rotation since arriving in Kandahar province in 2006. So much for IEDs not "getting" us anymore. As for our offensive operations, this diary has reported on almost daily combat and patrolling activity. Tell me, Ms. Wente, how does that square with your statement that we "no longer chase the Taliban"?

For some reason the CF will not forcefully respond to this distortion. If asked, the CDS will disagree. But there will be no attempt on the part of the Public Affairs people to contact reporters with facts to disprove what Ms. Wente has written. Instead, the CF will take it on the chin and soldier on. I suppose that to do otherwise might be seen as interfering in some way with the political process back home.

As I am speaking only for myself, I am under no such constraints. Ms. Wente, you were way out of line. You owe every member of Task Force Afghanistan an apology.

SEPTEMBER 14, MORNING | Emergency Ultrasound at the FOB

Those who know me professionally are aware of the role that emergency ultrasound has played in my career. When I first launched the EDE (Emergency Department Echo) course in Canada a decade ago, there was already overwhelming proof that this technique benefited patients. But the evidence mattered little: EDE was an incursion into "turf" that radiologists have always considered their preserve. The political battles I have waged to overcome this resistance are legendary in Canadian emergency medicine circles.

Much of the opposition has centred on the ability of emergency physicians to use ultrasound to detect serious injuries. The fear is that essential care will be delayed and the patient will deteriorate, perhaps fatally, if these injuries are missed.* Many emergency physicians

---

* To my knowledge, this has never happened in the decade we have been using ultrasound in emergency medicine in Canada. The organization formed to supervise the

also focus on the "positive" scan—one that shows the presence of an injury, especially an unsuspected one—when they begin to explore the use of this modality. The times this happens are marked indelibly in the memory of an emergency physician: a patient arrives at death's door and is saved only because an ultrasound scan guided therapy within seconds.

As dramatic and memorable as those cases are, they represent a tiny fraction of the ultrasound exams performed by emergency physicians. Today I was able to use EDE in a manner that is far more common and that ultimately has far more impact on emergency medical practice.

An ANA trooper had been struck by shrapnel from an IED and had some moderate lacerations on his face. They would be a challenge to repair, but they were not life-threatening. A far more worrisome injury was a small puncture wound in his right chest, right under his axilla. Even innocuous-appearing shrapnel wounds in the thorax can lead to life-threatening conditions. That could have been the case here. The patient was complaining of pain in his right chest, and there was a peculiar finding when I examined the side of his chest wall: feeling around the wound site, I got the faint impression that there were Rice Krispies beneath the skin.

Even the most junior emergency medicine trainee would have recognized that this was possibly "subcutaneous emphysema," or air trapped beneath the skin. In the current context, the most plausible explanation for this finding was that a piece of shrapnel had punctured the lung tissue and that air was leaking into the chest wall. If this was the case, a pneumothorax, or "collapsed lung," was a strong possibility. It would have been reasonable to insert a chest tube and call for helicopter evacuation. But the patient's vital signs were stable and he was breathing easily, so I elected to do an EDE instead. This test showed conclusively that there was no pneumothorax.

---

use of ultrasound in emergency medicine in Canada, the Canadian Emergency Ultrasound Society, has by far the most demanding requirements for certification of any such national body in the world.

I therefore felt comfortable not subjecting the patient to a surgical procedure (the chest tube) and not risking the lives of one of our helicopter crews to come and get him. I cancelled the medevac, and we spent the next hour repairing the patient's facial lacerations. During this hour, and for a couple of hours thereafter, I regularly rechecked the patient's chest with ultrasound. All these examinations were negative. Doing all these exams in a short time allowed me to demonstrate the technique to Corporal Girard. He quickly mastered both the manual ability and the image interpretation skills required to perform this exam.

After three hours of observation, the patient was still utterly stable. It was safe to send him back to his barracks.

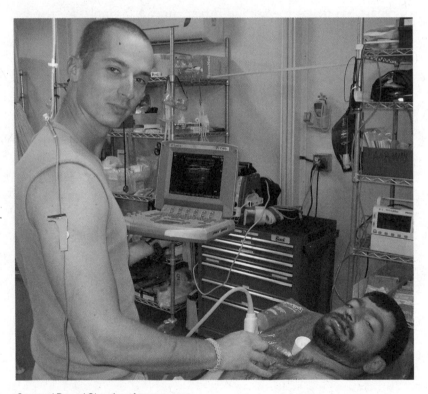

Corporal Pascal Girard performs an EDE

Addendum, September 15: The patient has returned for a follow-up visit. Repeat ultrasound scanning of his chest shows that a pneumothorax has not developed. "Negative" scans such as this one—scans that prove that the patient is not injured—have a great impact on the practice of an emergency physician. They represent more than 99 per cent of the EDE scans that we do, accelerating patient flow through our emergency departments and enhancing patient safety. This is where the most "bang for your buck" occurs with EDE.

SEPTEMBER 14, EVENING | My Right-Hand Man

I have not yet recognized the awesome contribution of Master Corporal Sylvie Guay. She is the most important member of my team, my UMS medic. We spent some time together at FOB Wilson when I first arrived, and she rejoined me here a couple of weeks ago.

Master Corporal Sylvie Guay, role model

When I arrived here in early August, the new UMS building had been in place for only a few days. All the gear was piled up in boxes in the corner. When Master Corporal Guay arrived, she worked tirelessly for several days to put everything in order: building shelves and labelling and sorting through a mountain of supplies.

It has been a very enjoyable professional relationship. At the end, she paid me the highest compliment an enlisted person can give an officer: she said she would be willing to come back to Afghanistan if she could be assigned to my UMS. I treasured the compliment, but told her that she was highly unlikely to ever come back here if that was the case.

What do you call a mother of two in her thirties who serves her country in war zone? "Role model" would be apt.

SEPTEMBER 15 | The Listeners

In an earlier entry I described the Taliban's espionage network. We too spend a lot of time gathering information, making extensive use of Afghan interpreters to eavesdrop on the Taliban. "The listeners" will sit for hours on end with a radio headset, telling us verbatim what they have heard. The Taliban know this and act accordingly. Often their exchanges go something like this:

Taliban A: "Did you get the big thing?"

Taliban B: "Yeah. I got it."

A: "Can you bring it to the place?"

B: "I have to get two guys to help me carry it. Can you send them?"

A: "Sure. I will send two guys to your house."

B: "Okay. When they get here, we will bring you the big thing to the place we said."

We intercept a lot of stuff like this, none of it particularly useful. But we keep listening. By doing so, we limit the enemy's ability to communicate. They have to use such stilted code that only limited amounts of information can be passed. And there is always the chance they will slip up.

Most of this work is done by our locally hired interpreters. The Taliban routinely try to infiltrate their followers into this group. So we have people who listen to the listeners to detect when someone's interpretation is intentionally misleading. When that happens, the interpreter is fired or, if we can make a case for espionage, arrested.

But where do we get native Pashto speakers we can absolutely rely on? In Canada. The CF places ads in media outlets that are aimed at the Afghan immigrant community. After a prolonged vetting process, an Afghan-Canadian who answers the ad can be granted a top-secret security clearance and sent to work with our intelligence people. I have met three of these individuals here, all of whom fled Afghanistan ten to fifteen years ago. They are pleased to be helping their country of birth get back on its feet. They would like to do more in the years to come.

Two of them are men with families. They are committed to the same values any other Canadian would be, including their daughters' education. They are profoundly grateful for what the Canadian Army is doing in their native land.

Even more interesting is a woman in her early thirties. She is happy to be able to help in the struggle against the Taliban, but she also laughingly admits she took the job for that quintessential Canadian reason: to pay off her student loans and start her own small business. She is doing work that is hard (and a bit dangerous) while she is young, to get her life off to a good start.

These people came to Canada from Afghanistan fairly recently, but they have all changed considerably in the interim. The woman, in particular, has gone through a remarkable evolution in a short time. She and I have gotten to be good friends, and she has shared with me her annoyance with an Afghan man who is currently pursuing her. She tells me he is quite attractive. Unfortunately, his exposure to Canadians has not caused much evolution in his attitudes towards women. Like any good friend would, I listened supportively but noncommittally as she talked about this man's advances. While many of the things she described would be considered very chauvinistic in Canada, I thought it was necessary for her to come to her own conclusions about him.

But then she revealed something that was so off-base that I was unable to hide my reaction. This Lothario has said he wants to marry her and that he will be faithful to her. However, on a number of occasions he has shared with her how much he enjoys the company of "white women." Seeing my facial expression upon hearing this, my friend came straight out and asked me what I thought about this statement. I replied that, from a Canadian perspective, she would be crazy to marry this guy. She agreed.

And another Canadian is born.

SEPTEMBER 16 | Last Day

LATE AFTERNOON

The sun is going down. I am sitting beside the hilltop observation post, looking out over Panjwayi district. There was a moderate dust storm this morning, and I am concerned that the weather may worsen tomorrow. The combat team is heading out on an operation in a few hours. I hope the weather does not make us "medevac red."

In twenty-four hours, I will be leaving the combat area. For all the danger and discomfort, the FOB has become so familiar that the thought of leaving is mildly unsettling. I didn't feel like this the last time. I was sad to leave my friends and worried about their future safety, but I was mostly very happy to be heading home. This time, I am experiencing something I have seen in combat veterans before.

Part of me likes being here. Life is simple. You get up in the morning. You do your job or you pass the time. Then you go to sleep. If you are still alive the next day, you do the same again. This differs markedly from modern life, in some ways you can anticipate and in one you might not. There is the meaningfulness of the work, the intensity of the emotions and the depth of the relationships—all that is to be expected. But the most striking difference, one that many young soldiers do not fully appreciate, is that there is so little choice here. You have one job to do, one place to eat, one group to hang out with. That's it. You don't have all the choices modern life in the developed world gives you.

I sometimes wonder if these endless choices have almost paralyzed us. We spend eternities examining various options—for a car, for a house, for a job or an outing—in the hopes of making the perfect decision. And when we finally make a decision, we often look back on it and wonder if it was the best one.

There is none of that here. Despite the risks, I have grown comfortable with the exquisite simplicity of my existence on the FOB. Fortunately, I have very strong bonds with my family and friends, bonds that more than make up for the intricacies of my life in Canada.

DAWN THE NEXT DAY

Major Jourdain is leading the combat team out on an operation. Just a few weeks left on their tour, and they are still going hard. True warriors, they are.

As I have done virtually every time some of our troops have left the FOB, whether for a patrol or for a full-blown operation, I got out of bed to wish the departing soldiers luck. And as always, I shook hands with the medic accompanying them (in this case Corporal Girard), giving him my usual injunction: "Bring them all back."

I began this practice after arriving here in June, and it has become a bit of a superstition. On my first tour, it seemed that my presence brought misfortune to Canadian soldiers: I was on the scene for the majority of cases in which Canadian soldiers were killed or seriously injured. This time, it has been the opposite. After 106 days on the FOB,

I have yet to deal with a single badly wounded Canadian, much less a dead one. I know that my telling the combat medics to "bring them all back" has had no impact on this. But there is no way I am going to change my routine at this point.

The combat team left in two waves. The first wave left on foot around 0130 and the second wave left at 0430 in LAVs. The plan was for the footborne troopers to approach silently and set up an ambush position before first light. The soldiers in the vehicles would then approach noisily and drive the enemy out of their suspected location and into the guns of the ambushers.

I am writing these final words a few minutes after I have said good-bye to the second, vehicle-borne wave of soldiers. Although I had slept only a couple of hours, I forced myself to get up to see them off. In all likelihood, this is the last time in my life that I will watch Canadian soldiers going into battle. I was so proud of them, and so proud of my country for having taken up this struggle.

The sun was coming up as they drove off. I kept watching the road for several minutes after they had disappeared around the corner leading away from the FOB. And I wept at the thought of the terrible risks these young people were taking.

SEPTEMBER 17 | Couturier

Couturier. It means "tailor" in French.

After seeing off the second wave of the combat team's operation, I was unable to go back to sleep. Despite having slept less than three hours the two previous nights, the thought of my imminent departure had me so excited that I stayed up. I finished packing, then wandered around the FOB. A helicopter was scheduled to take me back to KAF at 1300, and I thought I would sleep when I got there.

Corporal Vallières's section was heading out for a short patrol to a village close to the FOB. They invited me to come along with them, teasing me that my "inner infantryman" needed to go on one last combat patrol.

I admit that I was sorely tempted. As terrifying as my last combat patrol had been, the feeling of camaraderie that followed it had been intense and very rewarding. A big part of me wanted to experience that feeling again. Paradoxically, the fact that the risk of this patrol was only moderate argued most strongly against my participation. Because our troopers would be so close to the FOB, it was far more likely that a seriously wounded Canadian would be brought back to me rather than helicoptered from the battlefield to KAF. As much as I wanted to show these men that I was willing to assume the same risks they did, I had to consider the worst-case scenario. If I accompanied them, there was the possibility that an attack on the patrol would wound one or more Canadians while leaving me so incapacitated that I would be unable to care for them. Regardless of the physical wounds such an event would leave me with, the guilt I would feel for having failed to be there for these men would be unbearable.

During my other combat patrols, the danger I was exposing myself to was offset by the benefit of liaising with the local Afghan doctors or providing on-scene medical coverage to a patrol that otherwise would have none. No such justification existed here. It was simply a chance to "go out with the boys." As appealing as that was, I regretfully declined. An hour and a half later, the patrol returned. They had had an uneventful time and Corporal Vallières teased me yet again. It stung a bit, but I was nonetheless happy with my decision.

Major Jourdain arrived back with the first wave around 1100. They had performed a thorough sweep of the target area. Although they had failed to catch the big fish that had been in their sights, they had had a lot of contact with the locals. The major was pleased with the overall result.

After he had shed his weapons, gear and body armour, Major Jourdain went into the command post to monitor the return of the rest of his men. My helicopter was not due for several hours, so I kept him company. He jokingly offered to "buy me lunch" to celebrate my imminent departure as soon as the remainder of his team had arrived.

The members of the combat team still outside the FOB were the platoon commanded by Captain Lussier, accompanied by some combat engineers. They were only a few kilometres away from the FOB and had one last "vulnerable point" to cross before they would be home free. "Vulnerable points" are areas where there is a higher risk of IEDs. They include bridges, culverts and any other feature that can "canalize" our troops (that is, concentrate them in a restricted space).

Captain Lussier ordered most of his men to dismount from their vehicles to perform a VPS (vulnerable point search). They did so, and a thorough examination of the area failed to reveal any signs of enemy activity. The vehicles started to move forward again.

Then the IED went off.

An analysis performed after the blast revealed that the IED had been planted weeks, if not months, before. There was no way any of Captain Lussier's men could have detected it. The Taliban would have only observed the area from time to time, hoping to catch a Coalition convoy transiting the area. Today, they hit the jackpot. The blast went off under the driver of the leading LAV. It breached the armour, the force of the explosion concentrating itself in the driver's compartment.

I was chatting with Major Jourdain in the FOB command post when Captain Lussier reported that one of his vehicles had hit an IED. His voice was calm and matter-of-fact. Major Jourdain picked up a radio handset and began communicating with his platoon commander. Everyone else in the command post edged forward, listening intently to Captain Lussier's voice on the speaker. His tone remained professional and disciplined as he reported on the situation. First, he described the general scene. Then, as he approached the vehicle, he described the emplacement of the IED and the appearance of the vehicle that had been struck. Still entirely under control, he reported that one of his men was dead. Private Jonathan Couturier had been killed instantly.

Captain Lussier then went about organizing the helicopter evacuation of Private Couturier's body, his voice still unruffled and deliberate. Listening to him on the radio, I was amazed he was able to keep his emotions in check at a time like this. The depth of those emotions became clear less than an hour later when the platoon returned to the FOB. Major Jourdain, accompanied by the senior members of the combat team and me, went out to the vehicle marshalling area to meet them. Their faces were sombre, some of them streaked with tears. The emotions at play on Captain Lussier's face, however, were on another plane. He had done everything possible to prevent this from happening, but it was obvious that his heart had been torn out of his chest.

As hard as it was to see my friend suffering so badly, an even more difficult moment for me came when my medic, Corporal Girard, got out of his vehicle. With tears in his eyes, he told me: "I'm sorry, Doc. I didn't bring them all back." In that moment, I realized that the words I had used to wish my medics well had been poorly chosen.

Corporal Girard and I stepped away from the rest of the soldiers to discuss the case. It was obvious that Private Couturier's injuries had been so severe that he had been dead before Corporal Girard had gotten anywhere near the wrecked vehicle. I emphasized to Corporal Girard that there was nothing anyone could have done. Nonetheless, I could tell that on one level my medic felt that he had failed me. I had not considered this possibility before, and I regretted that my well-meaning, superstitious routine had had this unforeseen consequence.

I was still struggling with the emotions of the moment when I remembered that I would have to leave soon. I felt terrible at the thought of going home on a day such as this. Fortunately, I would not have to. In what I consider to be the greatest honour I have been paid during my service with the CF, Major Jourdain asked me to delay my return to KAF for twenty-four hours. Given the extent to which I had integrated myself into the combat team, he anticipated that a number of his soldiers would want to speak to me about our loss. I called my medical company commander at KAF, Major Annie Bouchard, and this request was immediately granted.

Chief Petty Officer Poulin returned later that afternoon, on the same helicopter that had been scheduled to take me back. Medical responsibility for the FOB was transferred to him, leaving me free (unless we got into serious trouble) to attend to the emotional needs of the troops.

Addendum, later that evening: Major Jourdain was quite prescient. Various members of the combat team, including some who had not been on the scene when Private Couturier was killed, have sought me out. I was also able to spend more than an hour talking with Captain Lussier.

The visits continued until well after midnight. The things these soldiers discussed with me are too personal and too painful to be discussed here. I hope I was able to mitigate some of the psychic wounds caused by this tragic event.

REQUIEM FOR JONATHAN

Of all the men we have lost over my two tours in Afghanistan, Jonathan Couturier was the one I had gotten to know best. Since arriving at FOB Sperwan Ghar, I had played countless hands of poker with him. In the last few weeks, I had taken to always sitting to his left, usually between him and "Beaver" Boisvert. My luck seemed better when I sat between the two of them.

It was amusing to play poker with Jonathan. He was good . . . until he tried to bluff. If he got called, he would get a hurt look on his face that immediately betrayed him. In between hands, I got to learn a bit about his girlfriend and a lot about his Mustang. While he clearly loved the former more, he talked incessantly about the latter. He was a great kid, quiet and thoughtful, unfailingly polite.

He was going home in six days.

SEPTEMBER 18, MORNING | The Elements, Part 4: Air

Before leaving for this tour, I had tried to comfort my wife by telling her that the arrival of Canadian helicopters in Afghanistan would reduce the risks I would face. I told her that I would be flying from FOB to FOB, high above the IEDs that kill so many of us. Things didn't work out that way. This would be the first and only day I would travel by air.

I woke up this morning still feeling the effects of having spent most of the past forty-eight hours awake. As groggy as I was, I tried to see as many people as possible to say goodbye to them individually.

I also stopped by the front gate of the FOB to see how our latest public relations venture was going. The festival of Eid-al-Fitr, which ends the Ramadan fast, takes place today. The combat team had put together some gift packages (blankets, food, cooking oil and so on) for some of the poorest families living near us, in accordance with Islamic tradition. Local elders were informed of this and had expressed approval at the way we were respecting their customs. It seems, however, that the Taliban do not share this opinion of our generosity. None of the gifts have been picked up, apparently because the Taliban have threatened the families. Coercing the poor so that they do not accept food for their families. Pathetic scumbags.

Around 1000, I dragged my gear over to the helipad. Captain Lussier's platoon would be flying out with me, along with Major Jourdain and Master Warrant Officer Lapierre. I had not been waiting long when I was joined by some of the members of the platoon. Vince Lussier came along after that and joined me at the front of the line. He asked what I would be doing when I got home and I replied with an off-colour joke. Vince laughed uproariously, evidently releasing some of the tension of the last twenty-four hours.

A Canadian Chinook arrived and we all boarded through the rear ramp. A few minutes later we lifted off. I wanted to imprint as many images in my mind as possible so I tried to look out the gunner's window at the Afghan landscape. I tried to reflect on what I have been doing for the past four months and what Canadian soldiers have been doing in this area for nearly four years. But I was unable to focus on the terrain. Something much closer kept drawing my eye.

As Vince and I had been at the front of the column when we boarded, we ended up sitting across from each other at the front of the

Chinook's passenger compartment. His face was clouded over and I could see that he was back in a very dark place.

We were met at the airfield by a bus which took us all back to the barracks where the troopers would be spending the night. I was then taken by truck to the headquarters building of my medical company. I walked in and went to Major Bouchard's office, dusty and rumpled, still carrying my rifle and pistol and wearing my protective gear. Outside of the barracks reserved for the battle group, it is unusual for anybody at KAF to be dressed this way. Major Bouchard did not recognize me at first. When she did, she said: "You look like a combat soldier!"

I had to agree with her. And I felt like one too.

SEPTEMBER 18, AFTERNOON | Saying Goodbye to Jonathan

After reporting to Major Bouchard, I went to the room in which I would be spending the next few nights. It contained two bunk beds and I had it all to myself—it seemed impossibly roomy. Chief Petty Officer Second Class Ray Racine, the sergeant-major of the medical company, had already arranged for my excess baggage to be placed there. These were things I had brought along only for the trip to KAF and back or for use during decompression. I began repacking my things for the trip home. Then the lack of sleep and the excess of emotion of the last three days caught up with me and I collapsed into bed.

At 1630 I returned to the troopers' barracks. Major Jourdain had asked me to remain with the platoon for the ceremony, and I was very grateful for that. Although I had a lot of respect for the people in my medical company, our relationship had only been an e-mail- and phone-based one. I was much happier remaining with the men of Combat Team Cobra for this ritual.

I had been to ramp ceremonies on my first tour and had always been impressed by how well they were conducted. Although agonizingly painful for the men closest to the fallen, the dignity and professionalism with which these events took place made them powerful mechanisms of emotional healing.

For those closest to the fallen soldier, the process starts an hour before the ceremony on the tarmac. We first went to a chapel, where Jonathan's casket had already been taken. For an hour, we sat with him in silence. Various senior officers came in, representing the other branches of the task force. They marched up to the casket, stood at attention for a minute, then expressed their condolences quietly to the combat team officers and to our company sergeant-major, who were seated in the first row of pews.

When this was over, we were taken to the airfield. We took our place beside the Hercules aircraft that would take Jonathan home. To our right, and therefore closer to the aircraft, would be the senior officers of the Canadian contingent and our padres. Across from us were the senior officers of all the other Coalition nations. To our left were the nearly two thousand KAF-based members of the Canadian task force. Facing them, and forming a passageway a couple of hundred metres long, were thousands of other Coalition soldiers.

When everyone was in position we were called to attention. The sun had gone down by this time. The night air was still. It was a perfect setting for such an occasion.

After the service, all the members of Combat Team Cobra marched into the Hercules in single file. One by one, we came rigidly to attention, saluted and then touched Jonathan's casket one last time. We then walked out and gathered together, where Major Jourdain addressed us for a few minutes. It could have been a perfect ramp ceremony. But it wasn't.

The service was performed by an anglophone padre. As this was for a francophone soldier, she tried to do much of it in French. But the quality of the padre's French was atrocious. Most of the words were mispronounced, and several French words were pronounced in English. Even the members of Jonathan's section, who had composed the "personal" part of the eulogy, were unable to recognize the words they had written.

As a French Canadian, I was enraged by this. After the ramp ceremony was dismissed, several members of the combat team angrily muttered about the way the eulogy had been performed. As I stood beside them, I noticed that the padre was standing close by, along with the senior padre of the task force. I walked over and asked to speak to her in private. We went to a point on the tarmac where no one else could hear us.

I proceeded to give this person the most thorough dressing-down I have ever delivered. I didn't raise my voice or use foul language, but I was as angry as I have ever been and my tone reflected this.

I joined Major Jourdain, and we made our way back to the barracks. He was absolutely livid. There had been four francophone padres lined up on the tarmac beside us. He thought it was unforgivable that the ceremony had not been performed by one of them.

When we arrived at the barracks where the platoon was being housed for the evening, several of the troops were still complaining about the eulogy. I described to the soldiers what I had done. The troops applauded so loudly that Major Jourdain, who had been at the other end of the building, came over to see what could possibly have cheered the boys up so much on such a sombre occasion.

After that, we celebrated Jonathan's short time with us. The army provided each man with two beers and all the pizza we could eat. As we drank and ate we laughed about Jonathan's obsession with his Mustang, his poker mannerisms and other quirks of his behaviour. The biggest laugh came when one of the troopers reminded us what the regimental sergeant-major had told us after the ramp ceremony. In a sincere but somewhat misguided attempt to comfort the platoon, he had told us to ask Jonathan to "protect us." The trooper relating this opined that Jonathan's reaction to this request on our part would be: "Not another fucking tasking!" That had us all laughing so hard we had beer and pizza coming out of our noses. Seeing the soldiers' faces as they chortled, I was reassured. I turned to Major Jourdain and said, "Your boys are going to be all right."

It was a legendary military wake, and it almost made up for the botched ramp ceremony. Almost.

Addendum, September 19: I warned Major Bouchard this morning about the run-in that I'd had with the padre the previous evening. She was as incensed as the rest of the French Canadians had been and told me not to worry about it.

Addendum, November 20: While I was at KAF, Major Jourdain informed me that he had lodged a formal complaint with the battle group about the padre's performance. In response to this, the senior padre phoned Major Jourdain at FOB Sperwan Ghar. After some discussion, she agreed that the way the ceremony had been handled was regrettable and that the combat team deserved an apology. She said that she would deliver the apology in person when the combat team returned from the FOB a few weeks later. She never did so.

Incredibly, it turns out that this was not a unique event. I have since learned that the ramp ceremony for Corporal Nick Bulger was mishandled in much the same way, only this time it was a near-unilingual francophone trying (and failing) to properly read an English text. True to its Canadian roots, the padre branch has fucked things up in both official languages.

SEPTEMBER 19, MORNING | A Farewell to Arms

Major Jourdain, Captain Lussier and the other Cobras were flying back to the FOB this morning. I went over to bid them farewell a half hour before they left. Once again, they cheered me for what I had said to the padre the night before. We all agreed that Jonathan had deserved as much.

I made one last round of handshakes, spending a little longer with Corporal Girard. After Vince, he was the one I was most concerned about. I was relieved to see that he appeared to be in good spirits. I then had the chance to have a longer conversation with Major Jourdain. I know he feels the loss of his soldier acutely, but when I asked him what came next, he answered with a steady voice and clear eyes: "We will soldier on." Then they boarded their vehicles and were gone.

I was no longer a member of a combat team. After 107 straight days in the combat area and over 2,500 consecutive hours "on call," I was no longer a FOB doc. Almost certainly, I will never be one again.

SEPTEMBER 19, AFTERNOON | Logistics

After lunch, I spent a couple of hours tearing through the KAF bazaar, where Afghan merchants come to sell all manner of textiles and handicrafts. I had a long list of people I wanted to buy gifts for, and very little time. My haggling, therefore, was limited and perfunctory. Several Afghan merchants did well today, but I was able to go to the post office this afternoon and ship home several boxes full of souvenirs. These will be distributed to good effect among friends and family. Wandering around KAF, I was reminded of a topic I had meant to write about earlier.

A chasm exists between those who serve at KAF and those who go into combat. There are two reasons for this. The first is the natural bravado of young combat troopers. With considerable justification, they see themselves as the elite. With less justification, they occasionally denigrate those who do not accompany them into the combat area.

The second reason has to do with the inevitable "bad apples" that appear in any group. Life at KAF is much more scheduled and orderly than life at a FOB. The FOB troopers can accept this. But they cannot accept being told that an item they require before they head out on a combat operation cannot be delivered to them because somebody at KAF has "gone home for the day" or is on "Sunday routine."

I am not making this up. Things slow down on the weekends at KAF. Most of the time, this is of no consequence to the people on the FOB. But the few times that it is, when someone who has never been shot at declines to work overtime to help us out, it provokes intensely negative feelings.

The reality, as in all these types of situations, is that the few bad interactions FOB people have with KAF people get reported and discussed endlessly on the FOB. That is unfortunate, because the soldiers in the "support trades" work hard in an environment where their contribution goes almost unnoticed.

In the June 3 entry's footnote I describe the way Master Seaman Carole Dubois detected an error in my pay for my previous tour, an error that had occurred more than a year earlier. When she told me I was entitled to these payments, I replied that there was no rush to pay me since I was headed to the FOBs and would have very little use for cash. She contacted me in August to sort through this issue.

This proved to be far trickier than she had anticipated, requiring numerous e-mails back and forth between us. After a few days, I noticed that it did not matter whether I e-mailed her at 0600 or at 2300; she would always reply immediately. This soldier was probably putting in longer hours than anyone else in the theatre of operations. And let no one say her work was not vital. Our soldiers are not rich. They and their families depend on people like MS Dubois to ensure that their pay flows smoothly into their bank accounts, so that there is always money for their families' mortgages, clothes and groceries. If this does not happen, the combat troopers will be unable to focus on their tasks and the impact on our combat effectiveness will be disastrous.

The same can be said for all the soldiers who serve in the support trades, such as logistics personnel, mechanics, cooks and many, many others. And yet, when these soldiers come home, they often get an almost embarrassed look on their faces when they are asked what they did. When talking to civilians, they will often use a generic term: "I was a supply technician" or "I worked in administration." Those same civilians will often look at the soldier quizzically. The unspoken message is that their service was less worthy than that of the combat troopers.

This is particularly unfair to those who serve at KAF but who risk their lives daily driving supplies out to the FOBs. They are exposed to a high degree of danger not only from IEDs, suicide bombers and

The best contribution of the support elements—great food!
(Surf-and-turf night on a FOB? Wow!)

ambushes but also from mundane accidents. A number of Canadian soldiers have been injured and six have been killed in such collisions.

So I would like to take a moment to recognize all those Canadian men and women who served in the essential support roles, without which the war-fighters would not have boots, beans or bullets. You will likely never be "mentioned in dispatches" nor receive any medals for bravery, but we could never win, or even fight, without you.

Addendum: Those wishing to learn more about the unprecedented challenges involved in keeping the CF combat troopers supplied in Afghanistan are encouraged to read Lieutenant Colonel John Conrad's *What the Thunder Said*.* Lieutenant Colonel Conrad ran the logistics for the first Canadian battle group deployed to Kandahar province

---

* Lieutenant Colonel John Conrad, *What the Thunder Said: Reflections of a Canadian Officer in Kandahar* (Toronto: Dundurn, 2009).

in 2006. The fighting was intense, and the infrastructure was a pale shadow of what it is today. The achievements of the logistics branch during that spring and summer were phenomenal.

SEPTEMBER 20 | Ultrasound, Again

The reward for good work is . . . more work.

I spent the morning dealing with a balky laptop that, after performing flawlessly on the FOB for nearly four months, began crashing every ten minutes. This was a problem because I had been asked to teach a course on advanced emergency ultrasound to the people at the KAF hospital. My presentations on the subject were contained in the malfunctioning computer. If I could not get it working again, the course would have to be cancelled.

It took three hours of intense CPR (computer programmer resuscitation) on the part of the good folks in the IT department, in particular Todd Doucet, to revive my abused laptop. They got me operational in time to supervise the outpatient clinic in the early afternoon, after which I went to the hospital to give my course. There is something admirable about a group of doctors who are so committed to their continuing medical education that they will sit in a dusty tent on the edge of a deafeningly loud airfield to learn new techniques from a visiting expert.

The course went very well. Having taught a course in basic emergency ultrasound at the Multinational Medical Unit (MMU) on my first tour, introducing advanced techniques to the same institution made for a nice continuation of the saga.

SEPTEMBER 21 | Out of Afghanistan

Last day at KAF.

I swung by the medical building to say my last goodbyes. While I had enjoyed my interactions with Major Bouchard, Sergeant-Major

Racine and the rest of the medical company, these had been long-distance relationships. There was none of the melancholy I had felt two days earlier when saying goodbye to Major Jourdain and the members of Combat Team Cobra.

I reported to the airfield at the prescribed time and then spent two hours in the waiting area before being called to board the plane. The army likes it when you're early for things like this.

The flight to Camp Mirage was uneventful and boring. I had forgotten to bring anything to read, so I sat there, trying (and failing) to sleep. Even with high-quality earplugs, a Herc is a very noisy place.

On arrival at Camp Mirage, the first order of business was to hand in my weapons. After my first tour, it had seemed natural to return my rifle and pistol. On this tour, I had been exposed to much more danger; on one occasion I had even been in a straight-up gunfight. As a result, I had grown attached to these firearms. They have been a source of comfort and security, and I was sad to part with them.

That feeling only lasted a few minutes, to be replaced by hunger. If I needed a reminder that I was off the FOB, I got it as I entered the mess hall. I was still wearing the Afghan scarf many of us wear in the combat area to shield our faces from dust. A lieutenant colonel took one look at me and got up from his table to inform me that I was improperly dressed. Considering that I had spent nearly four months wandering around the FOBs with the same scarf, that struck me as humorous. But military discipline asserted itself and I complied.

SEPTEMBER 22 | Mirage

I spent the day at Camp Mirage doing the last bits of out-clearance paperwork and getting my travel documents in order for the trip home. This is called a "buffer day," which I think serves to protect those leaving KAF from the vagaries of Hercules transports. Should your departure from Afghanistan be delayed by twenty-four hours, you will still be able to go on decompression on time.

It has been an unsettling day. On the one hand, I am extraordinarily happy that I have gotten out of Afghanistan alive and uninjured. But the feeling I had four days ago—the feeling that the FOB had become so familiar it was almost like home—has persisted. I feel disoriented.

I ended up wandering around the base, unsure of what to do with myself.

SEPTEMBER 23 | Decompression

Most Canadian soldiers who go on decompression are sent by plane to Cyprus. They stay together in the same hotel, watched over by counsellors of various stripes. These counsellors hold sessions in the mornings to smooth the reintegration of the soldiers back into Canadian society. They discuss ways of coping with post-battle stress, things to watch out for when reacquainting oneself with one's family and other challenges a returning soldier might face. The rest of the day is given over to recreational activities. Much of this recreation involves alcohol consumption. The hotel therefore outfits one room with padding to act as a drunk tank, and CF medical personnel are assigned to the local hospital to deal with the inevitable alcohol overdoses and fisticuffs.

By some fluke, no one else who was eligible for decompression left KAF at the same time I did. For a small group or, in this unique case, a singleton, it is not cost-effective to rent a plane. I would therefore be sent by myself in a car to a hotel on the shores of the Indian Ocean.

Well, not entirely by myself. The army feels that soldiers on decompression, particularly those who have been exposed to combat, must always have some kind of mental health person available to them should they wish to discuss anything. When I showed up for my pre-decompression briefing, I learned that I would be escorted on my decompression by . . . a padre.

I politely listened to his pre-departure briefing, an hour-long compendium of bromides about dealing with stress. The emphasis is on drinking less and talking more. There was one other soldier in the room with me for this briefing. He was a member of Combat Team Cobra whose behaviour in Cyprus last time had been so atrocious that he had been banned from the island. He would also be going to the Middle Eastern hotel I was headed for, but for some reason he was not leaving for several days.

Around midmorning, the padre and I got into a minivan and headed for our hotel. It was about a two-hour drive, and I knew the padre would want to try to talk to me. He seemed like a solid individual—cut from the same cloth as Captain Cholette, the "combat padre"—but I was still quite angry about the way the ramp ceremony had been handled and did not want to initiate anything. We therefore spent the first half hour in silence. Finally, the padre couldn't help himself and asked me how my tour had gone.

I decided to tell him in detail about the ceremony and how the troopers had felt about it. He agreed that the KAF padres had been extraordinarily insensitive. It felt good to hear that, but it did not make me want to spend my time off with him. When we got to the hotel I told him politely that I would see him in three days, when it was time to go.

I went to my room, got a book and settled in for a two-hour soak in the first bathtub I had seen in four months. I then went to a neighbouring hotel, where I spent well over one hundred dollars on an elaborate meal that lasted nearly three hours. And then to sleep, in a room all my own, in a bed twice as big as anything I had slept in since May.

SEPTEMBER 24 | Disconnected

This is weird. I am here by myself, surrounded by rich tourists from Europe and the Middle East. The room is comfortable, the food is amazing and it's fun to watch North American television again. But I feel cut off from my military family.

I have trouble imagining that anyone would think it would be a good idea to send a guy who has spent four months on a FOB to decompression alone. Almost certainly, my name and my time came up and a clerk booked my hotel reservation automatically. No one noticed I would be going by myself until yesterday morning.

The way I feel right now, I think it was a mistake for me to come. I should have asked the CF to send me home immediately. Barring that, I should have stayed at Camp Mirage. Being around other people in uniform would have been far more comforting.

SEPTEMBER 25 | We That Are Left . . .

I was wrong. Coming here was not a mistake. Something happened today, something that could not have taken place anywhere else, something that had to happen before I went home.

When Jonathan was killed on September 17, I went into "doctor" mode. My concern was for the men around me. I was in a unique and privileged position to be able to help them through this difficult time. My run-in with the padre had accentuated this by making me feel even more protective of these men, if that were possible.

This mindset persisted until I bid Combat Team Cobra farewell on the 19th. This disconnected me from my own grief. In the days that followed, the frenetic pace of my pre-departure activities kept me distracted. It wasn't until this morning that my own reaction to Jonathan's death bubbled up to the conscious level.

I didn't recognize it at first. I was only aware that I had no appetite for breakfast. So I went for a walk on the beach. I spent several minutes looking at the ocean. There was no one around me. In that setting of utter calm, my grief hit me full force. The pain was physical, an awful tearing feeling inside my chest that made it hard to breathe.

I don't think I've ever cried as much as I did this morning. This period of uncontrollable emotion lasted at least ten minutes. Perhaps it was longer. Thinking back on it several hours later as I write this, I cannot accurately gauge the time that passed.

Eventually, the emotional weight of the moment abated, and I began to be able to control the physical manifestations of my grief. As I achieved this control, my mind cleared and I began to look at

Jonathan's death more analytically. What came next was even more unpleasant. It provoked an intense wave of nausea, something I find even more disagreeable than pain.

Survivor guilt.

Jonathan was less than half my age. What right did I have to be going home to my family when he would not? What might he have achieved in his life, if he had had the chance?

The pure grief reaction had caught me by surprise. But my medical training allowed me to anticipate, if only by a few seconds, this next wave of emotion. Like Vince had on the helicopter, I went to a dark, dark place. Thankfully, I was not there all that long.

As soon as I could, I sought out the best remedy for these kinds of situations: hard physical effort. I spent the rest of the day hiking in the mountains inland from the hotel. I pushed myself as hard as I could, revelling in the feeling of the air coming into my lungs, the sun on my face and the sweat on my skin.

Standing on the hilltop, I knew I would grieve Jonathan's death, and the death of all my fallen comrades, for the rest of my life. I now viscerally relate to the veterans of World War Two who, more than sixty years on, shed tears on Remembrance Day.

But grief does not necessarily imply distress. I regret Jonathan's death, but I still believe in the cause for which he was fighting. And that makes all the difference.

By the time I came back down, I was famished.

And ready to go home.

SEPTEMBER 26–27 | Home

I spent a good part of the morning talking to the padre who had escorted me here. With part of my grief and anger processed, I was able to open up and have an honest conversation with him about my tour. It was very beneficial. He was an excellent listener and counsellor—the Canadian soldiers who spend time with him will be well cared for.

Mom and Dad and the yellow ribbon

Back at the Mirage base, I reported to the administration office to collect my passport and to complete the out-clearance procedures. I then spent the last few hours sitting quietly by myself, processing what I had been through yesterday.

The connections in Europe and Toronto were good, and it only took a little over twenty-five hours to make it all the way back home to Sudbury. I had flown from the Middle East in civilian clothing, as we must in order not to upset the "host nation." In Toronto, however, I changed into my combat uniform. I may have left as a civilian but I was coming home as a soldier.

When we landed in Sudbury, I called Claude on my cell phone to confirm that she had already arrived at the airport. A minute later, I was holding my wife and daughter in my arms. This gave me a more profound sense of well-being than I had ever experienced.

On the way home, Michelle could not get enough of me. She said that she'd had "tears of happy" in her eyes when she saw my plane land.

She insisted that I sit right beside her in the back seat. I was more than happy to oblige.

The drive home was the reverse of the drive to the airport four months earlier. We stopped at my parents' home, where the lamppost had been festooned with a gigantic yellow ribbon. Much hugging and handshaking ensued.

Then Claude, Michelle and I continued on to our house, where we spent the rest of the afternoon sitting in the backyard, talking and playing and laughing.

I have returned from my country's wars.

I am home.

Epilogue

2010

APRIL 30 | Looking Ahead

The seven months since my return home have been a roller coaster. The book tour for FOB *Doc,* combined with the pent-up demand for my ultrasound course, made the fall months exhausting. I had barely recovered from that when, in mid-January, we flew to Vietnam to adopt our second daughter. I am overjoyed to report that she has progressed faster than we could have dared hope. It is like watching infancy on fast-forward. At this rate, she will have caught up by the time she is ready to go to junior kindergarten. Best of all, Michelle has proven to be an extraordinary older sister. She is loving, kind, patient and invariably generous with her younger sibling.

Julianne has had quite an introduction to Canada. Six weeks after she arrived here, Prime Minister Stephen Harper came to Sudbury to attend an award ceremony put on for me by the local Rotary Club, in recognition of my service in Afghanistan and in emergency medicine. At the dinner, I could not help but reflect on my little girl's extraordinary journey. Less than three months earlier, she had been facing dire prospects in a heartbreakingly poor orphanage in the developing world. Now, she was having dinner with the prime minister

My Girlzzz

of Canada. I was extremely proud to be living in one of the very few nations on Earth where something like this can happen. We live in a great country!

I follow the news about Afghanistan as closely as possible, and worry a great deal about what the outcome will be. I can understand the emotion behind the desire of so many Canadians to have us withdraw in 2011, but I cannot see the logic of this course of action. If going to war in Afghanistan was the right thing to do in 2001, what will have changed in the intervening ten years to make that no longer the case? The enemy has not changed, and the penalty for failure now includes the nightmare scenario of the re-emergence of a hardline Taliban theocracy that goes on to destabilize Pakistan, the only nuclear-armed Islamic state. The consequences of a nuclear war, even if it is brief and limited to the Indian subcontinent, are unimaginable. The political consequences of a NATO/UN failure, which would be a failure of the world's democratic nations, would also be catastrophic.

Julianne, Claude, Prime Minister Stephen Harper, Michelle and yours truly—Sudbury, 2010

(Courtesy Deb Ransom, Official Photographer for the Prime Minister)

Much will depend on the effects of the American surge over the next two summers' fighting seasons, campaigns in which Canada will continue to play a very active role. As this book goes to the printers, the Canadian battle group is gearing up for a major push into the Taliban-infested areas of western Panjwayi. I am certain they will emerge victorious, but at what cost and to what long-term effect? While this war could be lost by a premature withdrawal of Coalition forces from the battlefield, it will not be won by foreign armies. Rather, success in Afghanistan will depend on three things.

First, the country must be independently militarily secure. To achieve this, the Coalition must maintain a robust force on the ground until the Afghan army is able to hold the Taliban at bay on its own. What I saw in 2009 confirmed what I had come to believe in 2007–08: the ANA would reach an acceptable level of competence in 2012. I feel our military pullout, therefore, to be a year earlier than it should be.

Second, the educational system must be nurtured and protected. This war will be won in the Afghan classroom, by giving the rural poor economic alternatives more attractive than a Taliban paycheque and by giving ordinary Afghans a world view that rejects extremism. The Taliban realize this, and will continue to do their utmost to destroy schools and intimidate, maim or kill teachers and students. They must be prevented from doing this.

Third, an Afghan leadership must arise that is worthy both of the Afghan people and of the sacrifice of the Coalition nations. Results in this area have been disappointing, to say the least. A flawed election was followed by a run-off election that was cancelled when the challenger felt he would not have a fair chance at victory. Everyone is questioning whether President Hamid Karzai is willing, or even capable, of curbing the corruption that plagues his government.

The political process did have a significant positive aspect, but it was one the media largely overlooked. The main challenger for the presidency was Abdullah Abdullah, the former minister of foreign affairs. Upon withdrawing from the run-off election, he committed himself to oppose President Karzai politically. This is a sea change for Afghanistan. For the past thirty years, any leader who has been pushed out of power has retreated to his ethnic power base and led an armed struggle against those who had forced him out of Kabul. Despite the weak mandate President Karzai obtained, not a single person who ran against him for the presidency has taken up arms. This lack of violence does not mean the political opposition is being docile. The country's parliament rejected 70 per cent of Karzai's first slate of ministerial candidates, forcing him to submit a second, more broadly acceptable list. It has blocked his attempts to gain more control over the independent Electoral Complaints Commission, which exposed much of the fraud in the August elections. At this writing, it is also fighting to retain control of the procedures for the Parliamentary elections scheduled for September 2010. All in all, the political opposition in Afghanistan is behaving much like a vigorous opposition in any other democratic country.

Could this be the beginning of a more peaceful Afghanistan? If Abdullah Abdullah and the other opposition leaders can agree to work within the political process even after they feel that they have been cheated of the presidency by fraud, perhaps many of the Afghans who oppose the government with violence can be convinced to enter into dialogue and negotiations, and give up armed resistance. Taliban supporters are not a monolithic mass. Many of them hunger for moral and coherent leadership, just like the rest of their countrymen.

Canadians will therefore watch events unfold in Afghanistan over the coming years with concern and trepidation. But regardless of the outcome, and regardless of how individual Canadians might feel about this war, all Canadians would do well to remember the names of Zhari, and Panjwayi, and Arghandab, and Shah Wali Khot. The men and women in uniform that you have met in these pages, and so many more in stories that have yet to be told, did Canada proud in those places. Canadians must be proud of them in return.

CAPTAIN RAY WISS, M.D.
Medical Officer, Second Battalion, Irish Regiment of Canada*
Emergency Physician, Sudbury Regional Hospital

---

* A reserve infantry regiment based in Sudbury, Ontario.

Glossary of Abbreviations, Acronyms and Initialisms

ANA Afghan National Army

ANP Afghan National Police

BIP Blow in Place

CBC Canadian Broadcasting Corporation

CCP Casualty Collection Point

CDS Chief of the Defence Staff

CF Canadian Forces

CFB Canadian Forces Base

CIA Central Intelligence Agency (U.S.)

CIDA Canadian International Development Agency

CIMIC Civil Military Cooperation

CNS Camp Nathan Smith

CPO Chief Petty Officer

CT Computerized Tomography

CPR Cardiopulmonary Resuscitation

DOW Died of Wounds

EDE Emergency Department Echo

EOD Explosive Ordnance Disposal

ESL English as a Second Language

ETA Estimated Time of Arrival

FBI Federal Bureau of Investigation (U.S.)

FLQ Front de Libération du Québec

FOB Forward Operating Base

FOO Forward Observation Officer

GP General Practitioner

HLTA Home Leave Travel Allowance

ICU Intensive Care Unit

IED Improvised Explosive Device

ISI Inter Services Intelligence (Pakistan)

IT Information Technology

IV Intravenous

KAF Kandahar Air Field

KIA Killed in Action

LAV Light Armoured Vehicle

MASCAL Mass Casualty

MMU Multinational Medical Unit

MRE Medical Rules of Eligibility

MRI Magnetic Resonance Imaging

MS Master Seaman

MULLE Mobile Unit Light Logistics Element

MWO Master Warrant Officer

NATO North Atlantic Treaty Organization

NCO Non-Commissioned Officer

NGO Non-Governmental Organization

NIS National Investigation Service (CF)

OMLT Operational Mentoring and Liaison Team

OP Observation Post

PA Physician Assistant

PBW Patrol Base Wilson

PPCLI Princess Patricia's Canadian Light Infantry

PPE Personal Protective Equipment

PRT Provincial Reconstruction Team

PTSD Post-Traumatic Stress Disorder

QRF Quick Reaction Force

RCMP Royal Canadian Mounted Police

RIP Relief in Place

RMC Royal Military College

RPG Rocket-Propelled Grenade

SAS Special Air Service (U.K.)

SEAL Sea Air Land (U.S. Navy)

SWAT Special Weapons and Tactics

TCCC Tactical Combat Casualty Care

TOC Tactical Operation Centre

UMS Unit Medical Station

UN United Nations

USD U.S. Dollars

VIP Very Important Person

VOIED Victim-Operated Improvised Explosive Device

VPS Vulnerable Point Search

VSA Vital Signs Absent

WIA Wounded in Action

WO Warrant Officer

The Fallen

THE PHOTOGRAPHS BELOW and on the following pages are of Canadian soldiers who were killed in action and who are mentioned in this book.

SERGEANT ROBERT SHORT
KIA October 2, 2003,
Infantry

**CORPORAL ROBBIE
BEERENFENGER**
KIA October 2, 2003, Infantry

CORPORAL JAMIE MURPHY
KIA January 27, 2004,
Infantry

Above are the official photos released by the CF when these three men were killed. These photos are lifted from impromptu photos taken by friends. They are low-resolution images, which become extremely blurry if I try to magnify them.

It was only when we came to Kandahar, and our dying became more frequent and predictable, that the CF began taking the formal, high-resolution pictures of our soldiers that appear on the following pages.

That is the picture I absolutely did not want to have taken of me.

CAPTAIN NICHOLA GODDARD
KIA May 17, 2006, Artillery

TROOPER MARK WILSON
KIA October 7, 2006, Armour

CAPTAIN JONATHAN SNYDER
KIA June 7, 2008, Infantry

WARRANT OFFICER GAËTAN ROBERGE
KIA December 27, 2008, Infantry

SAPPER SEAN GREENFIELD
KIA January 31, 2009, Engineer

TROOPER KARINE BLAIS
KIA April 13, 2009, Armour

PRIVATE ALEXANDRE PELOQUIN
KIA June 8, 2009, Infantry

CORPORAL MARTIN DUBÉ
KIA June 14, 2009, Infantry

CORPORAL NICK BULGER
KIA July 3, 2009, Infantry

MASTER CORPORAL CHARLES-PHILIPPE MICHAUD
DOW July 4, 2009, Infantry

MASTER CORPORAL PATRICE AUDET
KIA July 6, 2009, Air Force

CORPORAL MARTIN JOANNETTE
KIA July 6, 2009, Infantry

PRIVATE SÉBASTIEN COURCY
KIA July 16, 2009, Infantry

CORPORAL CHRISTIAN BOBBITT
KIA August 1, 2009, Engineer

SAPPER MATHIEU ALLARD
KIA August 1, 2009, Engineer

MAJOR YANNICK PÉPIN
KIA September 6, 2009, Engineer

CORPORAL JEAN-FRANÇOIS DROUIN
KIA September 6, 2009, Engineer

PRIVATE PATRICK LORMAND
KIA September 13, 2009, Infantry

PRIVATE JONATHAN COUTURIER
KIA September 17, 2009, Infantry

FOR THE FALLEN

They shall grow not old, as we that are left grow old.
Age shall not weary them, nor the years condemn.
At the going down of the sun and in the morning
We will remember them.

LAURENCE BINYON ·

At the going down of the sun
(Photo courtesy Master Corporal Ken Fenner)

We will remember them
(Artwork by Silvia Pecota)

(Photo courtesy Master Corporal Julien Richard)

CAPTAIN RAY WISS, M.D., is an emergency medicine specialist from Sudbury, Ontario, and a member of the Canadian Forces Reserves. In 2008, he was awarded the YMCA Peace Medal and the Ontario Medical Association Career Service Award. In 2010, he received the Rotary Club's Paul Harris Award at an event headlined by Prime Minister Stephen Harper. Also in 2010, he was selected to be the keynote speaker at the North York General Hospital Emergency Medicine Update, Canada's premier emergency medicine conference. FOB *Doc*, the book he wrote about his first tour, was one of Amazon.ca's "Editors' Picks: Top 100 Books" of 2009.

MIX
Paper from
responsible sources
FSC® C016245
FSC
www.fsc.org